IMAGES
of America

NORTH BEND

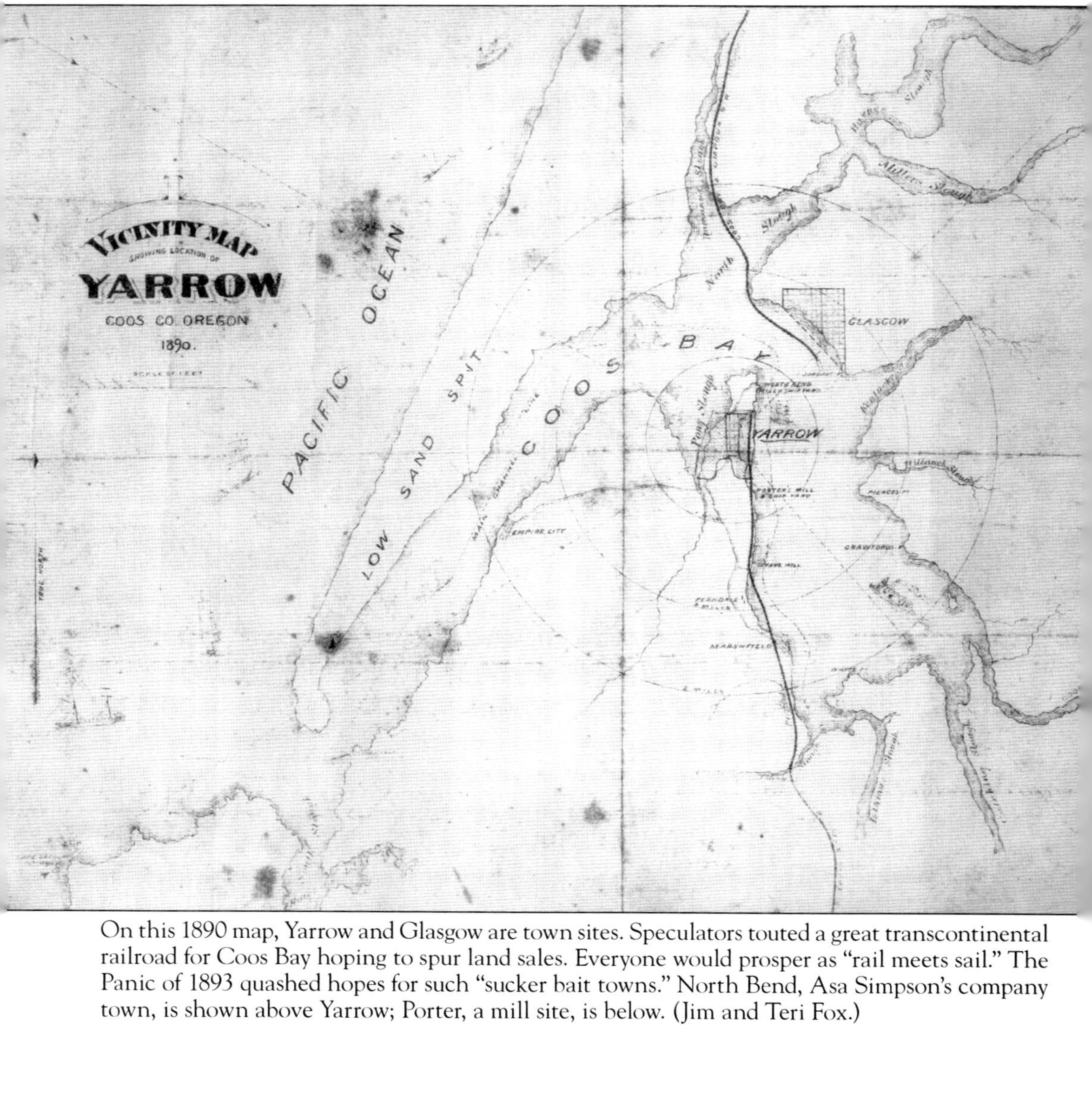

On this 1890 map, Yarrow and Glasgow are town sites. Speculators touted a great transcontinental railroad for Coos Bay hoping to spur land sales. Everyone would prosper as "rail meets sail." The Panic of 1893 quashed hopes for such "sucker bait towns." North Bend, Asa Simpson's company town, is shown above Yarrow; Porter, a mill site, is below. (Jim and Teri Fox.)

On the Cover: Auto racing was part of the Big Bridge Carnival in October 1915. This event celebrated the completion of the Southern Pacific's railroad bridge over Coos Bay. The auto race began at Sherman and Virginia Avenues. Vern Gorst, near center, held the starter's white flag. On the far left, the Star Theatre sign is visible. (CHMM 992-8-0914.)

IMAGES
of America

NORTH BEND

Dick Wagner and Judy Wagner
Coos Historical and Maritime Museum

ARCADIA
PUBLISHING

ISBN 978-0-7385-8135-4

Published by Arcadia Publishing
Charleston, South Carolina

Printed in the United States of America

Library of Congress Control Number: 2010926126

For all general information, please contact Arcadia Publishing:
Telephone 843-853-2070
Fax 843-853-0044
E-mail sales@arcadiapublishing.com
For customer service and orders:
Toll-Free 1-888-313-2665

Visit us on the Internet at www.arcadiapublishing.com

To the professionals and volunteers of the North Bend Fire Department

Contents

ACKNOWLEDGMENTS

No book is the sole product of its authors. Many hands, past and present, provide text and images for gathering, analysis, and organization.

At the Coos Historical and Maritime Museum, Vicki Wiese, interim director/collections manager, spent uncounted hours locating and processing images and information. Hannah Contino, museum assistant, also helped. They, like the museum's collection, are a wonderful resource.

Numerous individuals are due recognition. Gary Sharp, photographer extraordinaire, provided contemporary images. Chief Scott Graham of the North Bend Fire Department generously gave access to both department and family photographs. David Petrie, cultural director, and Jesse Beers, culture director assistant, of the Culture Department of the Confederated Tribes of the Coos, Lower Umpqua and Siuslaw Indians shared the tribes' collection and information. North Bend's recorder Joann Thompson and city administrator Jan Willis aided with the city's photographs. Mary Banks Granger, Sami Abboud, Pat Choat Pierce, Steve Greif, Patricia Richardson, Theresa Erskine, Joanie Johnson, Chris Byrne, Barry Hayes, Karen Hollingsworth, Jim Hillar, and Kimberly Hagner also contributed.

The late Victor West merits special mention for his lifetime photo collection of tall ships and other vessels as well as his detailed notes on local history from early newspapers.

We thank our Arcadia editors, Sarah Higginbotham, Donna Libert, and Devon Weston, for their guidance.

A photograph credit appears in parentheses at the end of each caption, except for those from the authors' collection. Abbreviations include CHMM for the Coos Historical and Maritime Museum; Confederated Tribes for the Confederated Tribes of the Coos, Lower Umpqua and Siuslaw Indians; NBFD for the North Bend Fire Department; and CNB for the City of North Bend.

INTRODUCTION

More than 10,000 years ago ancestors of the Coos Tribe arrived, most likely by sea, to the area now called Oregon. Details of their arrival are lost but the tribe's oral tradition, settlers' accounts, and government records give glimpses of life in more recent times.

The Hanis-speaking Coos spread out around the bay. Their villages were composed of numerous families, each with its own headman. The village chief came from those headmen. Permanent winter villages tended to be near rivers and streams where there was fresh water. Seasonal camps were upriver to follow salmon and eel migrations. Hunting, fishing, and gathering were the basis of the culture, with their language and technology evolving over the millennia.

Their world was full of spirits that inhabited every living and non-living thing. These spirits, made known through songs and dreams, influenced life and were a source of power. The shaman, or medicine man, was recognized as possessing many powers and was able to help others.

The natural world provided raw material for life—cedar trees for plank houses and canoes; rocks, animal bones, and antlers for tools, hunting gear, and utensils; and skins, grasses, and maple and cedar tree bark for clothing, baskets, and mats. Nearby waters were a year-round source of fish, mussels, and clams. The woods and meadows offered seasonal game, berries, and roots.

Early contact (1820s and 1830s) with European Americans introduced diseases that ravaged native populations. At the north bend of Coos Bay, villages like Gahakkich and Kolokaytch suffered. The Coos numbered several thousand in 1806 but only several hundred by 1876. Harsh treatment and insensitive government policies ensured their decline.

Settlers coming to the bay in 1853 valued the timber, newly discovered coal, and abundant fish and wildlife. There was little to prevent newcomers from claiming the land as their own. The takeover was aided in 1856 when the United States military, fearing the Coos would join the tribes engaged in the Rogue River War to the south, preemptively rounded up most of the tribe, moving them north to Fort Umpqua and onto a coastal reservation at Yachats. Coos women married to settlers were allowed to remain. Some men fled to the woods or were hidden by those in sympathy. After 1875, when the reservation closed, many surviving Coos returned to the bay area.

Asa Meade Simpson, a Maine shipbuilder, came west in 1850 for the California Gold Rush. He saw Coos Bay in 1855 and determined to build a sawmill and shipyard. In 1856, he sent a cousin, Alf Pennell, to scout a site. F. G. Lockhart's land claim passed through Frank Wilcox to the Aiken brothers, Glen and John. They sold the land at the north bend of the bay to Pennell (for Simpson) for $300. Simpson sent sawmill equipment. Soon a company town, North Bend, grew. Some Coos found employment at Simpson's sawmill and shipyard. Others worked side by side with European Americans in the lumber camps felling trees for the Simpson and Luse (Empire City) sawmills.

In 1899, Louis Jerome Simpson, Asa's firstborn, came to North Bend to work at his father's mill. He quickly became manager. While Asa was satisfied with a small company town, Louis had larger ambitions. He envisioned a new San Francisco around Coos Bay. He purchased "Yarrow," a platted town site just south of his father's land. In 1903, he incorporated Yarrow with his father's company town as the new City of North Bend. Many remarkable people came to help build the new city. Porter, farther south on Coos Bay, joined the new community.

The town grew quickly, real estate speculation ran rife, and rumors of a coming railway—spurred by Lorenzo Dow Kinney—fed the fury. Young Simpson became mayor, serving from 1903 until 1915. Beyond North Bend, L. J. Simpson purchased land along the coastal bluffs and built a large home there as a gift to his wife, Cassie. She named the property Shore Acres (today a state park and botanical garden).

The pulse of the new City of North Bend, born in 1903, quickened and then slowed. Four remarkable boom years were followed by five years of stagnation. The slowdown was largely the result of the national Panic of 1907. Furthermore, the area was resource dependent and its well-being hinged on the fluctuating demand for and price of timber and its products. The economic swings between affluence and adversity continued into the decade that brought the country into World War I.

Fires were a substantial threat to a town built of wood. Major destruction came in August 1908 when the Woolen Mill burned, in April 1909 when the waterfront warehouse was consumed, in July 1910 when the Coast House hotel burned, and in January 1911 when the Hotel North Bend and its Annex were engulfed in flames. Building fires and brush blazes regularly kept North Bend firemen engaged. Indeed, in 1919 the volunteer firemen threatened, then disbanded, until the North Bend City Council authorized a modern fire truck.

Asa Meade Simpson died in January 1915. Within a year, the Simpson Lumber Company's Porter Mill, timberlands, and other North Bend holdings were sold to Philip Buehner and Son. Other Simpson property, particularly real estate, was retained by the family-controlled Simpson Estate Company.

The August 1916 completion of the rail link between the bay area and Eugene was a notable event. The well-celebrated occasion marked the area's integration with Oregon and its decreasing orientation to San Francisco. Rail service was, however, a latecomer to the area. By 1916, the use of autos had expanded, organized groups lobbied for more and better roads, and as early as 1912, bay residents saw their first airplane.

The United States entry into the World War in 1917 gave the region a temporary boost with full employment. The United States Emergency Shipping Board, for example, contracted with Kruse and Banks' shipyard to build a number of large wooden vessels for its fleet. The yard's workforce expanded to about 650 men, becoming one of the county's largest employers. War's end in November 1918 brought retrenchment. In 1919 the shipyard cut back to 150 workers.

The peacetime readjustment period was also the time of a worldwide influenza epidemic. From 1918 to 1920, many area residents succumbed to the flu or its deadly complication, pneumonia. (Influenza returned in 1927 and again caused serious problems on the bay.)

Settlement of the L. D. Kinney land claims cleared expansion to the south. The Simpson Estate Company's sale of some lots to William R. Robertson (Robertson Land Company) allowed growth north in Simpson Heights. These were milestones in the city's growth.

By 1920, North Bend entered a new period of downtown construction and business vitality. In 1922–1923 all business fronts were occupied. Principal "fireproof" concrete construction included the Hotel North Bend, Independent Order of Odd Fellows building, Liberty Theater, American Legion Hall, Cutlip building, and Roosevelt School.

Early in 1924, all city streets were signed and houses numbered in preparation for the free home postal delivery service scheduled for October.

Peter Loggie, Henry Kern, Fred Hollister, Fred Magnusson, Dr. Philip Keizer, John Greves, Vern Gorst, Robert Banks, Henry Burmester, M. Sayle Taylor, and Lyle Chappell were some who played leading roles in civic life during the 1920s. Their work with the city council, North Bend Chamber of Commerce, hospital, schools, and fraternal groups helped North Bend develop.

Prohibition came to Oregon in 1915. A sizeable North Bend group opposed it. Selling liquor was illegal but personal possession was not. The law was widely flouted in Coos County. The day before Oregon's law took effect, Edgar McDaniel, editor of the *Coos Bay Harbor* (North Bend's weekly newspaper), made the rounds of the saloons collecting his printing bills. Booze sold at half price, so McDaniel took wagonloads of "in kind" payment back to the large basement under his printing office. Years later, whenever the "Do It While Living Club" gathered for cards and conversation in the printing office back room, McDaniel furnished the liquid refreshment. The McDaniel family, like many others in town, made their own home brewed beer. They produced five gallons a week, bottled by the quart—bottle caps being the most costly part of the process.

National Prohibition, 1920–1933, reinforced the demand for forbidden products delivered by boat from Canada or by car or truck from private South Slough stills. Bellhops at the Hotel North Bend knew where to find liquor for hotel guests and furnished information on the local bordellos as well. "The Sheridan Rooms," 1840 Sheridan, were especially notorious. Certain float houses, tied to the Montana Street Bridge and at the foot of Washington Avenue, were also suspect.

Garages and gas stations, fueling the spread of the auto, commanded more and more business locations in the 1920s, 1930s, and into the 1940s; for example, Gurnea's on the northeast corner of Sherman and Washington, and Sunrise on the northwest corner of Sheridan and Washington. Later, the northwest corner of Sherman and Washington, now a city parking lot, hosted a Mobil station. Gilmore Gas was first located at Union and Virginia in 1935.

North Bend's good times ended with the February 1926 fire that destroyed Stout Mill A (formerly the Porter mill). Immediately, several hundred men were out of work and the economic consequences rippled through the community. In July, the Stout Company also closed Mill B, a result of the lumber market decline. A local recession was underway, one that would deepen and lengthen with the 1929 stock market crash and the national Great Depression of the 1930s.

The First National Bank of North Bend closed, in order to prevent failure, well before the national "bank holiday." It held many mortgages and other loans on which payments were not being made. With the bank closed, and many people hoarding money, including gold and silver coins, local businessmen had the city council do what other communities across the land were doing—issue emergency money.

Depression scrip, like North Bend's 1933 "myrtlewood money" (denominations printed on circular blanks of myrtlewood), were used in communities as ready cash. While unconstitutional (only the U.S. Congress can authorize the printing of money), the need was such that no one cared about technicalities. The *Harbor* in March 1932 ran a notice that Tenino, Washington, was using wooden money. That probably inspired Mayor Edgar McDaniel to champion the idea. Local businesses ran ads declaring that "myrtlewood money is good money." They would accept it and use it. The City of North Bend stood behind the issue and would still redeem any pieces returned to it today.

Local scrip, though useful, did not prevent the crippling losses caused by the Depression. The newspapers of the 1930s were filled with lists of property that Coos County seized from owners whose taxes were too far in arrears. Indeed, the county made 1933 property tax free to lessen the taxpayer's burden. As unemployment grew, so did crime such as theft. At its worst time, North Bend let the streetlights go dark because the city could not afford electricity. Yet even in the gloomiest years, there was an occasional flicker of hope, like the pilchard fishing boom in the mid-1930s.

Recovery from the Depression came in fits and starts. The Works Progress Administration offered employment and a flow of money to communities by funding projects that helped restore commercial life. Along the Oregon coast, five major bridges were built. The largest and most impressive, the bridge over Coos Bay, was completed in 1936. This bridge permitted the retirement of the ferries used to connect the Roosevelt Highway (U.S. Highway 101) between North Bend and Glasgow. North Bend City Hall also benefited from federal public works funds. Yet another project, an outgrowth of the 1930s, was the airport at North Bend. In 1942, the navy took over the facility for wartime use and made many improvements before returning it to the city postwar.

During the 1919–1941 period, North Bend prospered, faltered, and with federal assistance, recovered. Her citizens rebuilt her commercial center and kept faith with the city despite numerous setbacks. The next generation enjoyed great prosperity and growth.

A recurring local political issue came to a head during the Second World War. For years area leaders had discussed consolidating all the small towns around Coos Bay into one city. By general understanding, the title City of Coos Bay was reserved for that union, and not to be taken by any until all joined. In 1943, an election was held to consolidate North Bend and Marshfield—the latter the largest community on the bay. Benders overwhelmingly rejected the notion, by almost 10 to 1. Marshfield approved. However, majorities of each community had to approve before consolidation could occur. After this rejection, consolidation leaders in Marshfield secured their electorate's approval to rename Marshfield as Coos Bay. While other elections have been held—several very close in the 1960s—more recent elections in 1983 and 2004 found North Bend citizens generally 70 percent in favor of retaining their independence.

After wartime prosperity, North Bend's waterfront U.S. Highway 101 connection with the new City of Coos Bay was made a four-lane highway. Weyerhaeuser built a large sawmill south of the old Porter Mill and the economy flourished. The 1950s were mostly very good years. Sam Choat constructed the Skyline Apartments along south Sherman Avenue. Oregon Homes developed the Airport Heights area. Edgewood Terrace, adjacent to Newmark Street, came later. In the 1970s prosperity meant new construction in places all around North Bend.

With the creation of Pony Village Mall by Walt Kraus in 1960, downtown North Bend began a decline. The Hotel North Bend closed, renting only its Sherman Avenue storefronts. Other locations on Sherman and Union became vacant, some derelict. Buildings were torn down, especially in the 1960s when no preservationist movement existed. Even today, there are wooden structures downtown whose useful life cannot be cost-effectively salvaged. Yet developers like Wayne Schrunk and the Umpqua Community Development Corporation have each brought older buildings back to life.

Community pride expressed itself in an indoor swimming pool built in 1957 (substantially refurbished in 2009), and the fire hall finished in 1965. The former International Woodworkers of America union hall, completed in 1966, became the new community center in June 1991. Other improvements included a new public library built in 1989, the high school athletic field (improved with a large private donation for new grandstands, scoreboard, etc.), the City Hall reconfiguration improving police facilities, and the recent waterfront improvements including a boardwalk finished in June 2010.

Citizens of all ethnic origins, from the Coos tribal members whose ancestors first peopled this area, to more recent Hispanic immigrants, have a part to play in preserving the area's heritage while improving its physical and economic environment.

Contemporary North Bend, in the words of Mayor Rick Wetherell, is both "a city that works" and "a city that believes in itself." His motto is "TGWB"—"Thank Goodness We're Benders." Its citizens strive to achieve a good life harmonizing the balance in nature practiced by the earliest Coos people with the developmental goals promoted by L. J. Simpson, founder of the city.

One

The Coos Endure

Descendants of the first people had mostly peaceful contact with the traders and travelers visiting the bay area. In 1852, the Coos aided those stranded by the *Captain Lincoln* shipwreck and in 1853 tolerated settlers from Jacksonville who established Empire City among their villages. One exception was the Lockhart family—the first to take Coos land that became North Bend. The unwelcome Lockharts returned to Empire.

Attempting to open Native American lands for settlement without hostilities, the federal government negotiated the 1855 Empire Treaty with many coastal tribes. Treaty provisions allowed Indian land rights to be "extinguished" in exchange for compensation. The U.S. Senate never ratified the treaty. Newcomers took the land anyway.

In 1855–1856, the Rogue River War to the south pitted vindictive miners and Oregon Volunteers bent on extermination against Indian people. The Coos were not involved, but the United States Army rounded up a majority of the tribe and held them in a camp near Empire City. In the summer of 1856, they moved to Fort Umpqua and were eventually marched to confinement at Yachats.

Years of deprivation followed. Inadequate food, poor shelter, disease, and lack of medical care weakened their bodies and brought early death for many. Separation from their homes and sacred places eroded spirits. When the reservation closed in the mid-1870s many returned to the bay, especially South Slough.

Returnees had little money or land and faced restrictions on traditional hunting and fishing practices. Some women married white men or worked in white households. Men worked in the woods or found jobs in sawmills and shipyards.

Despite all the hardships, the tribe's quest to have promises honored continued. In 1916, the Coos confederated with the Lower Umpqua and Siuslaw Indians to strengthen their struggle for redress.

Over generations, in the face of a prolonged 1930s court case and disheartening turns in federal policy such as termination of tribal status, tribal leaders like Russell Anderson of North Bend kept alive the fight for recognition and land claims.

In 1984, Congress restored tribal status to the Confederated Tribes of the Coos, Lower Umpqua and Siuslaw Indians. Since restoration, the Confederated Tribes have focused on improving the lives of their people and recapturing their history and culture.

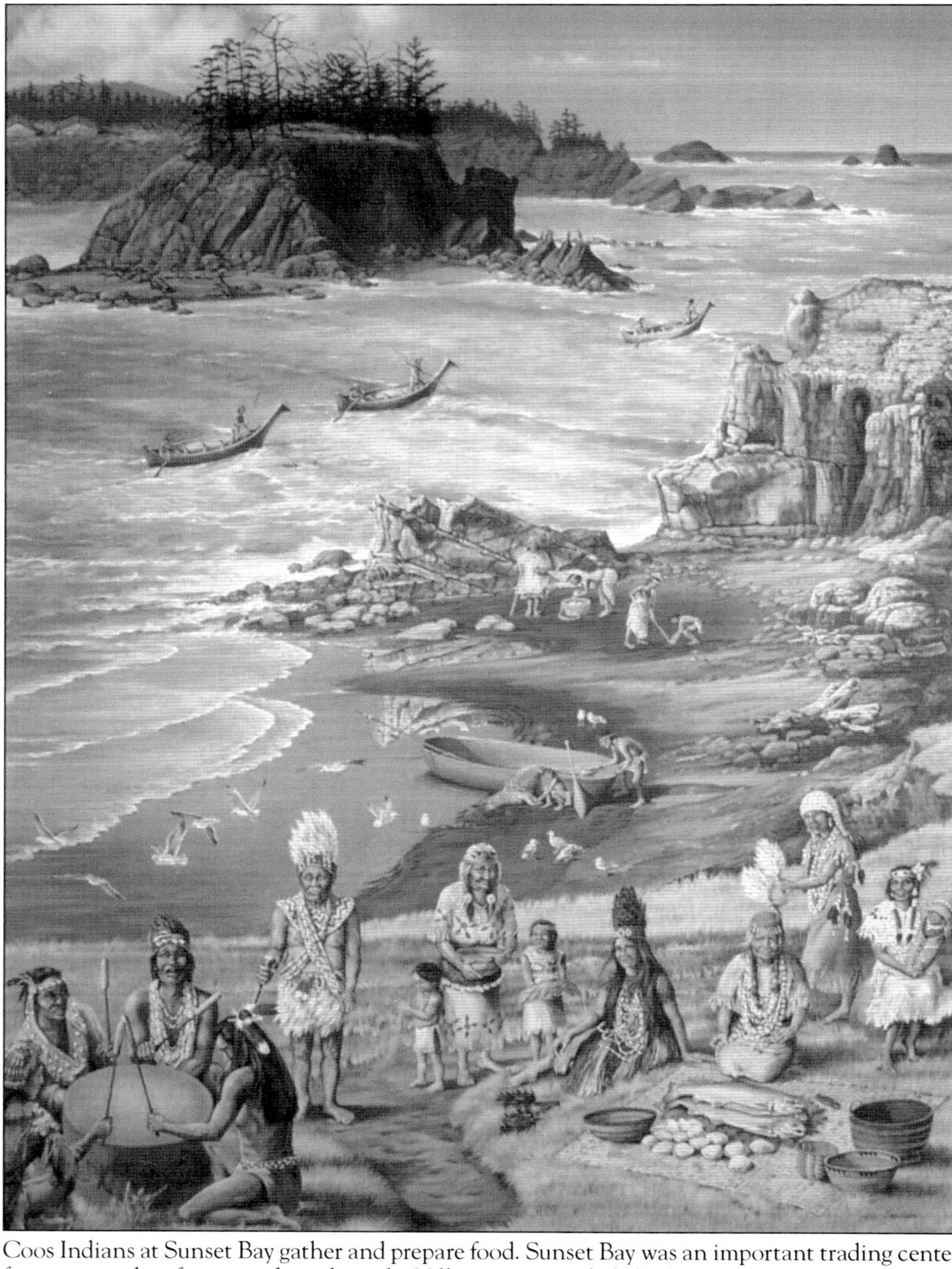

Coos Indians at Sunset Bay gather and prepare food. Sunset Bay was an important trading center for native tribes from north and south. Villages surrounded the bay and were located up Big Creek. Deerhead canoes for fishing and transportation are shown in the water. Two traditional plankhouses are at top left. Confederated Tribes member Pam Stoeshler painted the original full color historical representation on display at tribal headquarters. (Confederated Tribes.)

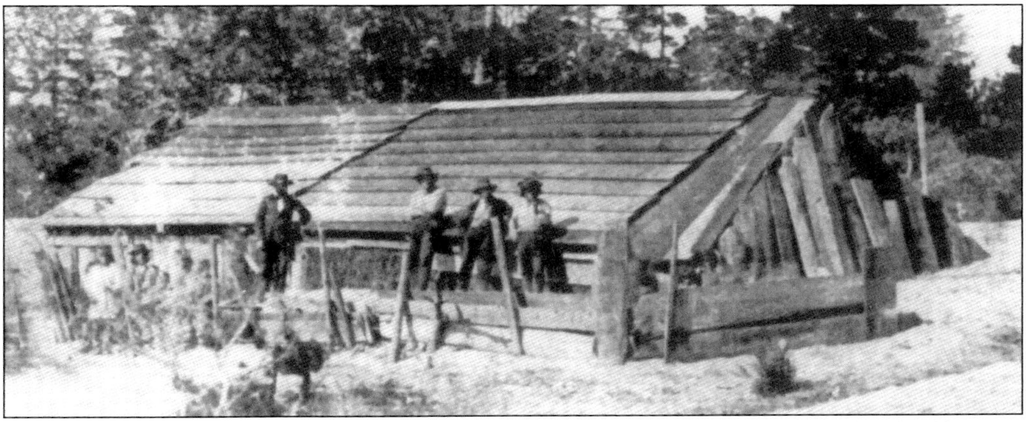

Coos Indians dug down several feet to construct subterranean hand-split red cedar plankhouses. (Horizontal planking is unique to our area.) The roof had a hole (with rain cover) for venting cooking fire smoke. Dirt floors were covered with tule reed or other matting. Both Coos and Lower Umpqua peoples occupied this 1856–1859-era Fort Umpqua plankhouse, built with sawed lumber, during confinement. (Confederated Tribes.)

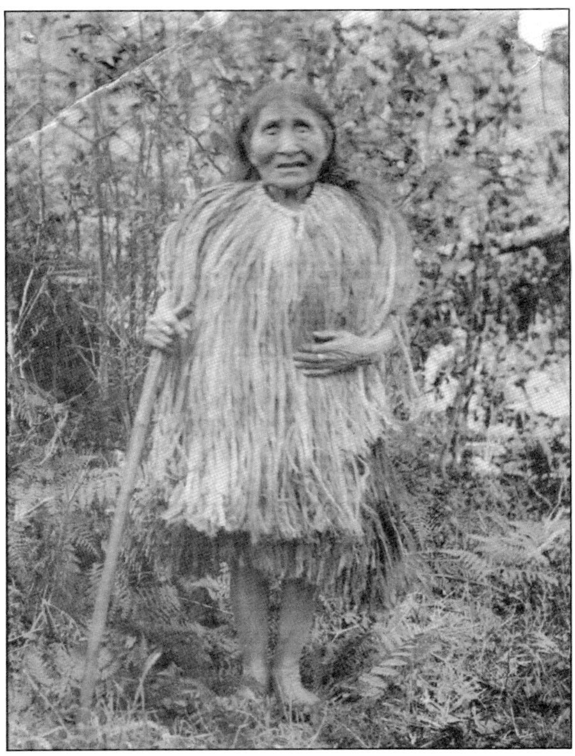

A Coos woman, "Old Kate," wears a traditional winter garment with cedar clasp. The cape and fringed cedar bark skirt is waterproof and comfortable. The inner surface of peeled cedar bark is smooth and silky to the touch. Bark was stripped from cedar trees only in the spring when it peeled easily. Traditional Coos society was matriarchal, with lineage coming through the ancestry of the mother, rather than the father. (CHMM 959-246n.)

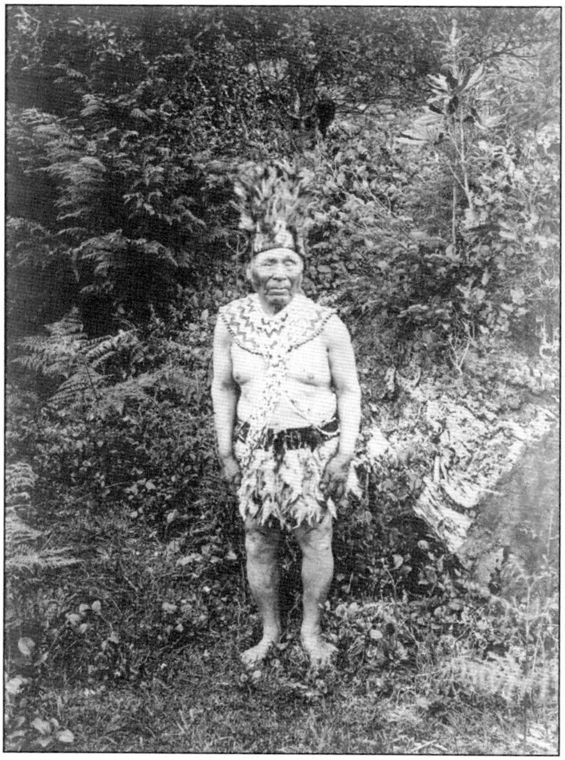

Chief Doloose Jackson, the last hereditary Coos chief, wears a woodpecker scalp headdress, shell ornaments, and a man's beaded and feathered apron. In later years he was a familiar figure in North Bend, dressed in a bowler hat, vest, coat, and pants typical of the time. At his death in January 1907, the Simpson Lumber Company purchased a lot for his burial in Marshfield's cemetery. (CHMM 975-73La.)

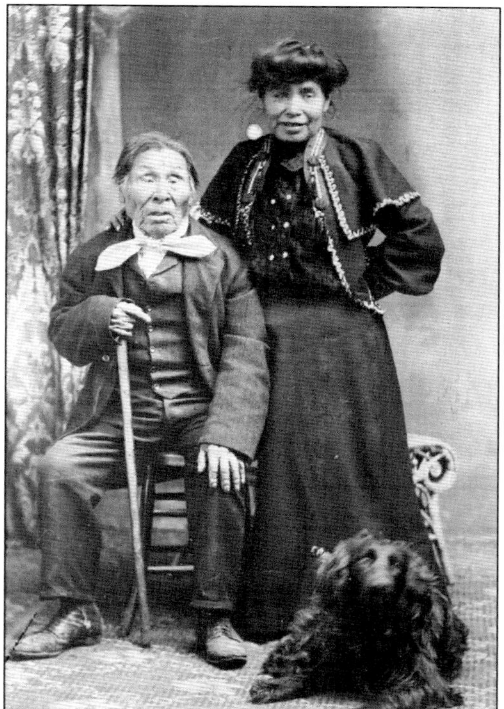

Coos Chief Doloose Jackson (born about 1843 at Hanistitch village—Empire today) poses with daughter, Lottie Evanoff, about 1905. Her grandfathers were chiefs—both murdered over the issue of friendship with whites. She, a child of the Yachats' reservation, in later years provided researchers with stories of family relationships as well as matters of everyday life including gathering plants and berries and drying salt and seafood. (CHMM 992-8-3153.)

Annie Miner Peterson (c. 1860–1939), a strong and resourceful woman, spoke both Coos languages—Hanis and Miluk. She was the last speaker of Miluk. In the 1930s, she shared her knowledge of Coos languages, stories, myths, and history with University of Washington ethnologist Melville Jacobs. Together they preserved her information for future generations. (Her headband is post-1875 Plains Indian influence. The Coos traditionally wore caps.) (CHMM 989-P201.)

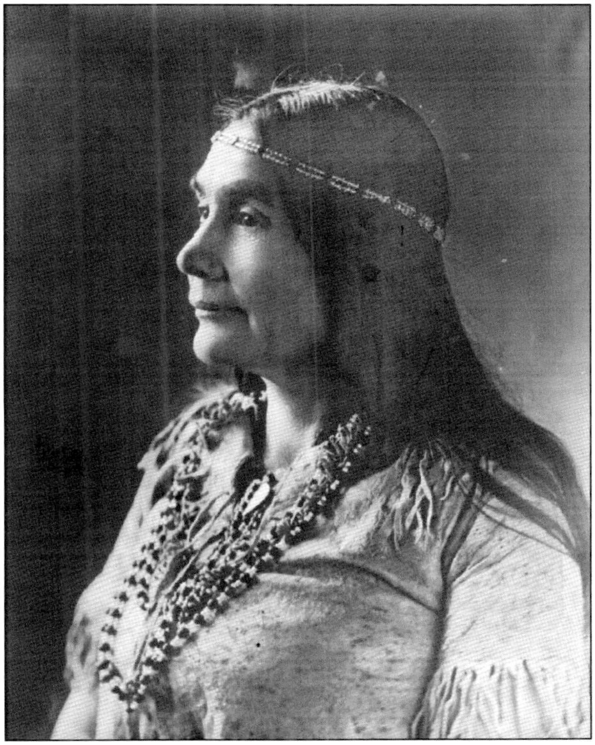

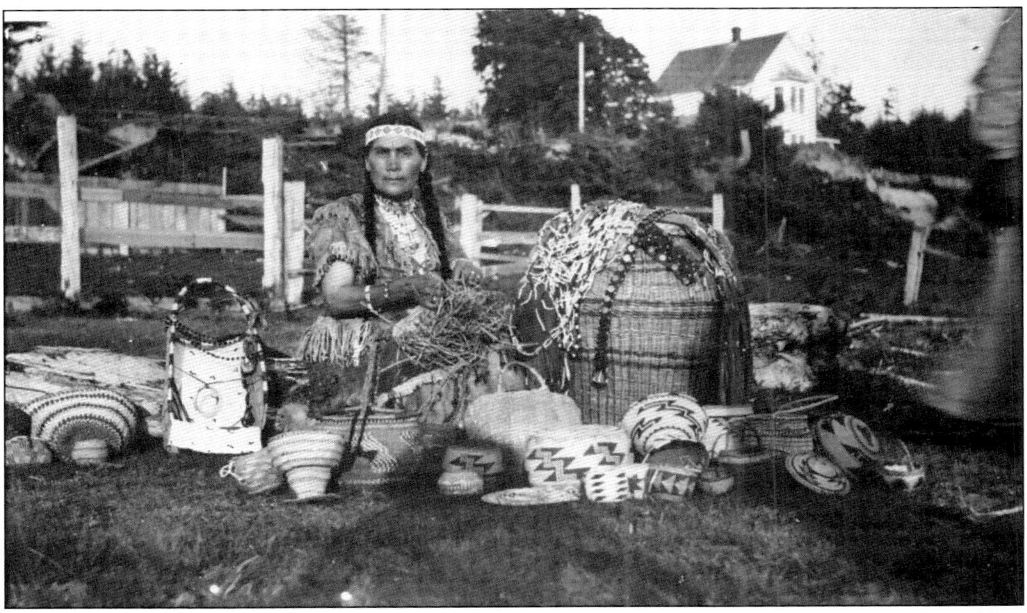

Annie Miner Peterson displays an array of handwoven baskets, beads, and other parts of her collection. She wove some baskets, others were acquired in trade. Basket sales helped her earn money. Strung on the tall basket beside her are many dentalia shells (from Vancouver Island) once used as money. This photograph was taken at Empire in 1914. (CHMM 922-8-3150.)

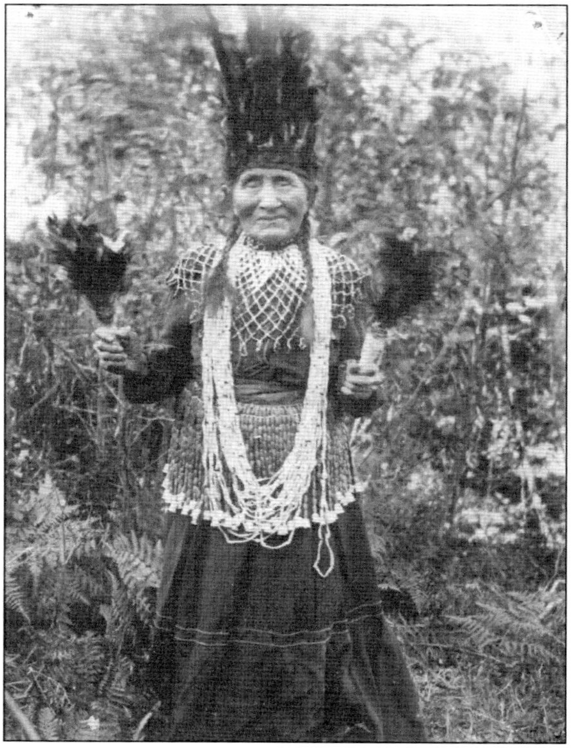

"Old Kate," holding feather dance wands, is pictured wearing strings of dentalia with a beaded collar or cape and a dance apron of pine nut beads and trade thimbles. Her display of dentalia suggests both wealth and privilege. Her skirt is contemporary cloth. (CHMM 995-D184.)

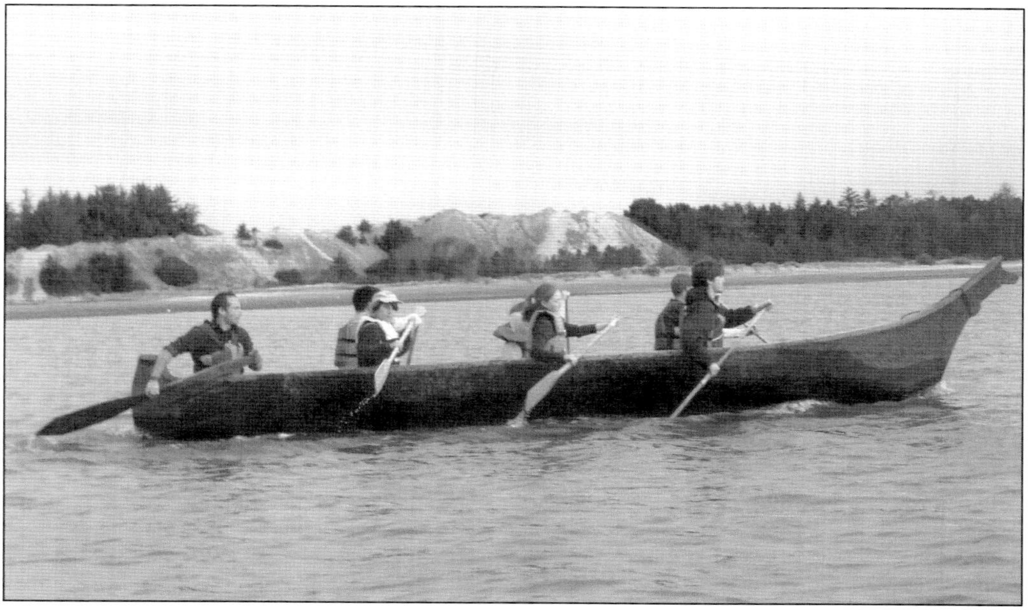

Confederated Tribe members paddle on Coos Bay near Empire in their replica ocean going deerhead canoe. Past Chief David Brainard, using both traditional and modern techniques, crafted this canoe from redwood in 2003. Coos canoes could be California redwood, found on the beaches, or local cedar. Today Confederated Tribe members regularly meet other tribal groups for various competitive events. (Confederated Tribes.)

Two

Asa Simpson's Company Town

Captain Asa Meade Simpson purchased land on the north bend of the bay from Glen Aiken in 1855. Simpson built and began operating a sawmill in 1856—the second on the bay—and soon added a shipyard.

Simpson saw the plentiful supply of coal found in the region in the early 1850s. He needed a sawmill to provide the deck loads of lumber necessary for shipping coal. His shipyard built the vessels to carry the product; his tugs provided escort over the bar. Simpson was not interested in development beyond his company's settlement. His North Bend consisted of the mill, shipyard, worker housing, cookhouse, company store, miscellaneous outbuildings, and later a schoolhouse. Supplied with local fish, game, and produce as well as goods shipped in, its inhabitants were self-sufficient.

In 1860, Simpson hired Charles Merchant to manage the company store. Merchant refused the job unless alcohol was banned from sale. Simpson agreed, approving the result. In consequence, thirsty millworkers had to walk the county road—the sawmill trail—to Empire City saloons.

Coal waned and timber's importance grew but the extraction of natural resources to fulfill company contracts servicing Simpson retail businesses in San Francisco, Sacramento, and Stockton remained the reason for North Bend's existence. Her orientation was seaward and the strongest ties were to San Francisco, Captain Simpson's home base. Primary transportation was by sailing ship and later by steamer.

Around 1889, Thomas and Leticia Symons purchased adjacent property south of Simpson's North Bend from Charles Eckhoff. (Thomas D. Winchester acquired the land from the government in 1863. Winchester sold to Charles Merchant in 1864, who sold to Eckhoff in 1865.) The Symons platted "Yarrow" in 1890, touting it as the "maritime, manufacturing and commercial metropolis of Southern Oregon." Yarrow failed.

In 1899 happenstance set the stage for a dramatic change in North Bend's destiny. The captain's eldest son, 21-year-old Louis Jerome Simpson, newly married and with much to prove, brought his wife, Cassie, to North Bend. Young Simpson's philosophy differed greatly from his father's. Optimistic and expansionist, Louis favored development and diversity.

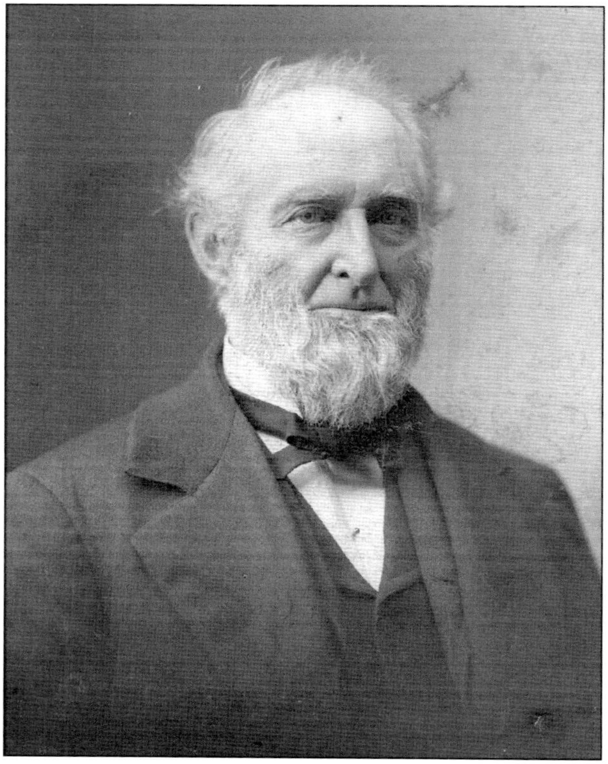

Asa Meade Simpson (1826–1915), a Maine native, came west for California gold. He made his fortune in lumber and ships, buying timber and sawmill sites, constructing mill towns with shipyards at West Coast locations including Hoquiam and South Bend in Washington, and Gardiner and North Bend in Oregon. (CHMM 972-18c.)

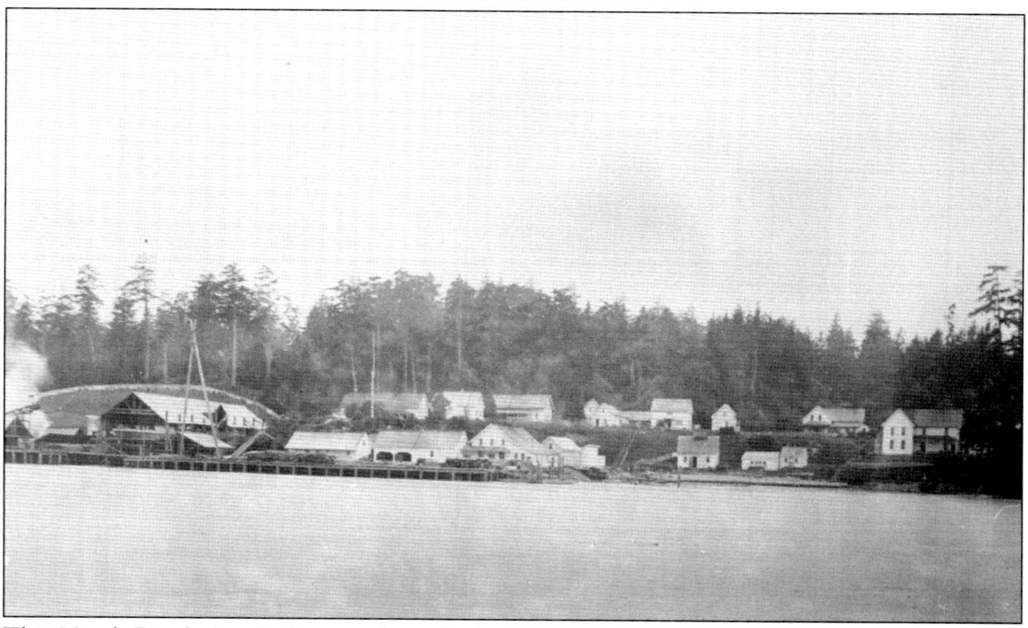

This North Bend view looks west from the bay. The major feature is the covered ship shed on the left. The company store is the last dock building to the right. The larger house on the far right possibly belonged to Captain Robert Simpson, Asa's brother and partner, who represented Simpson Brothers Lumber Company here in the 1870s and 1880s. (CHMM 009-16-1408A.)

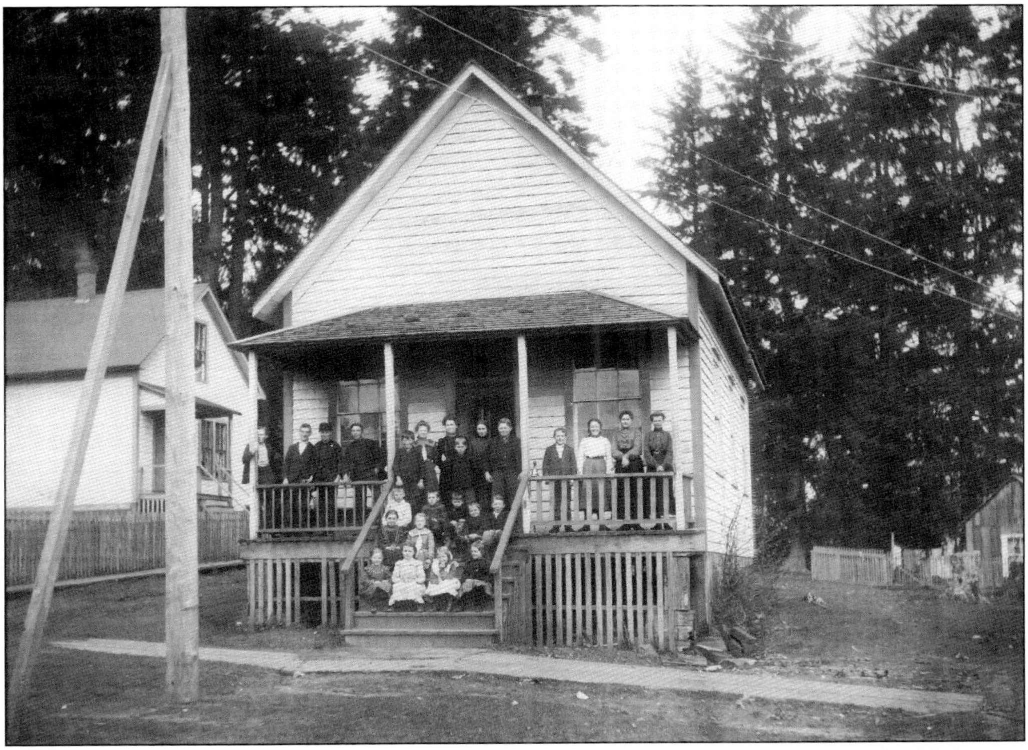

John Kruse built North Bend's schoolhouse in 1862, before Simpson sent him to build ships at Gardiner, Oregon. By 1867, Kruse was back in North Bend. The schoolhouse also was used for community and church functions—the Presbyterians first worshiped here. (CHMM 989-P192.)

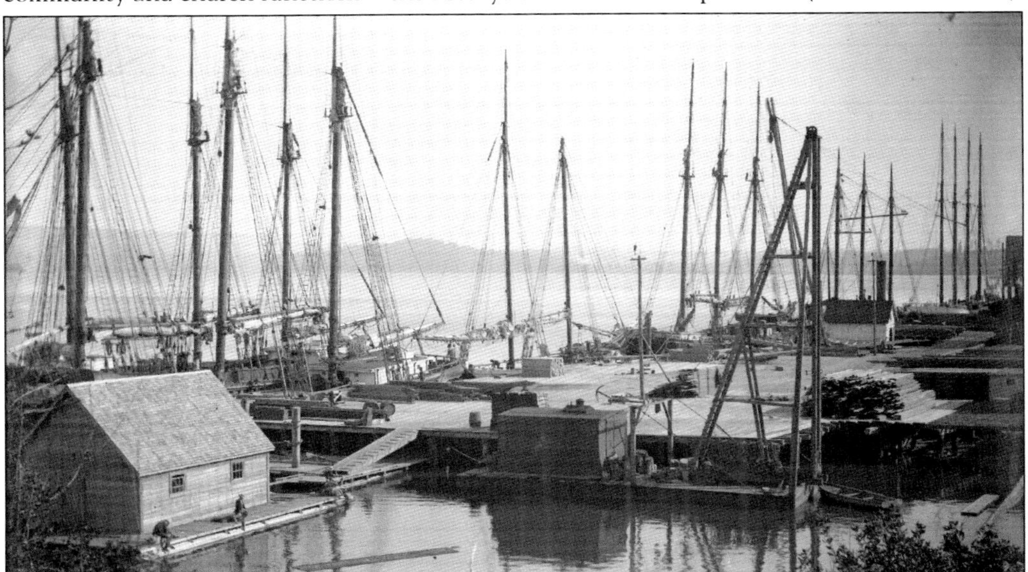

Six ships, including two berthed side by side on the left, make a dramatic company town dock scene. The view looks south. For a sense of scale, note the two men on the small floating house at left. (CHMM 992-8-3553.)

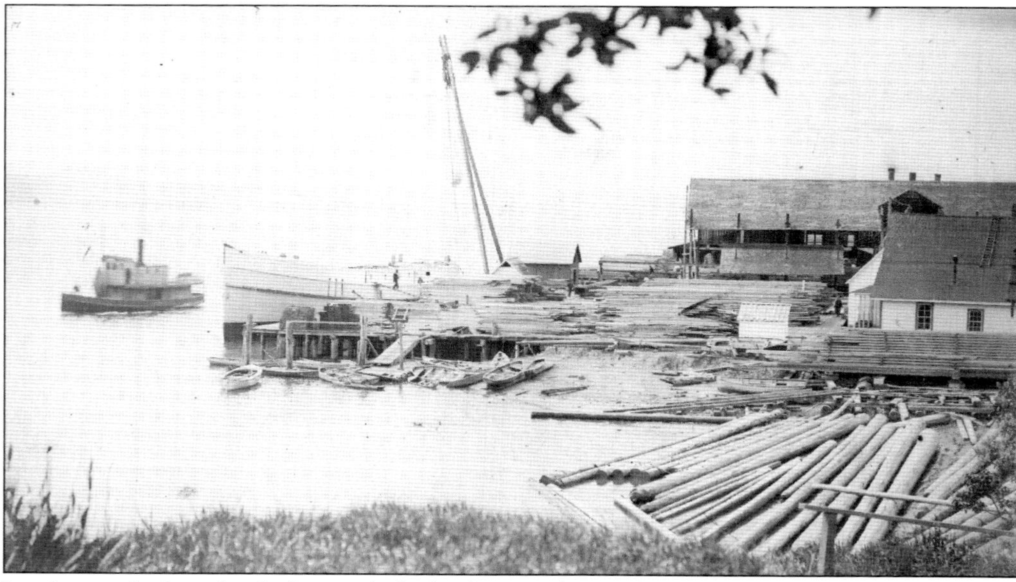

Lumber stacked on the dock is ready for loading on the newly finished (April 1898) steamer *New Brunswick*. Her engine and steam equipment was added when she reached San Francisco. The company store is to the right and the shipway is beyond. (CHMM 998-2.11.)

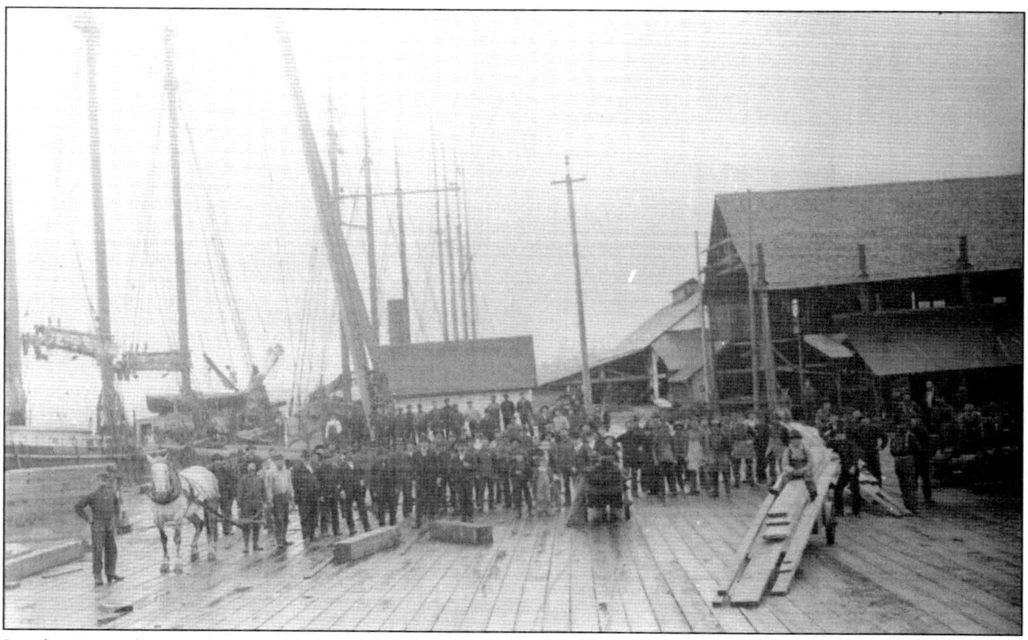

In this North Bend dock scene, around 1900, Old Joe the company workhorse is visible at left. The shipway, an open-sided structure, is in the foreground with the sawmill in the background. The people gathered on the wharf suggest a recent ship launch. (CHMM 009-16-1412.)

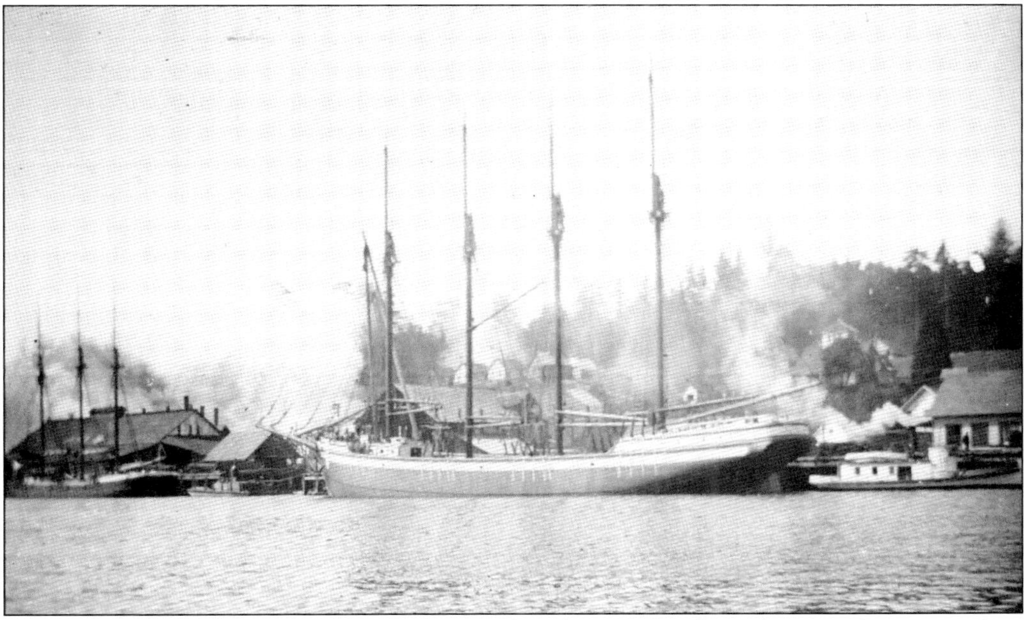

This image shows the four-masted schooner *Admiral*, center, and another vessel awaiting their lumber loads at North Bend. The *Admiral* was started by Emil Heuckendorff and finished by K. V. Kruse in 1899. She was lost in 1912. The sawmill stands at left. (CHMM 009-16.41.)

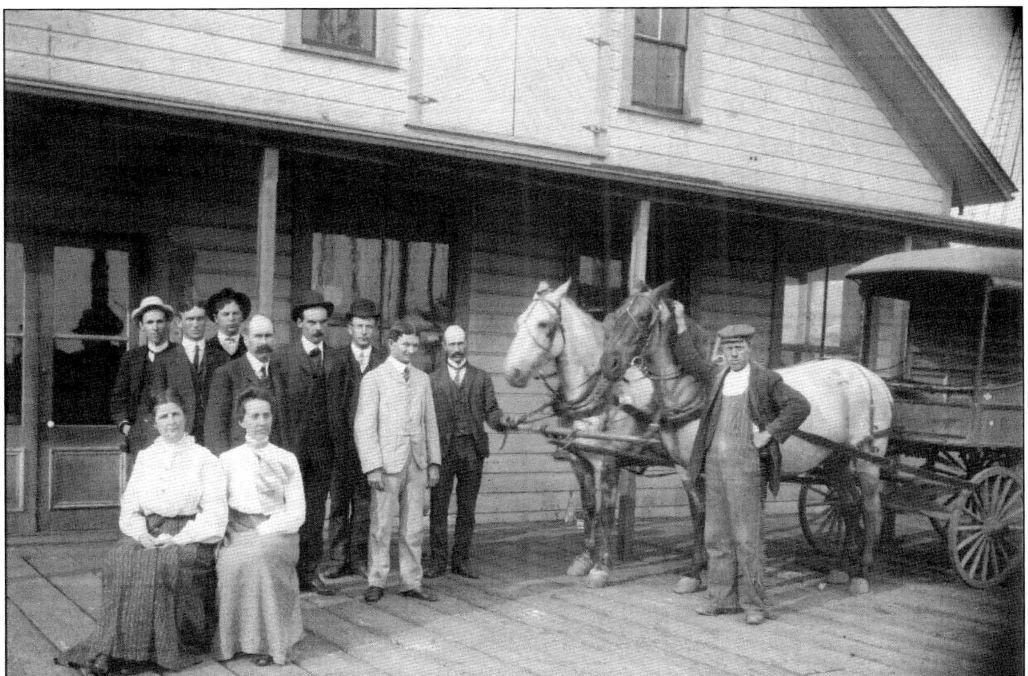

Employees of the Simpson Lumber Company's store are shown in front of their building around 1905. C. M. Byler, store manager and longtime friend of Louis Simpson, holds the reins of a delivery wagon horse. (CHMM 958-568a.)

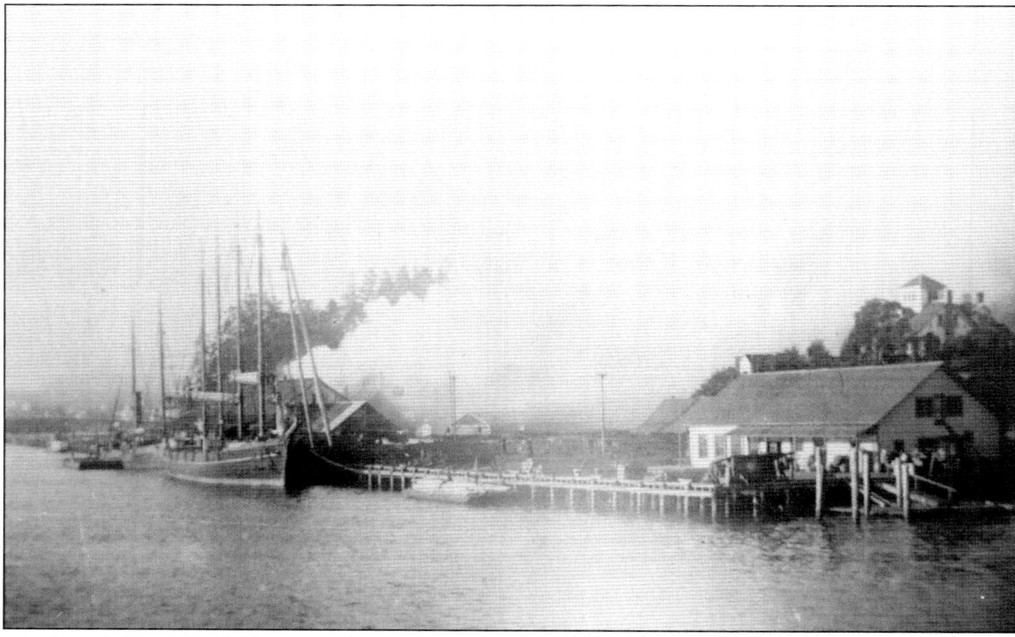

The North Bend dock shows lumber storage where the shipbuilding shed once stood. The shipway was torn down in August 1903. Smoke from the sawmill blows toward workers' housing. The company store is on the right. Above the store is the "cupola house," so called because Louis Simpson added the cupola in 1904 to the house he and his wife, Cassie, occupied. (CHMM 009-16-1412A.)

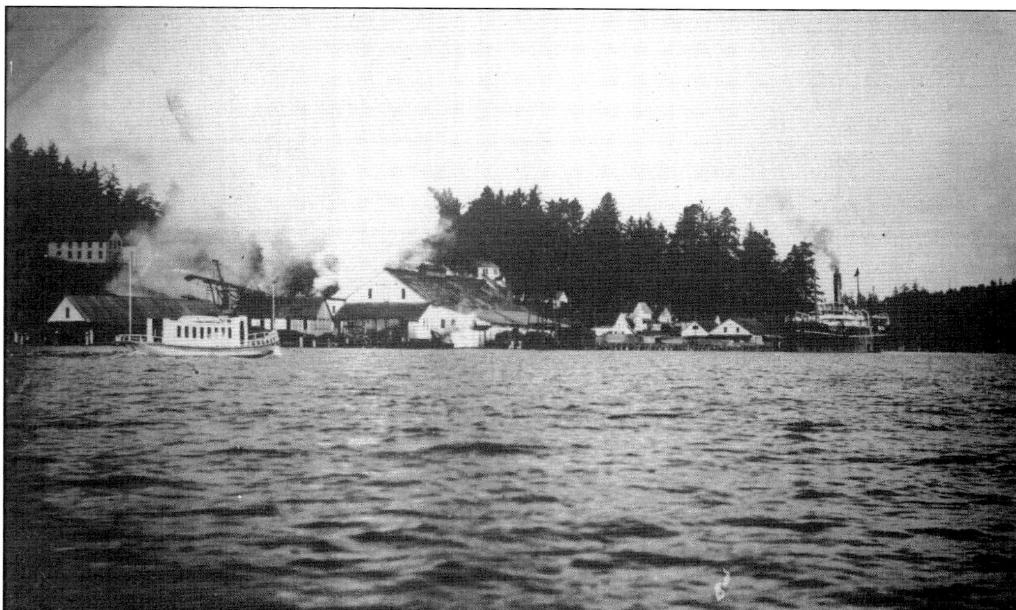

This is a view of "Old Town" around 1910. The City of North Bend is "new town." The launch *Eagle* is on the left, with the sawmill at the center. The company store building is visible on the dock, next to an unidentified steam ship. (CHMM 992-8-0848.)

Three

Simpson Shipyard

Asa Simpson established his North Bend shipyard in 1858, the first on the coast north of San Francisco. Elbridge G. Simpson, Asa's brother from Maine, supervised building the first vessel, *Arago*, a two-mast brigantine. Fifty-five ships followed. Other early builders included T. McDonald (of Hoquiam, Washington fame), W. C. Robinson, and J. H. Howlett.

Shipyards were located adjacent to mills for a ready source of lumber. Skilled craftsmen using hand tools built ships from the bottom up. Keel blocks—on the ways—held the keel, or backbone, of the ship. Frame ribs curved upward from the keel. Frame planks (usually of fir or white cedar) were attached to the ribs both outside and inside. Oakum, a tarry fiber, was pounded between the planking to make the fit watertight. Interior bracing, decking, spars, and rudders as well as masts came before the rigging. Machinery and painting were last.

John Kruse began building ships for Simpson in 1864 at Gardiner, Oregon. In 1867 he came to North Bend where at least 30 ships, including the famous clipper *Western Shore*, are credited to him. Kruse endured because he built ships exactly the way Asa Simpson wanted them. *The Coos Bay News* called his *Dare*, built in 1882, a "naval beauty." Kruse also helped build a schoolhouse that was used for celebrating weddings as well as for entertainment. He built the *Omega* in 1894, supposedly Simpson's last ship, but Simpson changed his mind and in 1895 Kruse began construction of the four-masted barkentine *Addenda*. Illness then forced him to retire. He built more ocean-going vessels than any other Oregon shipbuilder.

The final Simpson ship constructed at the original North Bend shipyard was the *Marconi*, built by Peter Loggie in 1902. The last Simpson ship built at one of its own shipyards was the *Alpha*, finished in 1903 by Emil Heuckendorff on the ways at Porter.

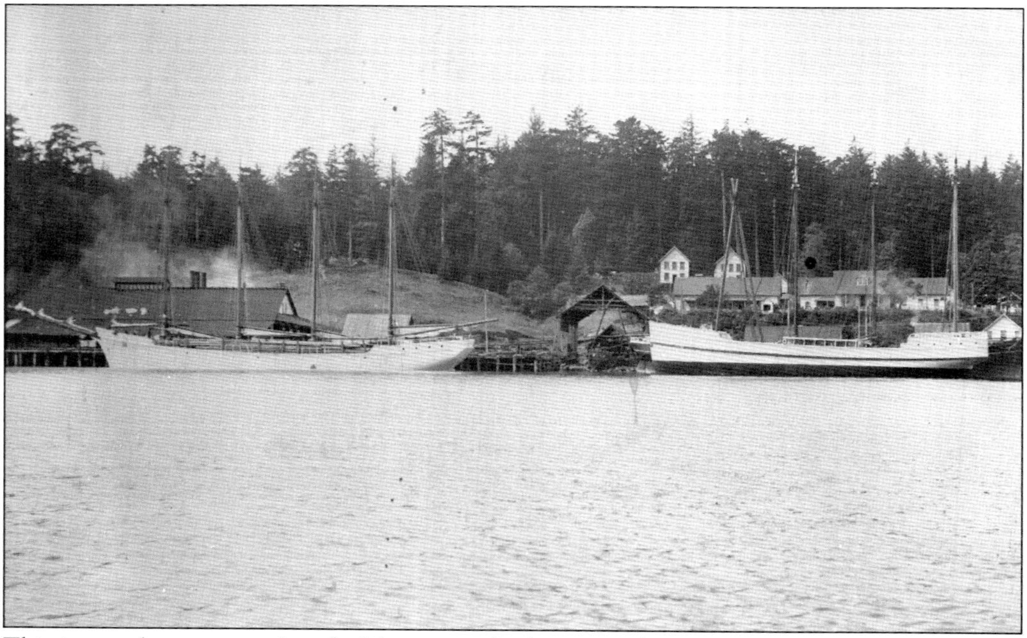

This image shows an unidentified four-masted schooner at left in front of the sawmill, another unidentified vessel under construction on the ways (under the shed), and the hull of the newly constructed steam schooner *Mandalay* at right. The *Mandalay* was launched in April 1900 and was lost at sea in October 1918. (CHMM 992-8-0840.)

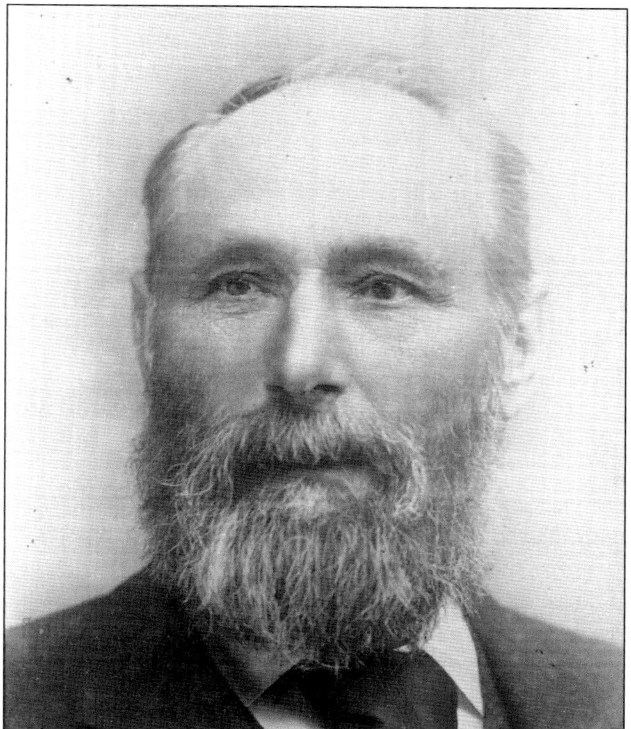

John Kruse (1835–1896) came to America in 1854 from Denmark. He worked for Simpson both at North Bend and Gardiner. He did most of his building at North Bend but while at Gardiner is credited with the *Wm. F. Browne* (1864) and the *Pacific* (1865). Kruse built ships the way Simpson ordered, endured, and became Oregon's most prolific builder of oceangoing vessels. (CHMM 922-8-3131.)

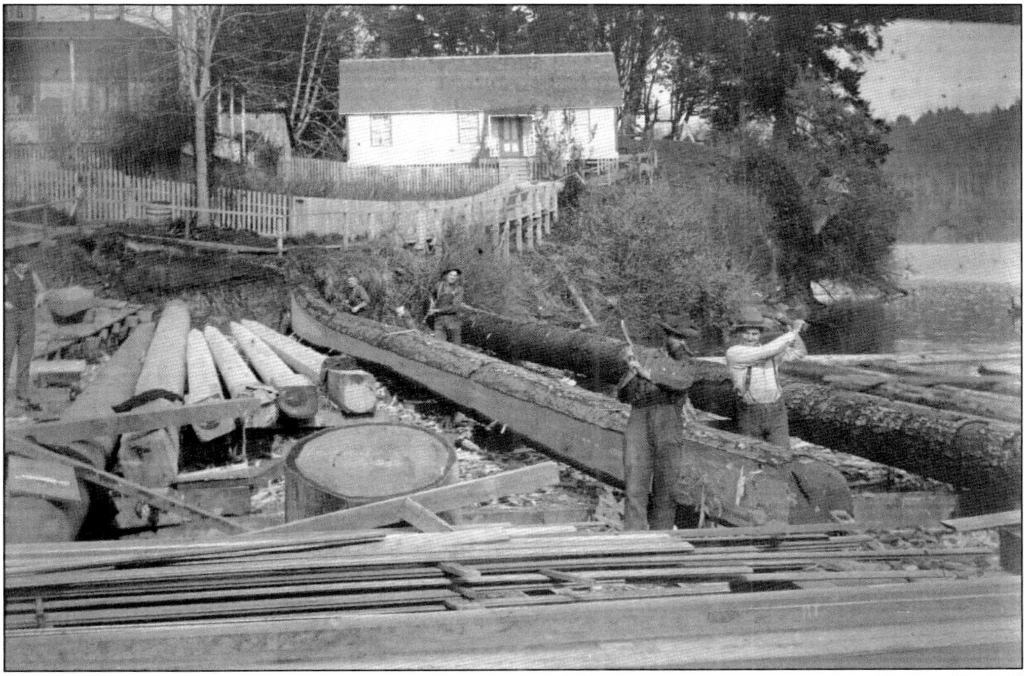

The Simpson spar yard at North Bend, just north of the company store, is viewed here. Skilled axmen hewed out yardarms and spars from timbers. The larger home, upper left, may have been that of Captain Robert Simpson, Asa Simpson's brother. (CHMM 992-8-2588.)

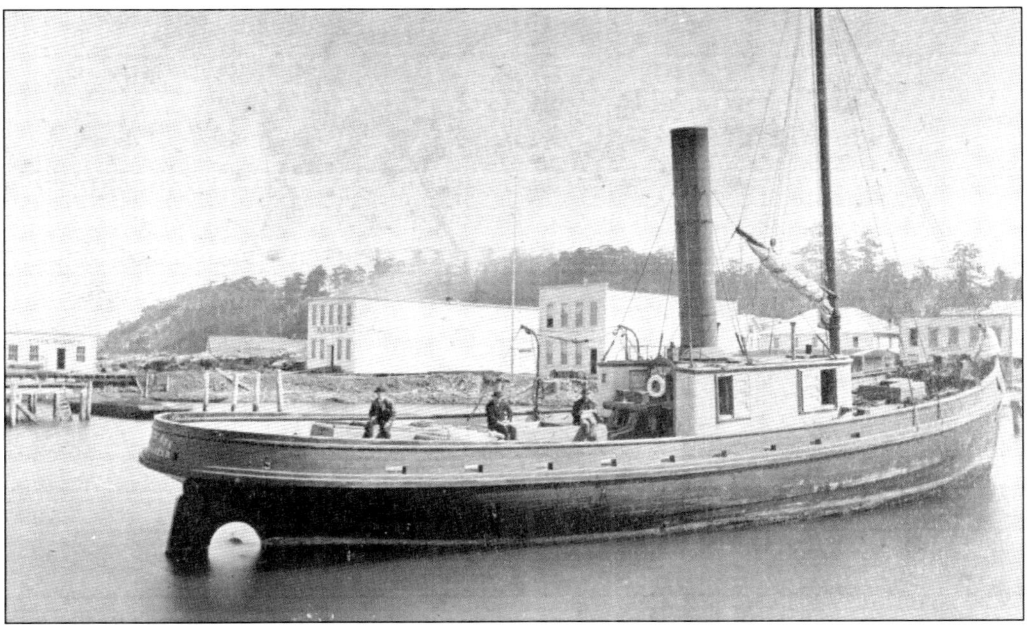

The second tug *Fearless* is docked at Empire City on Coos Bay in 1875. The first *Fearless* was wrecked near present day Charleston in 1873. Simpson Lumber Company used these tugs to move schooners safely in and out over the Coos Bay bar. When not used for North Bend mill purposes, the tugs were rented to other shippers around the bay. (CHMM 992-8-2375.)

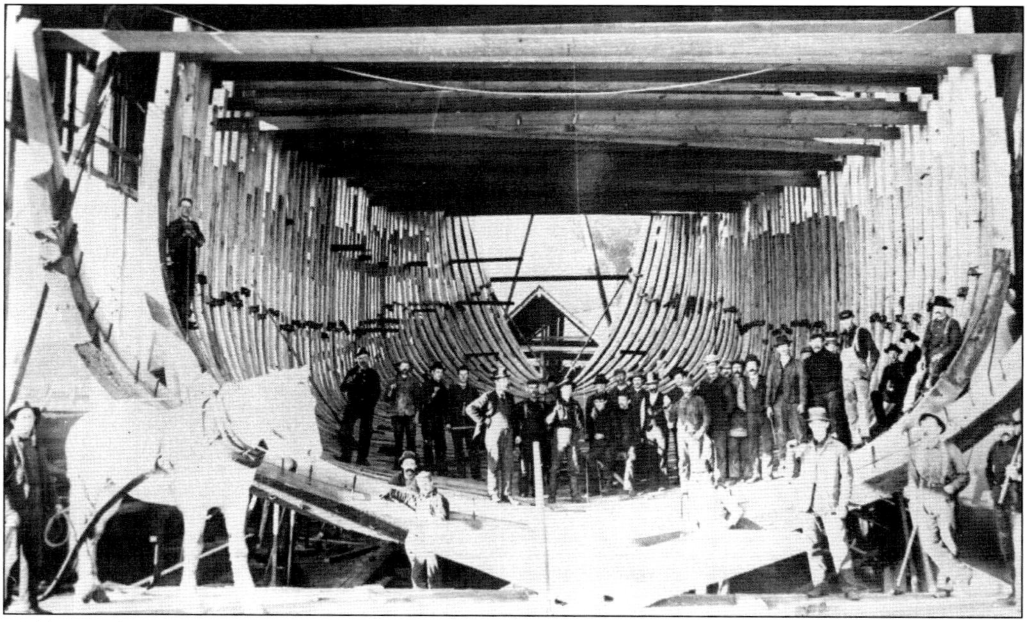

"Old Joe" the company shipyard horse is pictured with Emil Heuckendorff's shipbuilding crew and the ribs of an unidentified ship under construction at the Simpson yard. When the horse died after more than a decade of service, the *Weekly Coast Mail* of April 11, 1903, eulogized the hardworking animal for his "kind and obliging disposition and thorough reliability." (CHMM 009-16.10.)

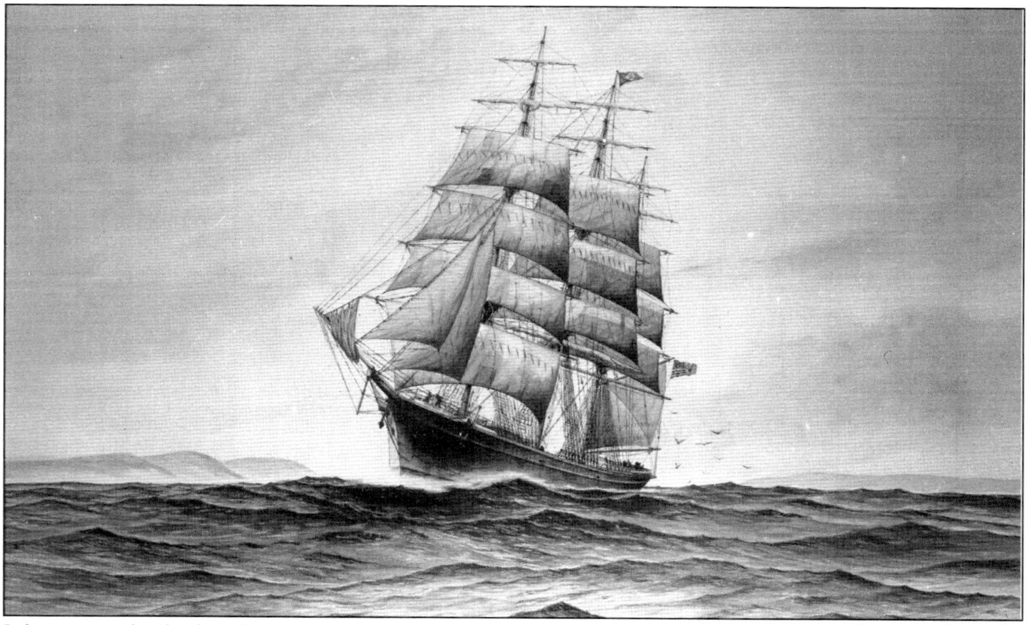

John Kruse built the clipper ship *Western Shore* in 1874. Asa Simpson designed the hull. Robert W. Simpson drew the sail plan. She set speed records from Oregon to Liverpool, England. The Simpson flag, the "Diamond S," floats atop her along with her name pennant. She wrecked in 1878. No photograph of Oregon's only true clipper ship is known. This painting is attributed to W. S. Stephenson. (CHMM 992-8-3039.)

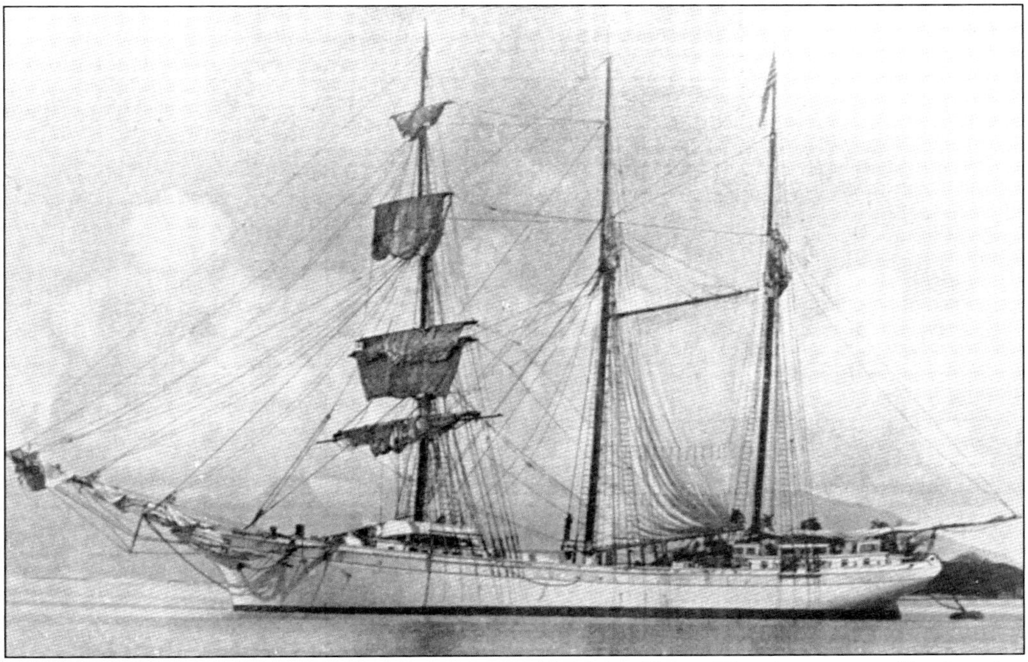

The *Tropic Bird* was built in 1882 by master shipbuilder John Kruse. The three-masted barkentine (347 tons) was constructed for Andrew Crawford. Based in San Francisco, she plied the South Seas carrying cargo and passengers. In Tahiti the vessel was known as "Te Manu"—the bird. She was lost in 1907 off Perula Beach at Chamela Bay, Mexico. Charles Robert Patterson (1878–1958), noted maritime artist, painted her. (CHMM 009.16-11.)

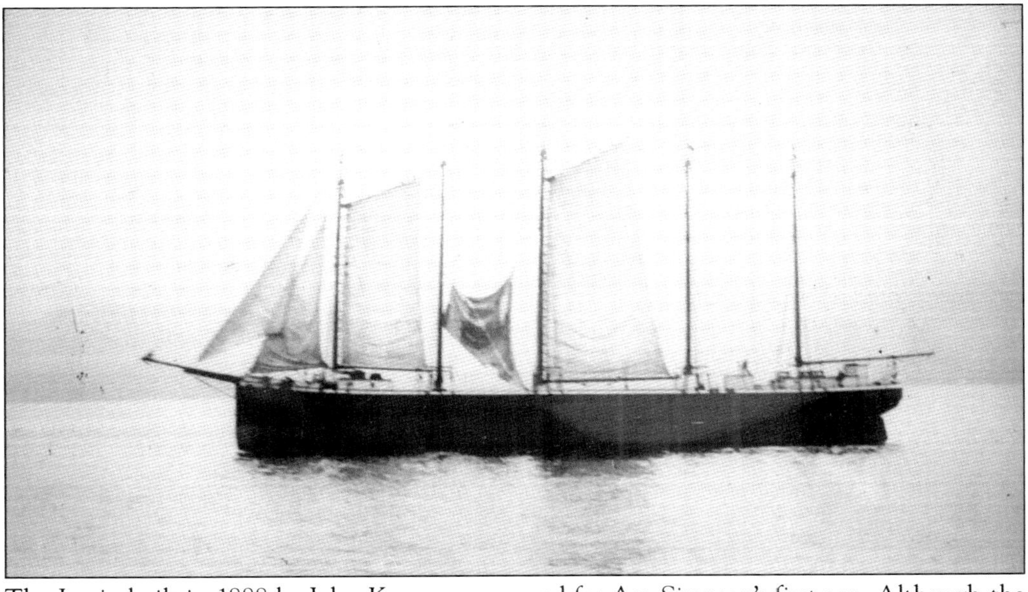

The *Louis*, built in 1888 by John Kruse, was named for Asa Simpson's first son. Although the *Louis* was intended to be a steamer, she was first rigged as a five-masted schooner for use in the Pacific coal trade. Asa kept her rigging and she became the first five-masted American schooner used in salt water. She wrecked in 1907—a bad year for Simpson vessels. (CHMM 009-16.22.)

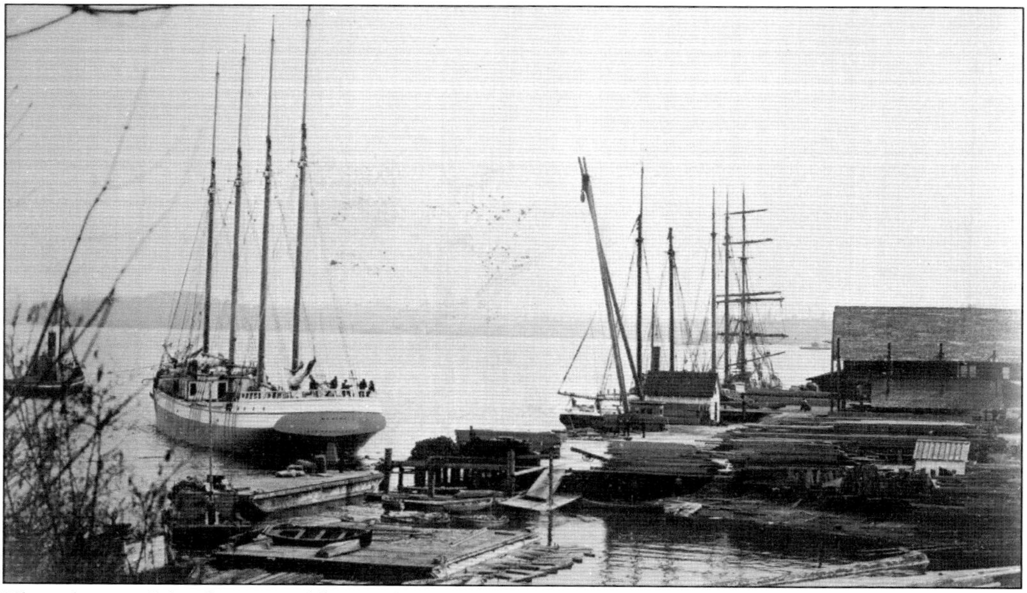

The schooner *Manila* is towed by tug from the Simpson docks. She was built by Emil Heuckendorff and launched on March 1, 1899. Sold in 1916, she was captured and burned in the South Seas by the German raider *Seedler* on July 8, 1917. (CHMM 992-8-0844a.)

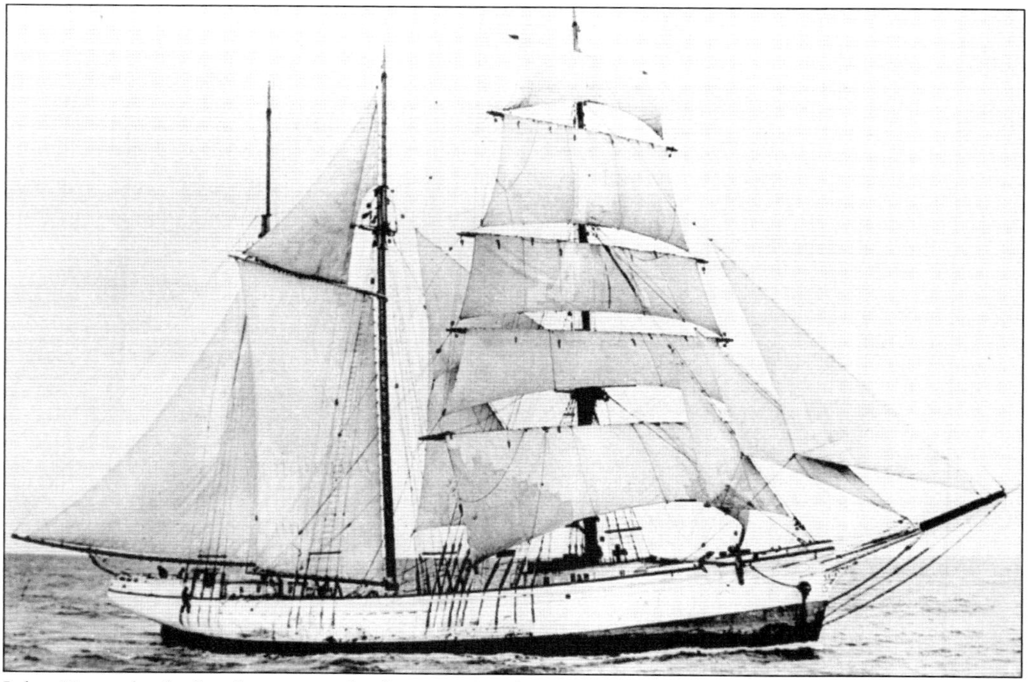

John Kruse built the four-masted schooner *Gardiner City* in 1889. She was re-rigged a few years later as a three-masted barkentine. After being damaged during a 1904 gale at Redondo Beach, California, she was repaired. In 1911, she collided with another ship whose anchor cut every rope on her starboard side, tearing down her masts. She was jury-rigged and went to San Francisco, never to sail again. (CHMM 009-16.24.)

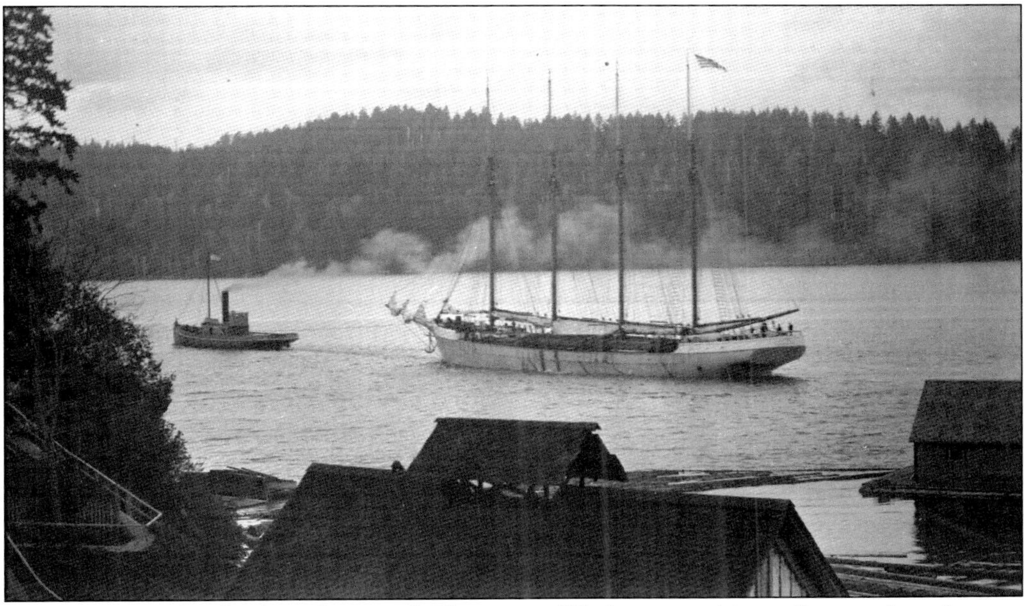

The tug *Columbia* (built at Simpson's Knappton, Washington shipyard) tows the schooner *Churchill*—loaded with lumber for Australia—away from North Bend. Built by Victor Anderson, the *Churchill* was launched on March 4, 1900. In 1917, she stranded on French Frigate Shoal, northwest of Hawaii. Her crew of 14 was rescued. (The distinctive roof of the blacksmith shop is visible in the foreground.) (CHMM 992-8-0853.)

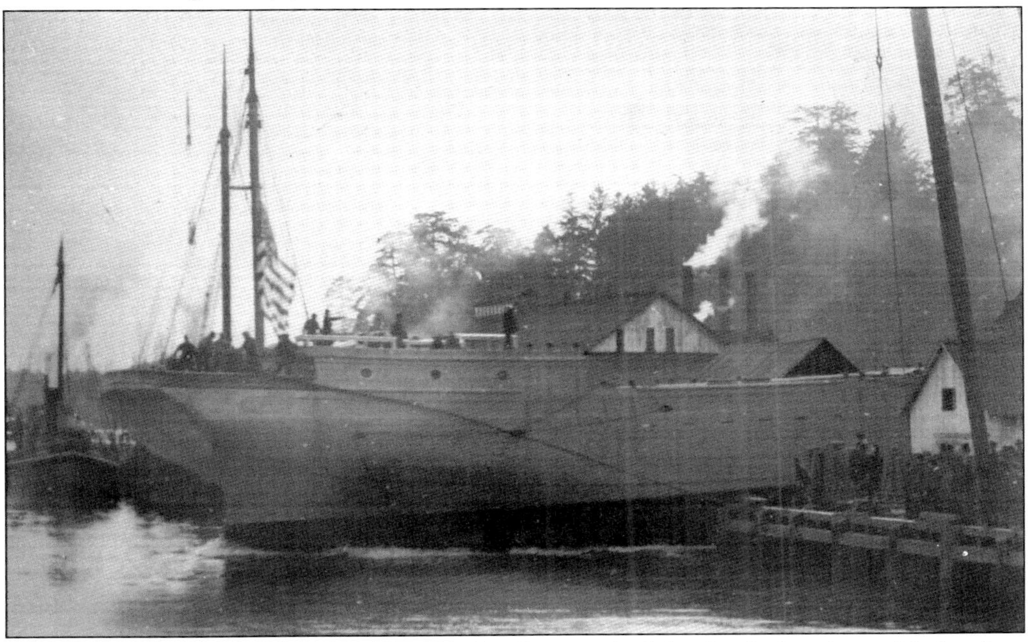

The *Alumna* was launched on April 6, 1901. Asa Simpson had the ship built to honor his daughter Edith's 1900 graduation from a private finishing school in New York City. The ship later became a floating brewery in Alaska. She also served as a fish processing plant and a barge in British Columbia during her working life. (CHMM 992-8-2589.)

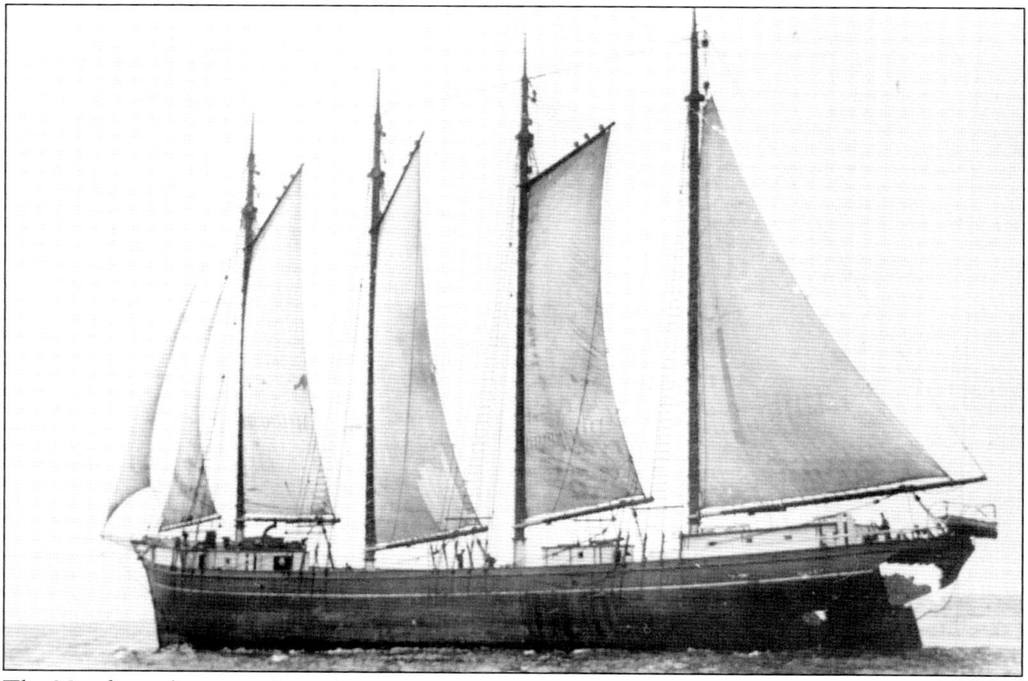

The *Novelty* is shown under sail. Built by John Kruse in 1886, her name reflected her originality. She had no bowsprit and was "bald-headed" (no topmasts.) She was the first four-masted schooner built on the Pacific. In later years a short bowsprit was added. The *Coos Bay News* opined that her name should have been "Oddity." (CHMM 009-16.15A.)

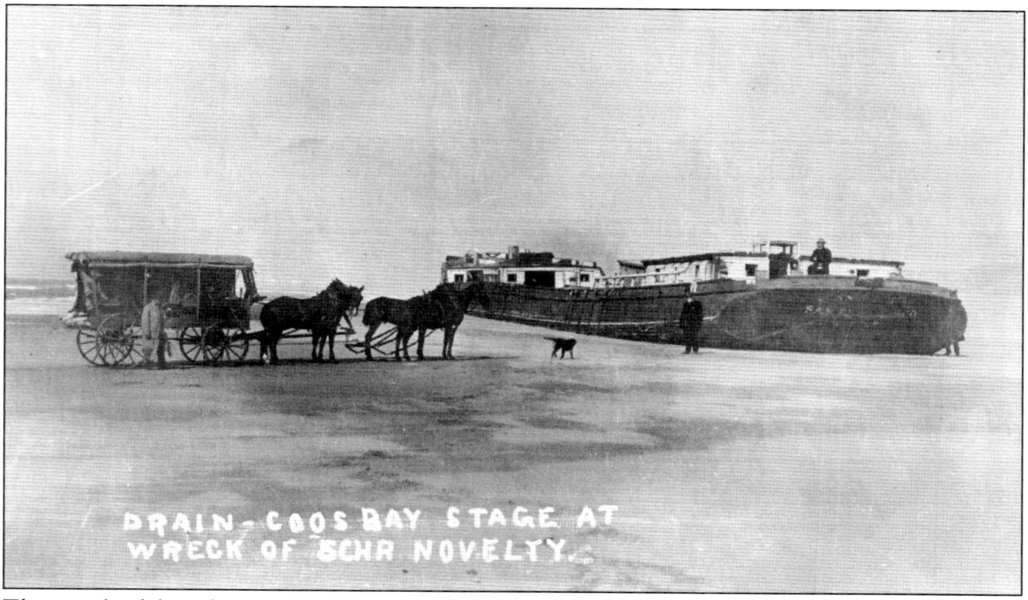

The wreck of the schooner *Novelty* is pictured. She was coming from San Pedro in October 1907, missed the fog-bound entrance to Coos Bay, and ran ashore north of Ten Mile Creek. All the crew walked away. For some time after, the stage to Drain that traveled along the beach would stop so passengers could see the stripped and abandoned vessel. (CHMM 007-25.62.)

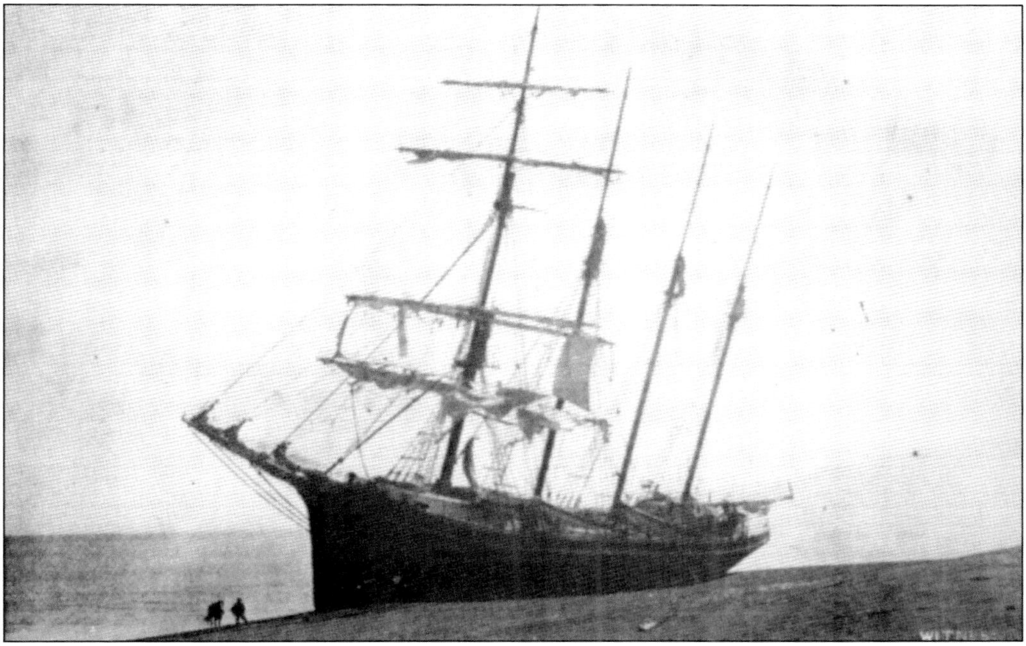

The four-masted barkentine *Addenda* was started by John Kruse and finished by Emil Heuckendorff in 1895. The *Addenda* stranded in 1904 on Palliser Bay near Lyttelton, New Zealand, during a storm. Her crew was saved but the ship was a total loss. (CHMM 009-16.409.)

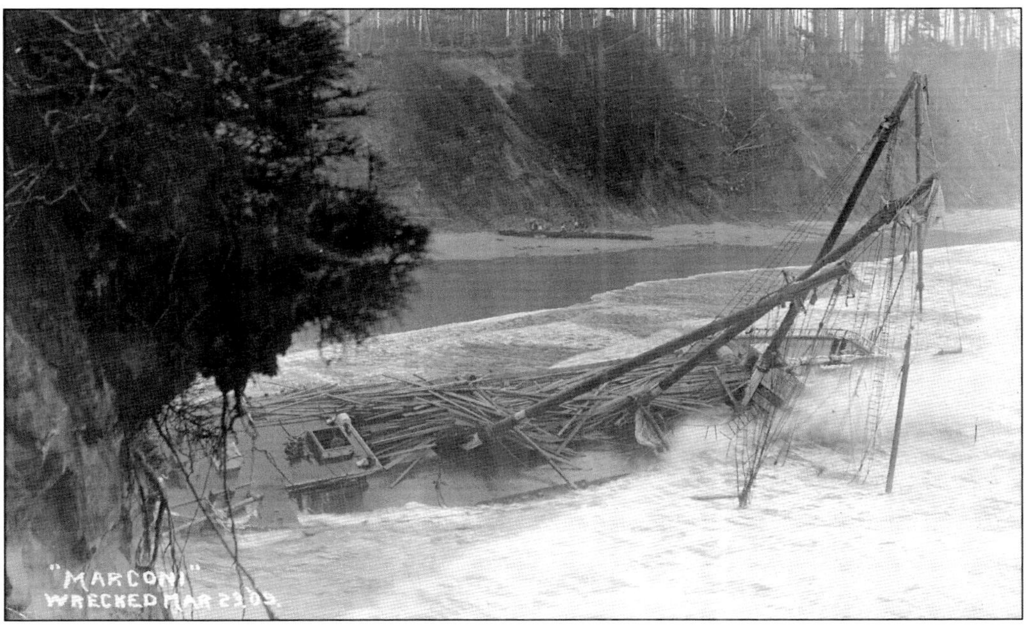

Peter Loggie built the *Marconi* in 1902—the last ship to come from the yard at "Old Town." In March 1909, while being towed out over the Coos Bay bar carrying a full load of lumber, her hawser broke. Heavy seas pushed her onto the rocks of the south spit, where she broke up. (CHMM 006-27.36.)

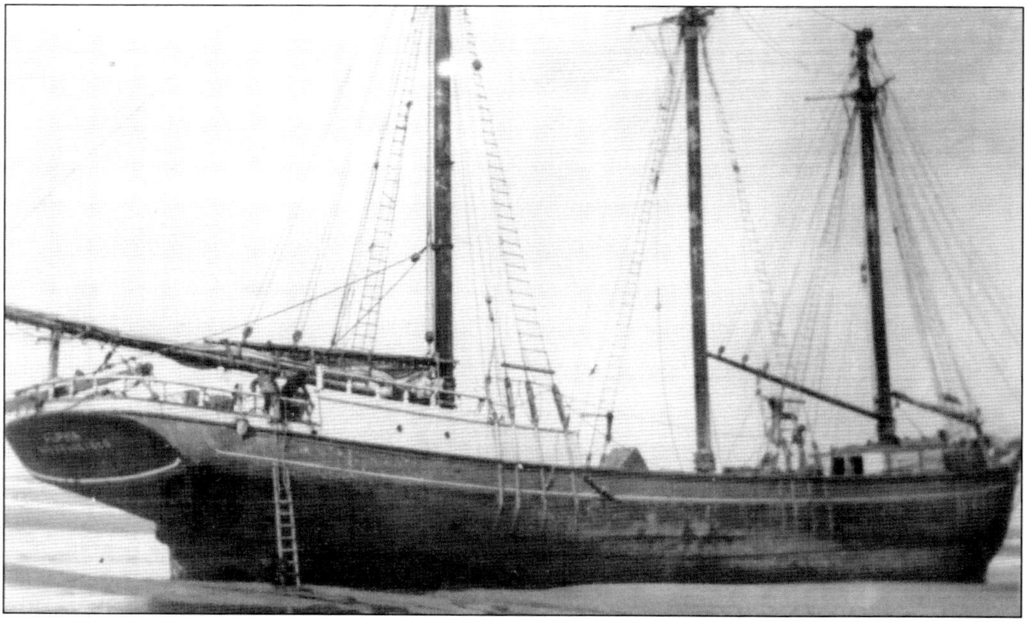

The three-masted schooner *Alpha* was wrecked in 1909, blown off course and stranded on the beach 9 miles north of the Umpqua River. The schooner, named for the Greek alphabet's starting letter, was the first vessel built at the Porter shipyard, next to the Porter sawmill, at the south end of North Bend. Emil Heuckendorff constructed her in 1903, the last ship from a Simpson shipyard. (CHMM 007-25.348.)

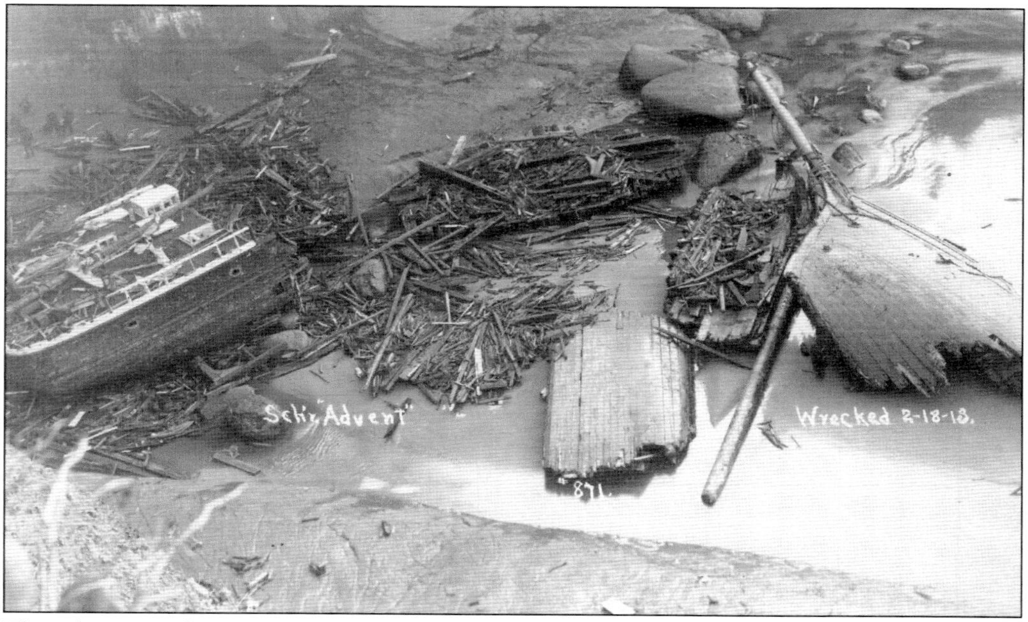

The schooner *Advent* was built in 1901 by K. V. Kruse and wrecked in February 1913. She was crossing the Coos Bay bar when the wind died, her anchors failed, and she drifted helplessly onto the South Spit, where she broke up. The men of the Coos Bay Lifesaving Station rescued her captain and crew. (CHMM 008-45.46.)

Four

Louis Simpson's City

In 1902, Louis Jerome Simpson purchased the Yarrow town site from the Symons for $25,000. He filed the plat with Coos County and in December 1903 the state officially recognized the City of North Bend. Simpson became mayor and served until his resignation in 1915. Although his father's mill site was taken into the city, there was a distinction made between Old Town and new town North Bend. A 1902 pavilion built at Old Town was an early community center for parties, dances, and theater.

Simpson furnished free land for waterfront industries in new North Bend. Soon there was a woolen mill, iron works, grocery warehouse, and a sash and door factory. Wooden buildings constructed along Sherman Avenue included a hotel, bank, rooming houses, hospital, saloons, grocery, hardware, and clothing stores. The city thrived. Additionally, the Simpson Lumber Company purchased the sawmill at Porter, midway between old North Bend and Marshfield. Now the city stretched from pavilion to Porter.

Simpson constantly promoted his city. The growth surge and real estate speculation drew interesting people. Charles Winsor, recruited to manage the Bank of Oregon, became Simpson's friend and business partner. L. D. Kinney touted a never-to-be transcontinental railway and streetcar line. J. A. O'Kelley, the "boat king," ran regular waterfront service to Coos Bay communities. C. M. Byler ran a grocery store. Vern C. Gorst, with a partner, opened a bus service between North Bend and Marshfield. Gorst's inventive mind created various air, land, and water machines.

Simpson's old town home was a social mecca but it was his father's creation. During 1907–1908 Simpson built a large oceanfront house (Shore Acres) for his wife, Cassie, suitable for large parties and hosting visiting notables. After ending his mayoral duties in 1915, Simpson and Cassie moved permanently to Shore Acres.

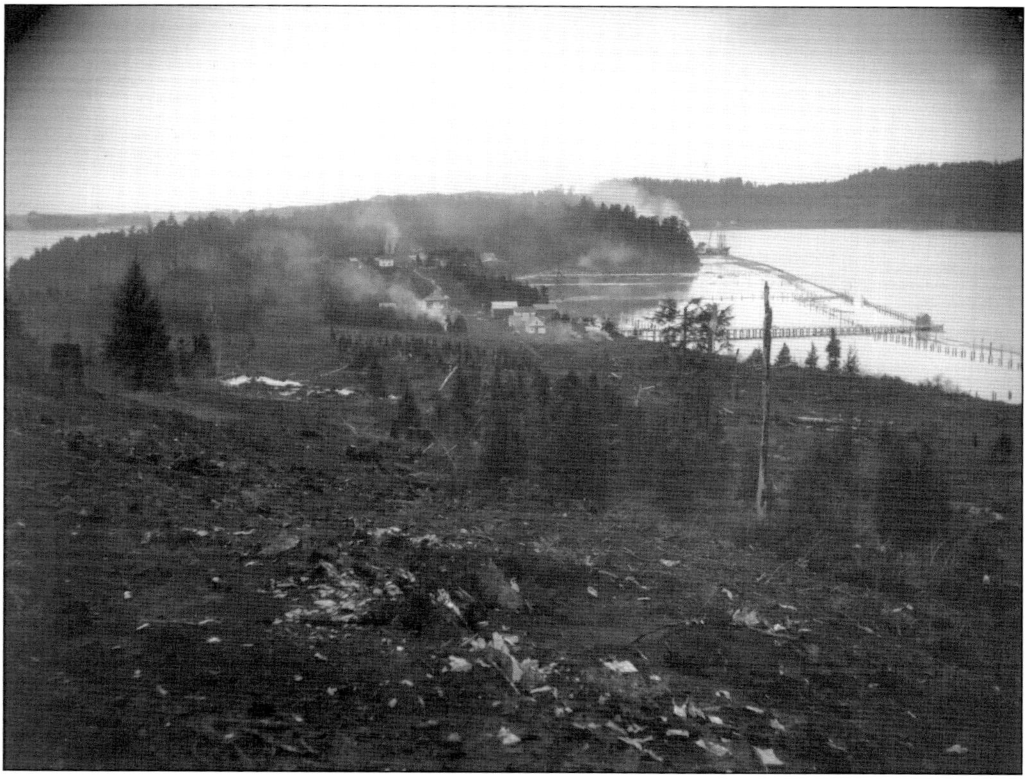

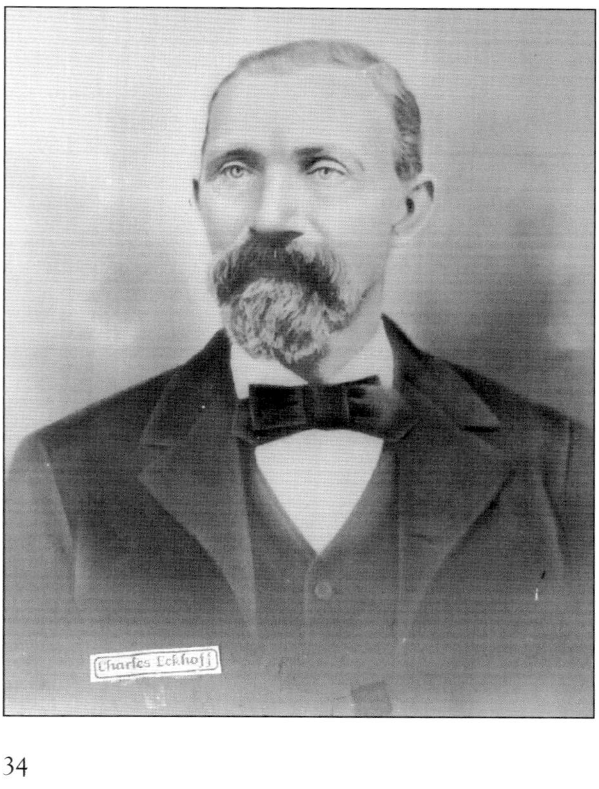

This is Yarrow around 1902, when young Louis Simpson purchased it for $25,000. The photograph shows the wooded peninsula with the clearing for downtown North Bend. The log pen Symons rented to Simpson Lumber Company is to the right, as is the pier and dock that footed on Eckhoff (now California) Avenue. The shed at pier's end, with a painted "Y" and arrow, marks the boat landing. (CHMM 992-8-3768a.)

Charles Eckhoff (1831–1911), father of 11, was an early settler, county road builder, logger, and land buyer. His $400 purchase of future downtown North Bend from Charles Merchant was sold to Thomas Symons for $16,000 and became the Yarrow town site. L. D. Kinney bought another Eckhoff holding on Pony Slough's west side for his Bangor town site. (CHMM 008-53.65.)

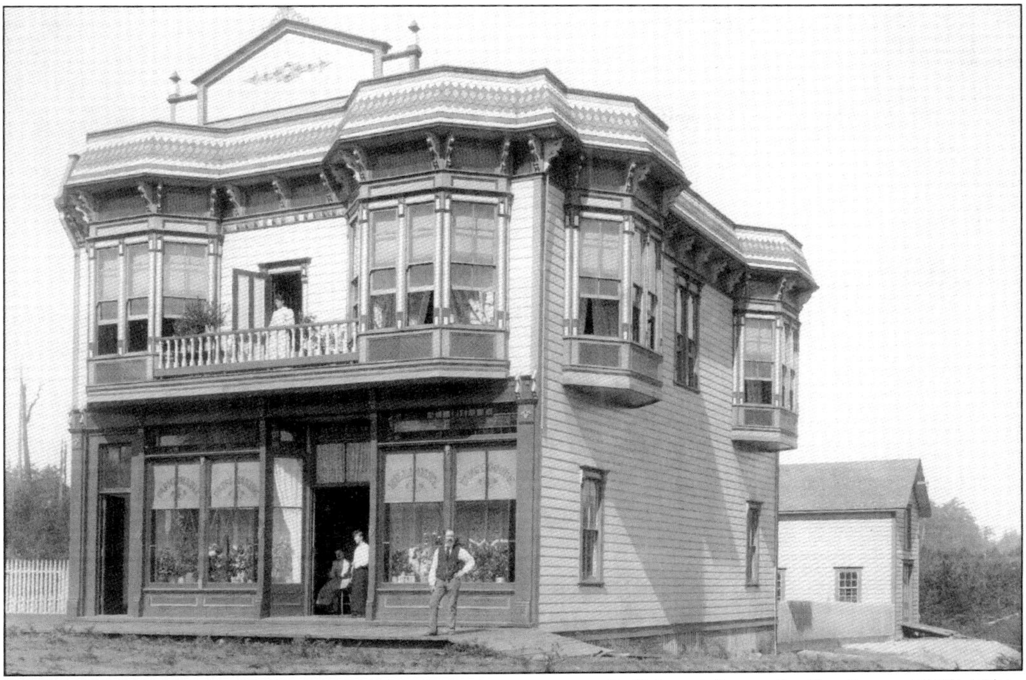

Eckhoff's Yarrow home (facing Eckhoff Avenue—now California) was built about 1890. This lovely Victorian had bay windows on the east side, but an unadorned west side. After Louis Simpson purchased Yarrow, Eckhoff's family lived upstairs and the ground floor was rented to various merchants. (CHMM 008-53.43.)

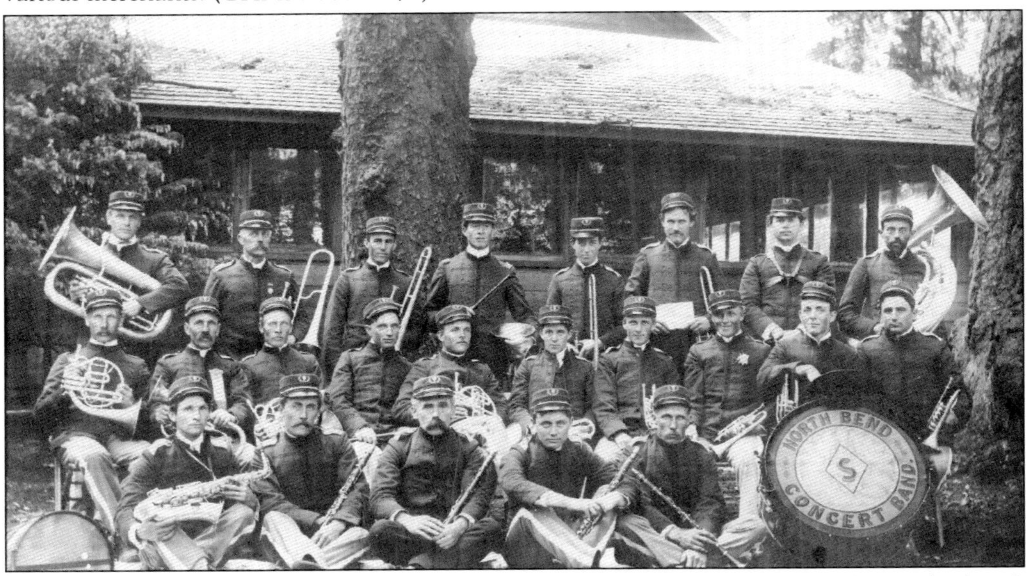

The North Bend Concert Band, led by Charles Kaiser, poses before the pavilion. The band, supported by Simpson, and bearing the Simpson "Diamond S" logo on its drum, formed in 1900. Uniforms and instruments were purchased in 1901. The pavilion was built in 1902 for dancing, but Simpson soon had it enlarged and enclosed. It served as a community center useful for social events. (CHMM 958-5688.)

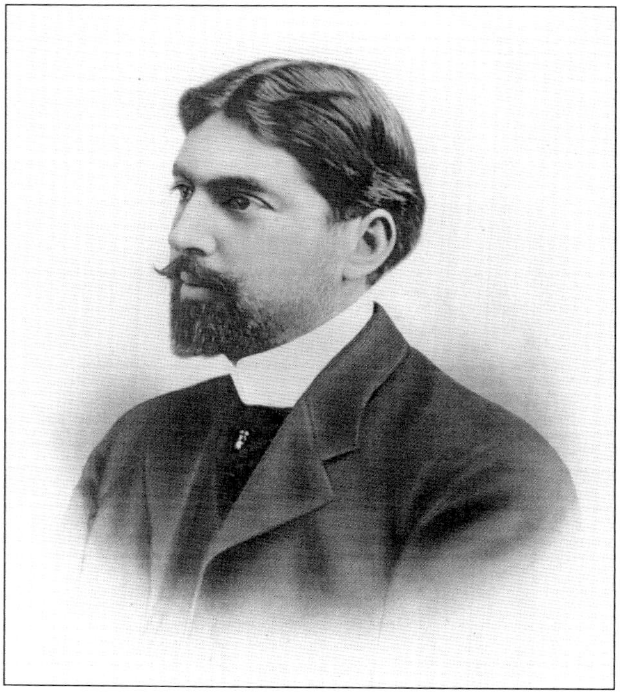

This 1904 portrait of L. J. Simpson, age 27, shows him with moustache and Van Dyke beard. He was North Bend's developer, first mayor, and industrial entrepreneur. In 1899 he married Cassandra Stearns, whom he met at Hoquiam, Washington. He built the large home on the ocean, Shore Acres, for her. (CHMM unnumbered.)

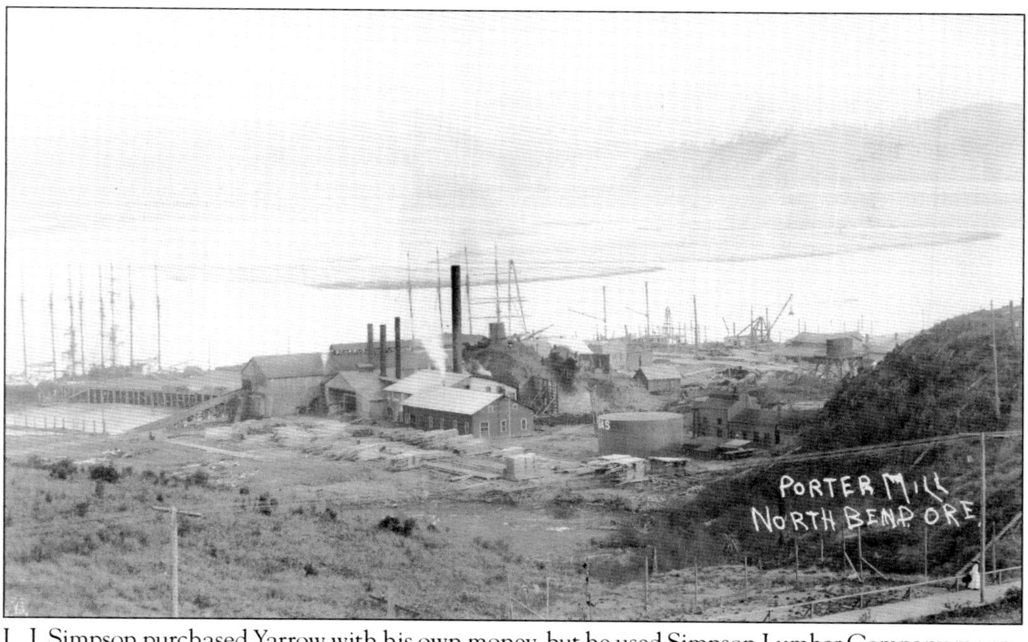

L. J. Simpson purchased Yarrow with his own money, but he used Simpson Lumber Company money to purchase the Porter mill, south of town, from California interests in 1902. When electricity was first generated for North Bend, the town was lit "from pavilion to Porter." (CHMM 010-2.4.)

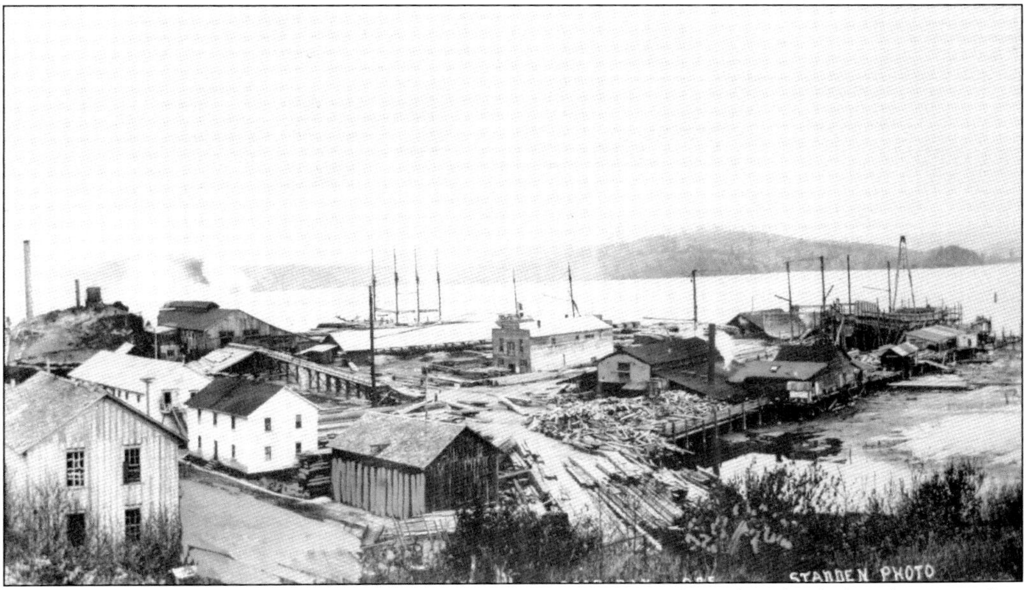

The Porter mill and shipyard is shown with a ship on the ways and another, loaded to the gunwales, in the bay. The California Lumber Company built the Porter mill in 1888. It was vacant for several years prior to Simpson's 1902 purchase and reopening in January 1903. (CHMM 009-16.1419.)

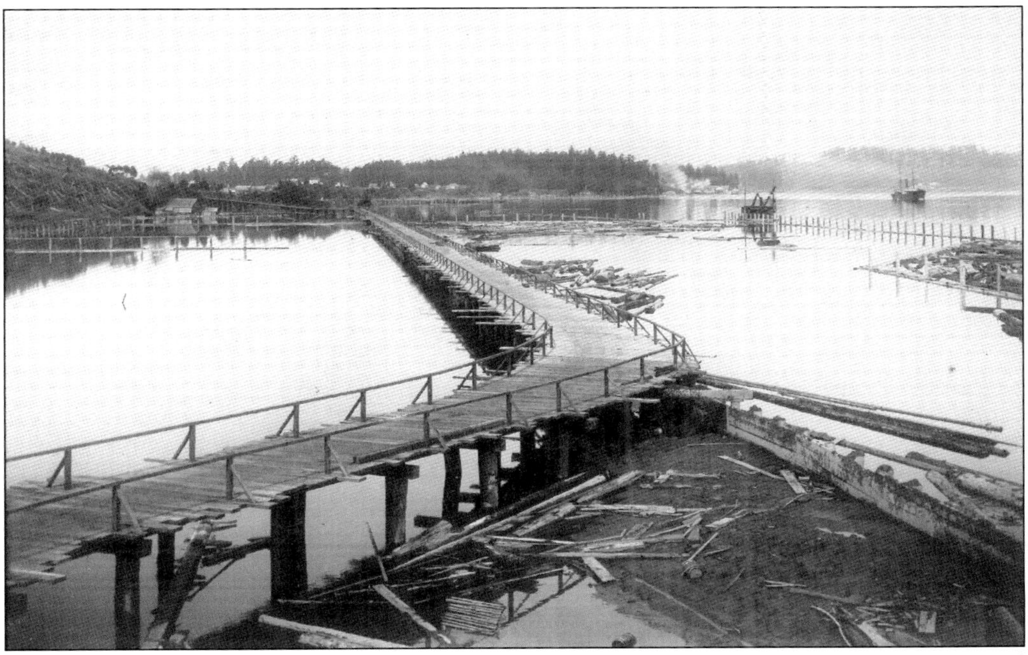

L. J. Simpson, no doubt using his father's money, authorized a wooden roadway out on the mud flats at the Porter mill to connect to his newly acquired Yarrow. The roadway was wide enough to accommodate a horse and wagon. This view is from the Porter site looking north toward Yarrow. In the distance, where smoke rises, is the Simpson company town, the first North Bend. (CHMM 958-55.)

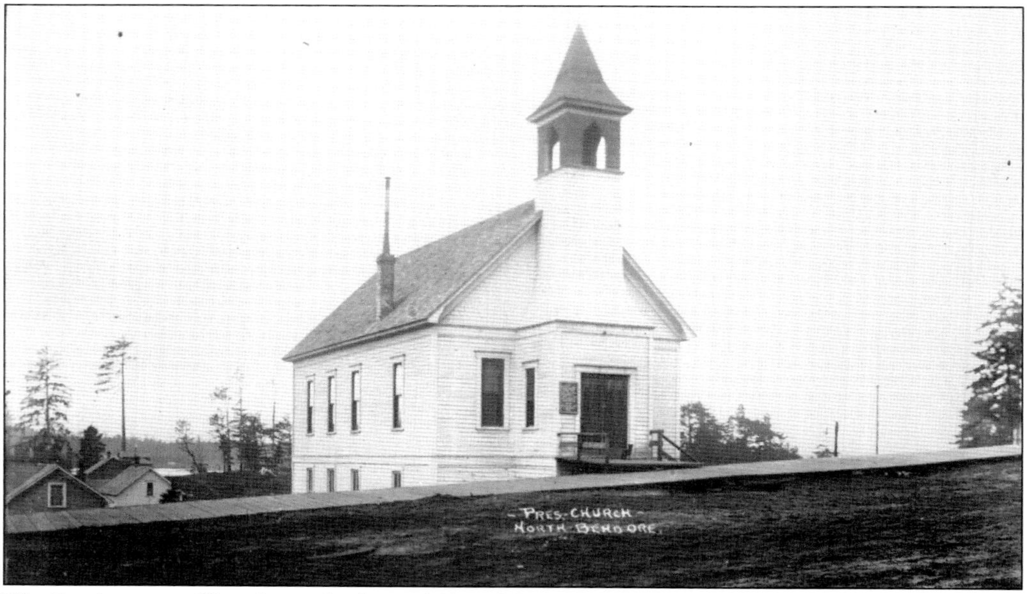

The Presbyterian Church was built in 1903 on Union, just south of Montana. L. J. Simpson gave the land for this and other early North Bend churches. Reverend Duncan McRuer was the first pastor. With volunteer labor and some donated materials, the cost of the 26-by-40-foot building was about $500. Space in the church was leased by the school district until Central School was built. (CHMM 992-8-0958.)

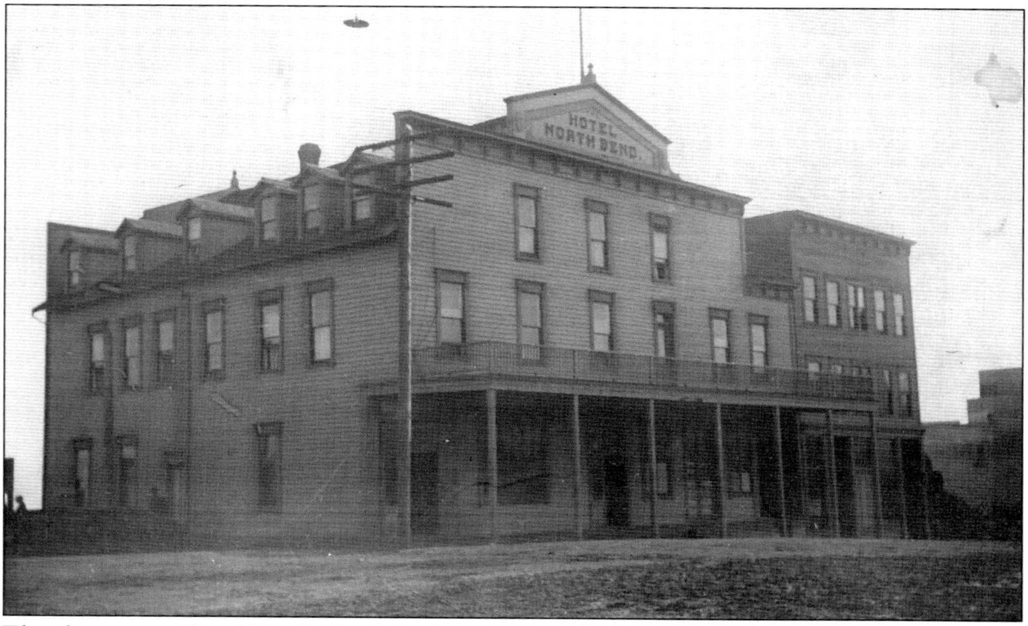

The three-story Hotel North Bend, built in 1903, was on the southeast corner of Sherman at Connecticut. Robert Marsden owned the building, which had 50 rooms plus a dining facility. In 1905 the Annex, on the right, added 38 rooms and an expanded bar, "The Antlers," decorated with 18 pair of deer and elk horns. In 1907 Marsden offered the hotel for sale for $10,000. He had no takers. (CHMM 962-57E.)

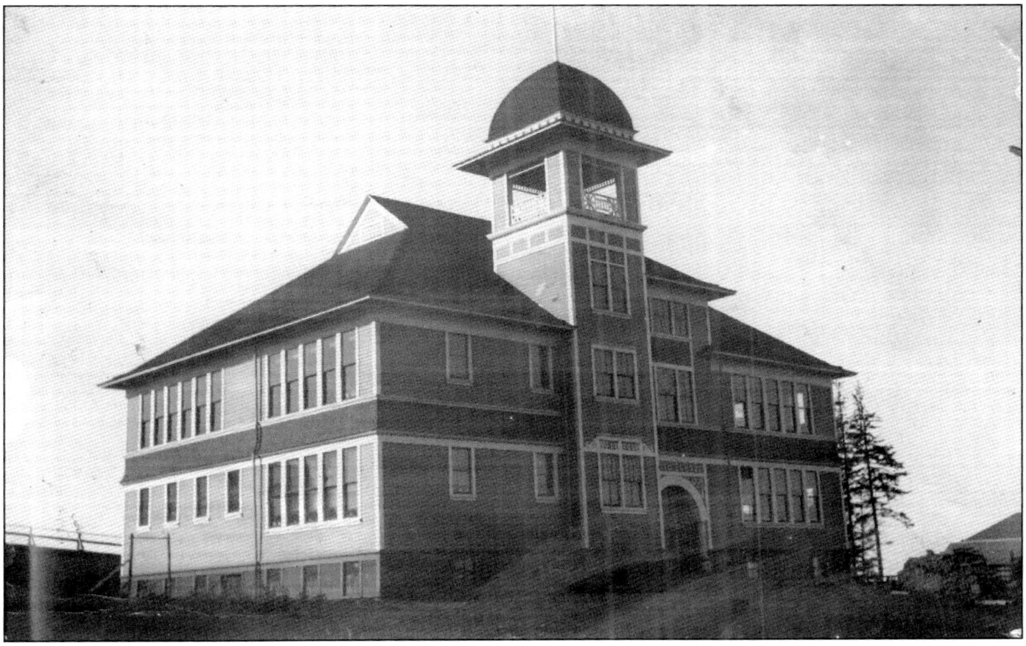

Central School, North Bend's elementary, was constructed in 1904. It had eight classrooms and living space for a janitor. E. B. Fish, contractor, got the $22,000 job. In 1906–1907, teachers were paid $70 a month (men) and $50 (women). The janitor had to light fires, mop muddy floors, right overturned privies, and keep the physical plant in good order. Central School closed in 1948 when Hillcrest School replaced it. (CHMM 962-57C.)

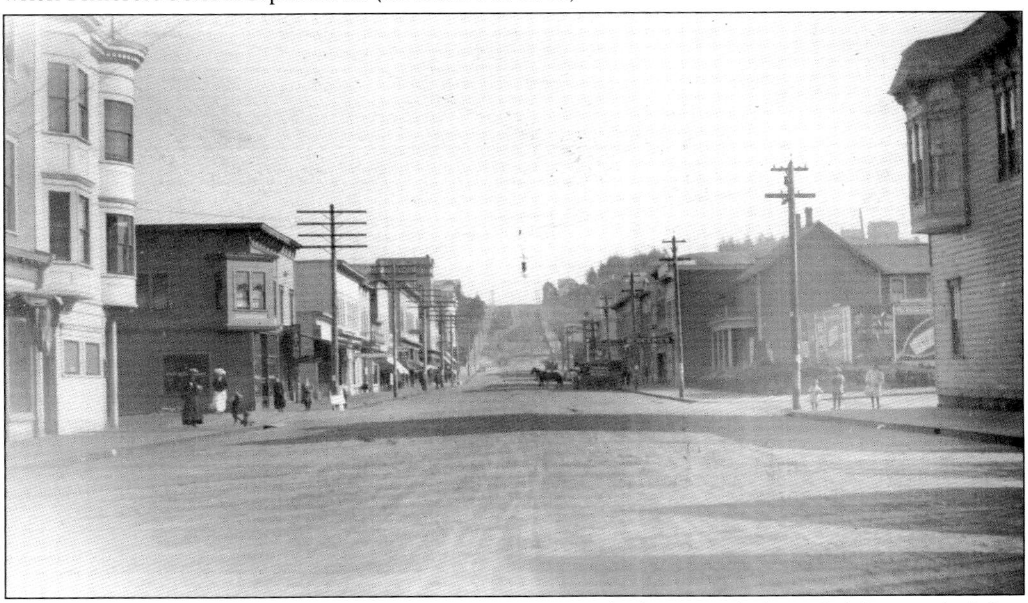

This is a post-1908 picture of a planked Sherman Avenue looking south from California. At left is the Grand Saloon building and across California the Rush building, built about 1906. On the right is the edge of the Eckhoff home. Across California is a sign-filled lot, and next the Dorchester, a rooming house that was built around 1902 and burned in 2008. (CHMM 975-34h.)

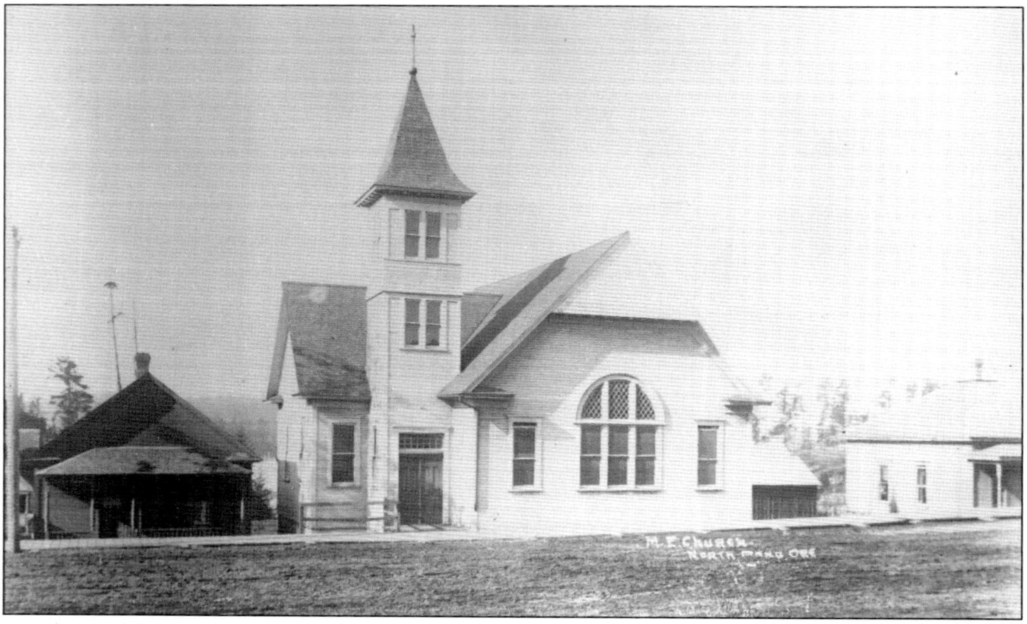

North Bend's first Methodist Church stood at 1956 Meade Avenue on lots donated by L. J. Simpson. Thomas Vigars, a realtor, drew the architectural plans, and a contract for the $1,800 building was let to Vigars in November 1904. The structure was completed in March 1905. A concrete foundation, modern heating plant, and electric lights came in 1917. (CHMM 992-8-0957.)

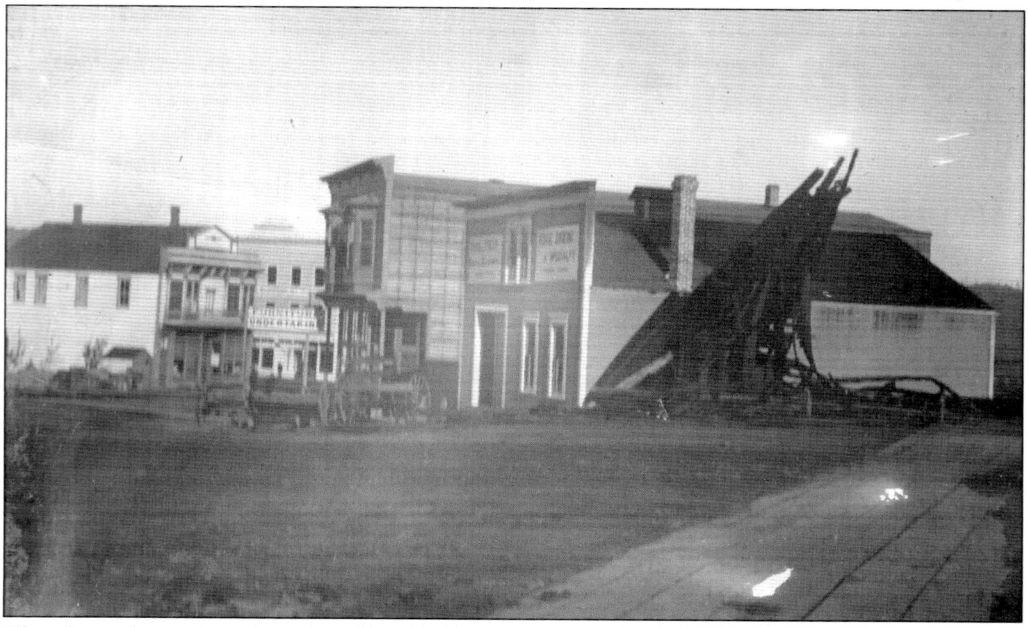

The charred remains of the first City Hall and adjacent *North Bend Citizen* are shown after the September 22, 1905, fire. City Hall was rebuilt at the same Grant Circle location (Union at California). Fire equipment was on the ground floor. City offices and the council chamber were upstairs. The sign to the left is for a furniture and undertaker's store—caskets were "furniture." (CHMM 962-57P.)

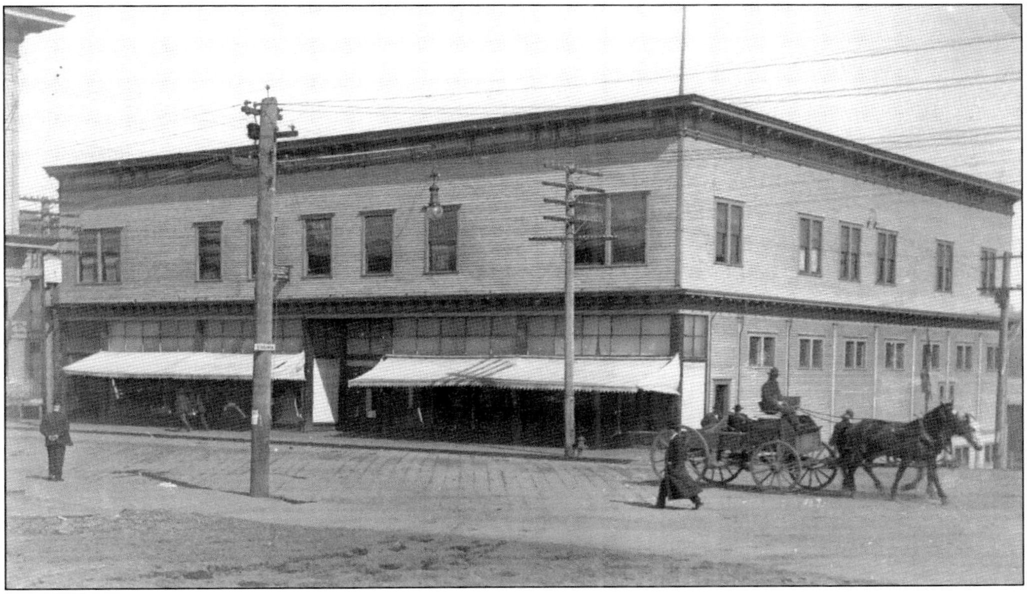

Simpson money built the Simpson-Myers building at Sherman and Virginia Avenues in 1906 to house the A. W. Myers department store. Today this is the site of the concrete Independent Order of Odd Fellows building. This photograph was taken after 1908, when Sherman was first planked. The sign on the telephone pole is an early street sign, reading Virginia. (CHMM 958-563a.)

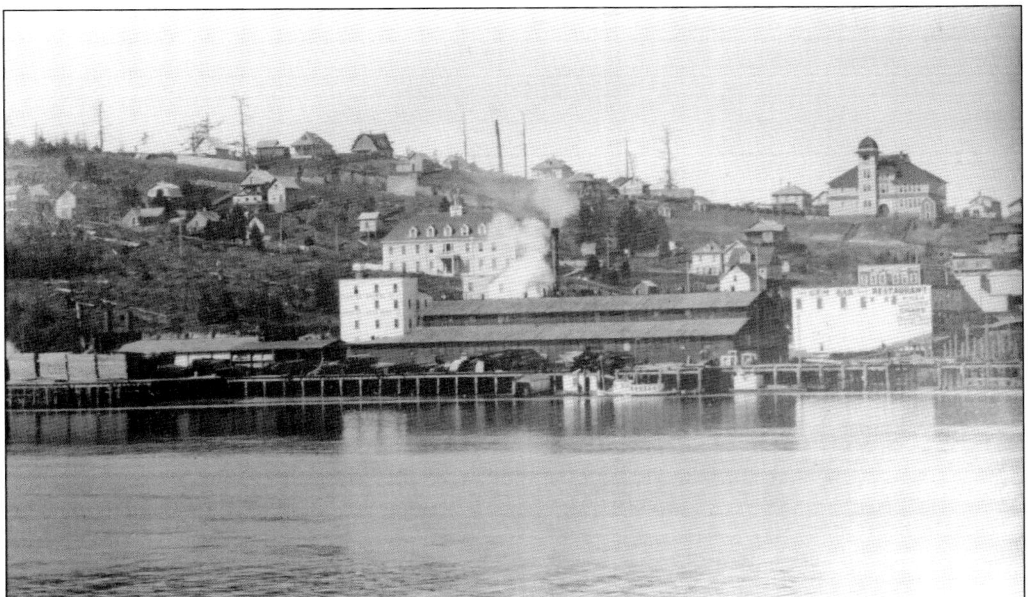

This is North Bend's Sherman hill, viewed from the water, showing the infamous Gem Bar and Restaurant—Jay Wilcox's brothel—on the right. Moving left are North Bend Manufacturing's sash and door factory, then the brewery, and above it Mercy Hospital. Central School is at top right. (CHMM 007-25.216.)

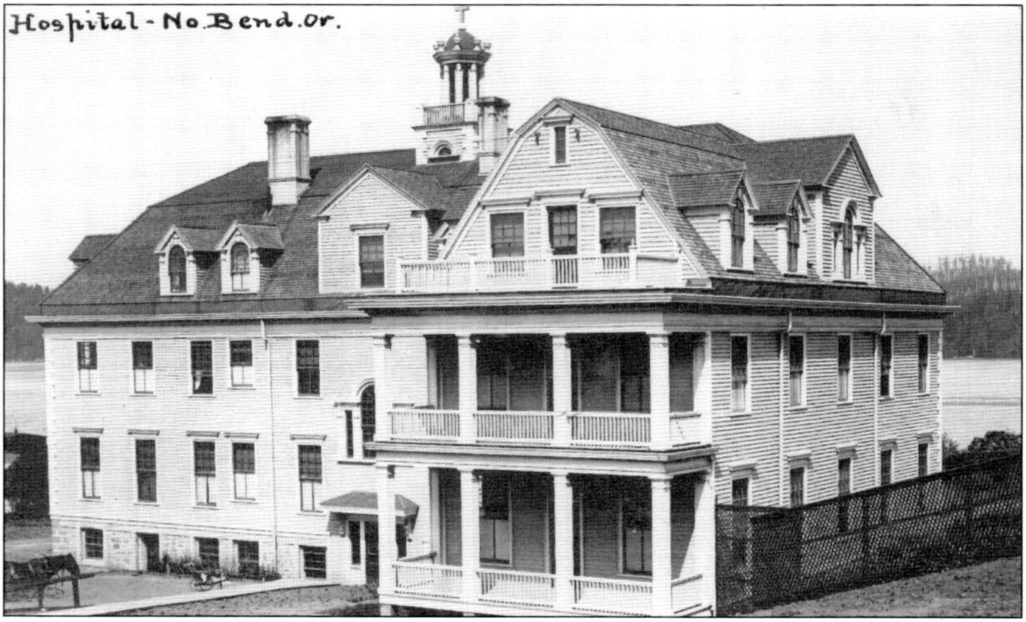

In 1903 L. J. Simpson gave 16 lots on Sherman hill to Father Edward Donnelly for a hospital. Newport, Rhode Island architect David B. Emerson had drawn plans. The cornerstone of the large $30,000 building was laid in 1904. Mercy Hospital, staffed by the Sisters of Mercy, opened in 1906. Holy Redeemer Catholic Church was built next to the hospital in 1914 at a cost of $3,800. (CHMM 990-31.)

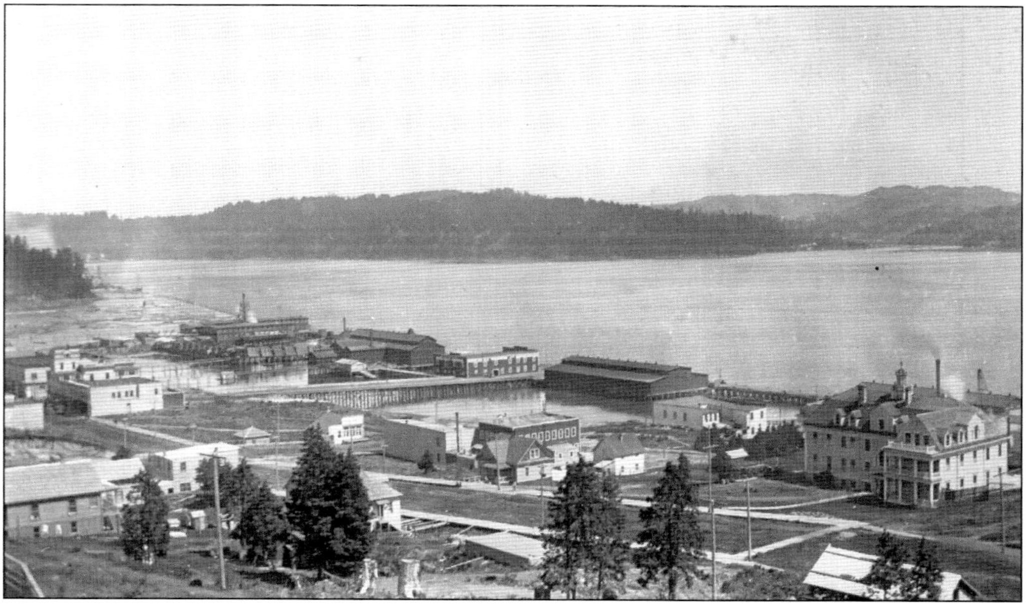

This view from Union hill shows Mercy Hospital to the right, then the city's dock with the sash and door factory hidden below the hospital. To the left along the waterfront are the city warehouse, the wholesale grocery warehouse, the woolen mill, and last, at far left, the furniture and veneer factory. (CHMM 992-8-0950.)

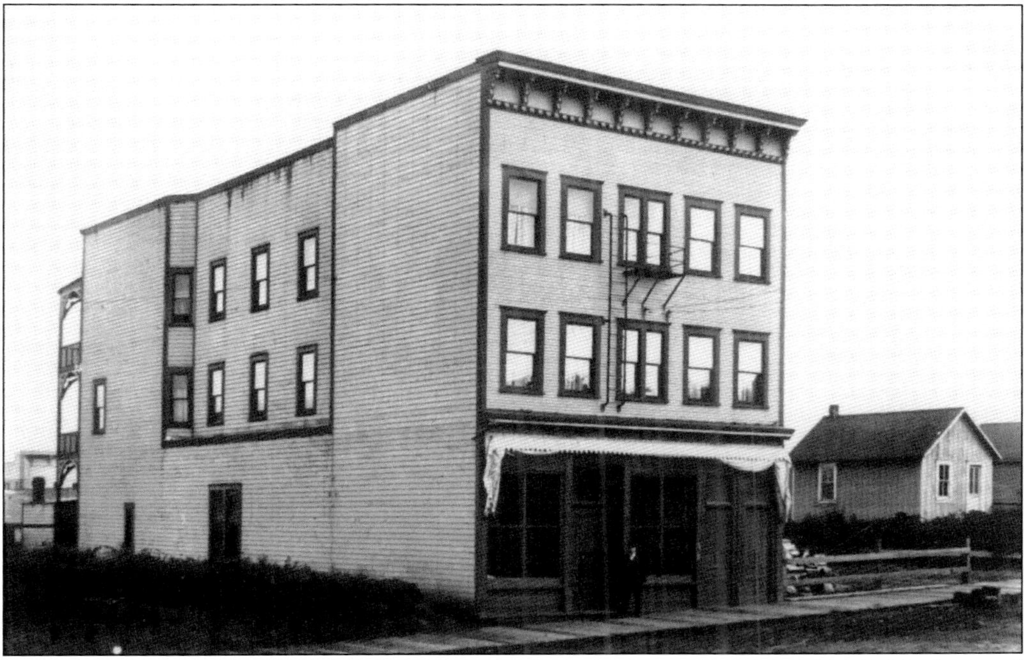

The Hotel Oregon was at 2043 Union Avenue. Built for owner S. Rogstad in 1906, the hotel was, more accurately, a large rooming house with a dining room. A man smoking in bed was the most likely cause of the fire in June 1953 that destroyed the hotel. The porches on the bay side are sometimes visible in photographs taken from the east. (CHMM 007-25.473.)

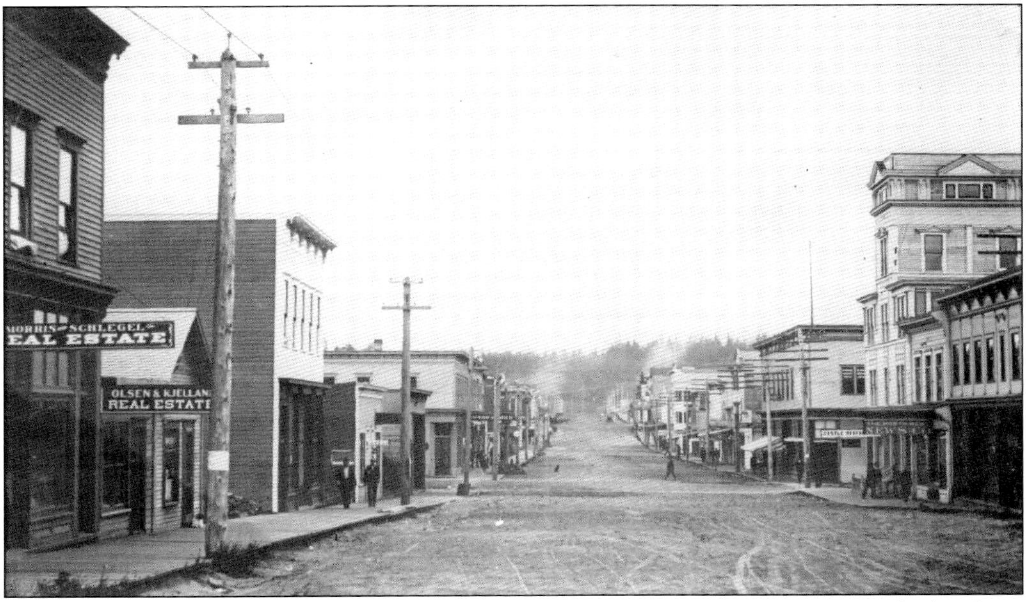

This view is of Sherman Avenue looking north about 1907. The buildings on the right (east) are the Coos Bay Grocery, the smaller newsstand building, and the four-story Winsor building. The poles and wires served both the original Pacific States Telephone and Telegraph Company and the electric utility. (CHMM 963-83h.)

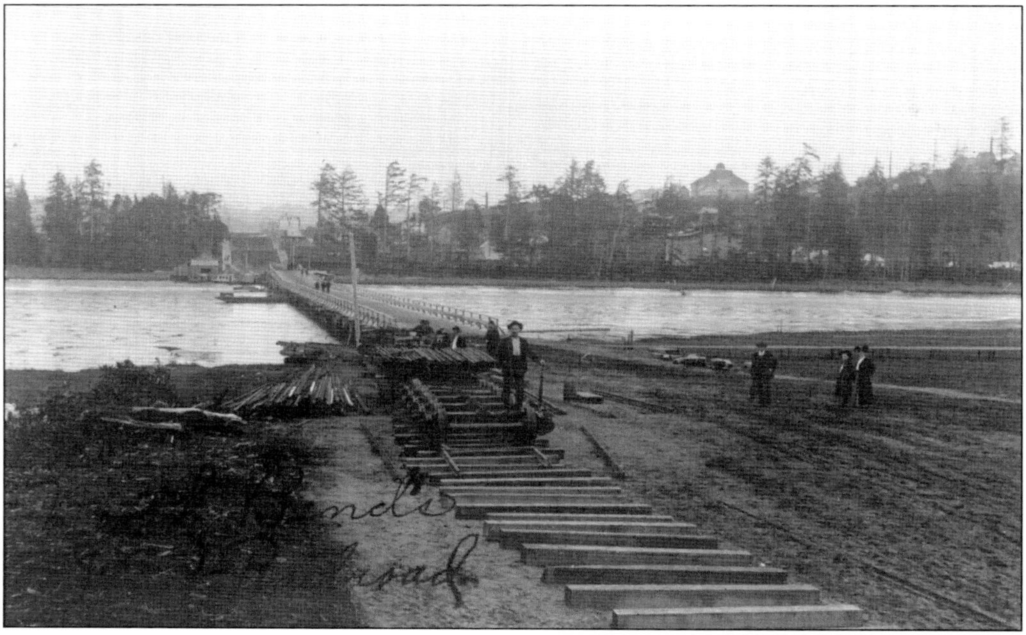

The Virginia Avenue Bridge was under construction in 1907. This bridge connected North Bend to Bangor. The photograph is from the Bangor side looking east across Pony Slough with Central School on the hill to the right. This photograph is humorously marked "North Bend's first railroad." The rails were used to get logs to the slough, where they were floated to a mill. (CHMM 992-8-0819.)

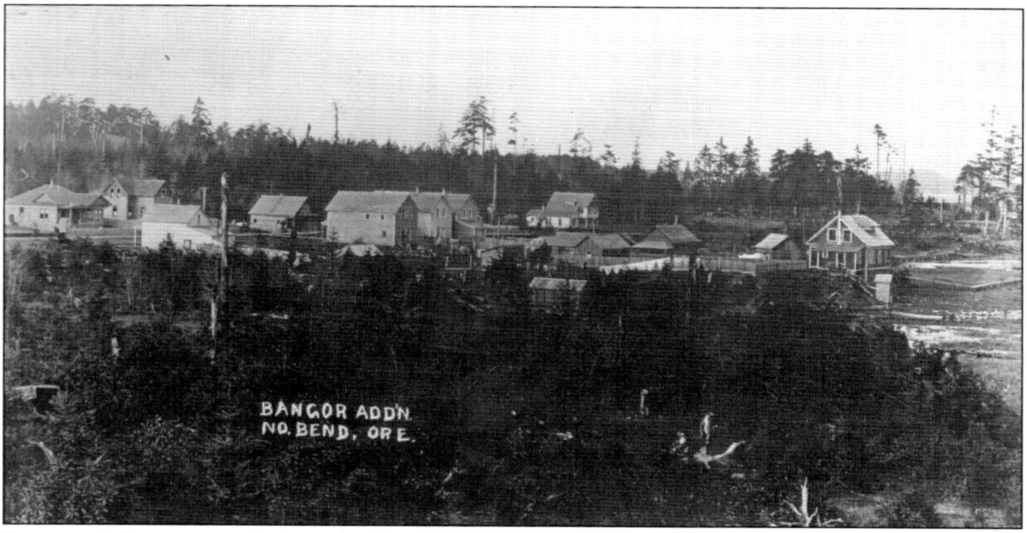

Some early homes were built in the Bangor Addition to North Bend. Three William James houses, built in 1907, still stand in a row, as does the house across the street at the corner of Marion and 12th Streets. L. D. Kinney platted Bangor in 1902, declaring that as Bangor, Maine was second only to Portland, Maine, so his Bangor would be second only to Portland in Oregon. (CHMM 992-8-0955.)

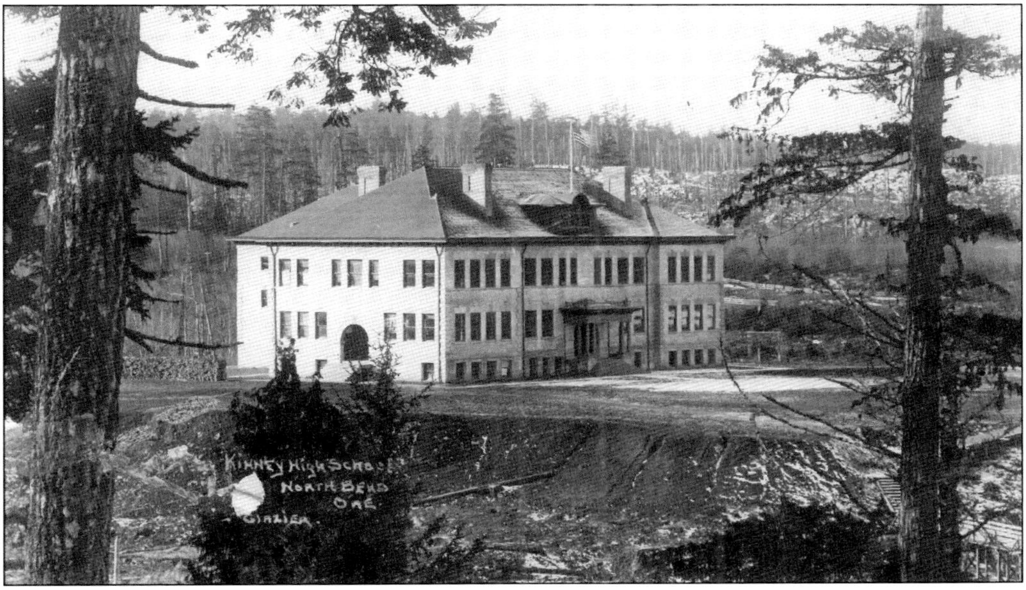

Kinney High School was one of two early brick buildings constructed in North Bend. L. D. Kinney gave four acres (which he did not own) to the school board. Construction began in 1908 on the $57,000 structure that opened in 1909. For two years the school bore Kinney's name. Classroom pressure was so great on the elementary school that some young students were sent here. The building was demolished in 1967. (CHMM 989-P219.)

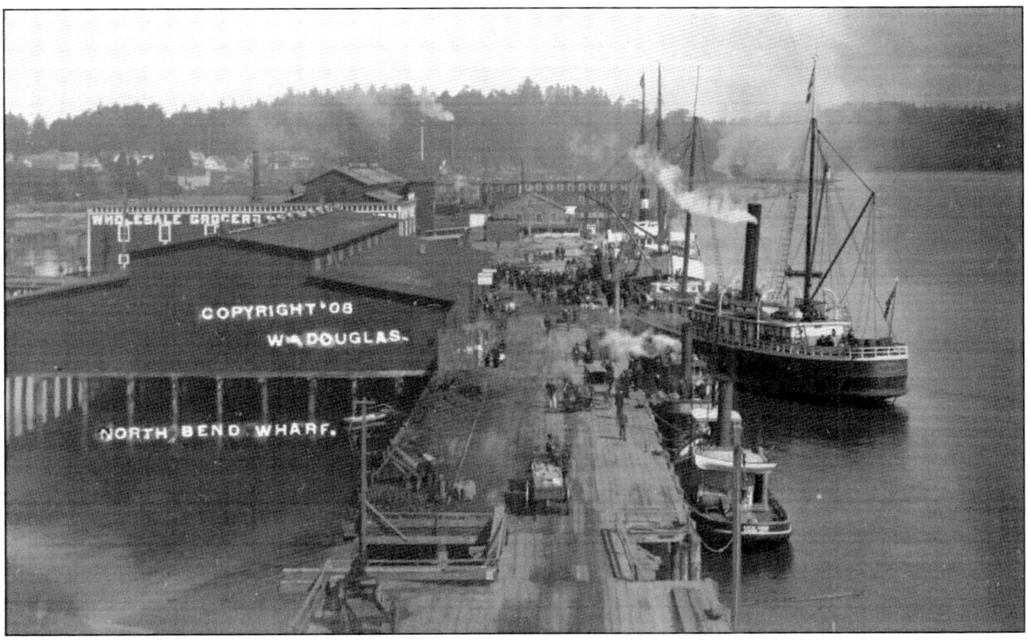

This view of the North Bend waterfront in 1908 shows the commercial activity on the water, including warehouses, a wholesale grocery operation, the unsuccessful woolen mill, and the Coos Bay Manufacturing Company's box factory. Ships at the dock include the coastal steamer *Alliance*, the *Homer*, and the tug *Katie Cook*. (CHMM 992-8-0828.)

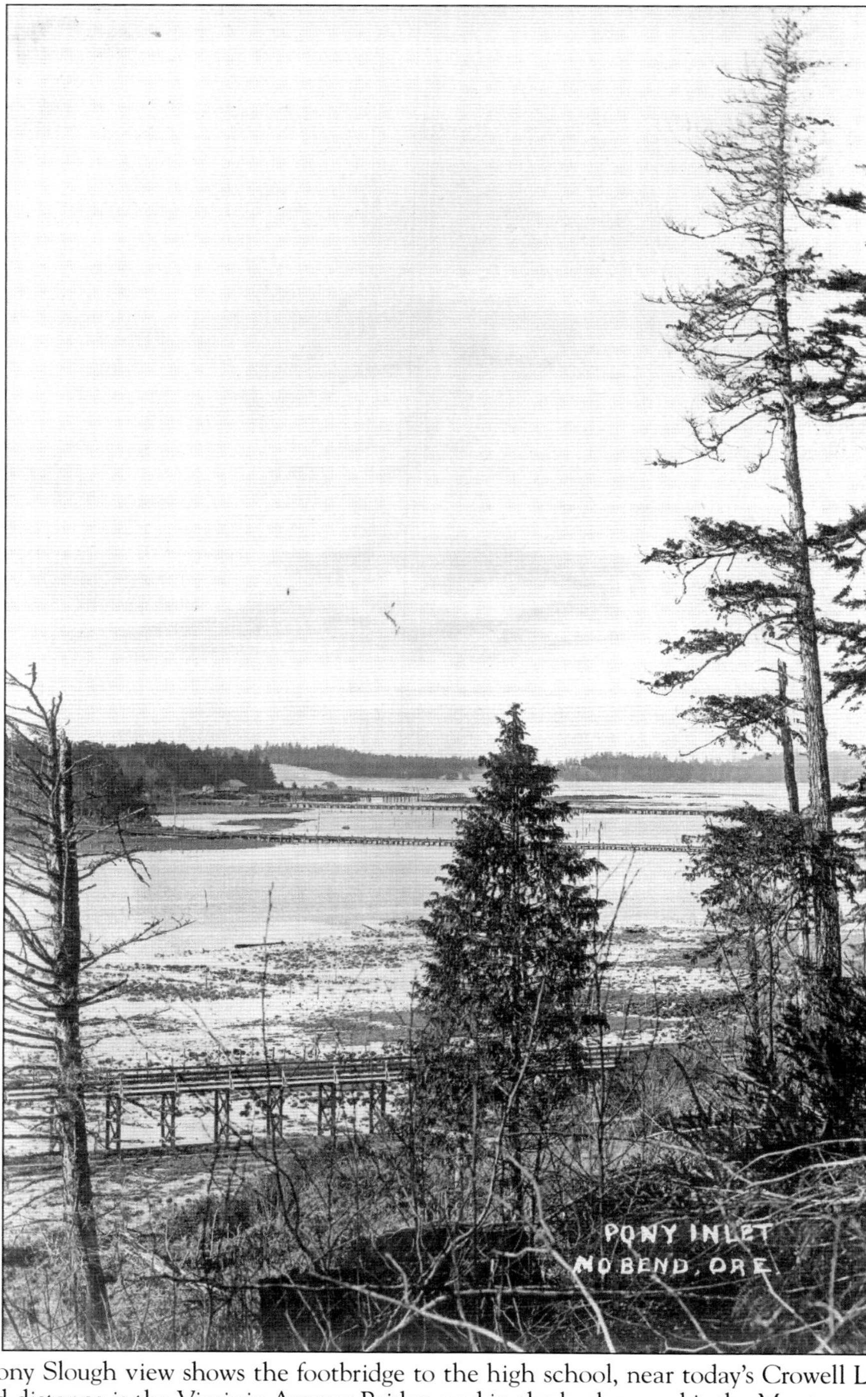

This Pony Slough view shows the footbridge to the high school, near today's Crowell Lane. In the mid-distance is the Virginia Avenue Bridge, and in the background is the Montana Avenue Bridge with the Reynolds sawmill on the west side. The privately built Montana Bridge was never transferred to the city and, as the bridge deteriorated, liability concerns caused the city to tear up the approaches and abandon it.

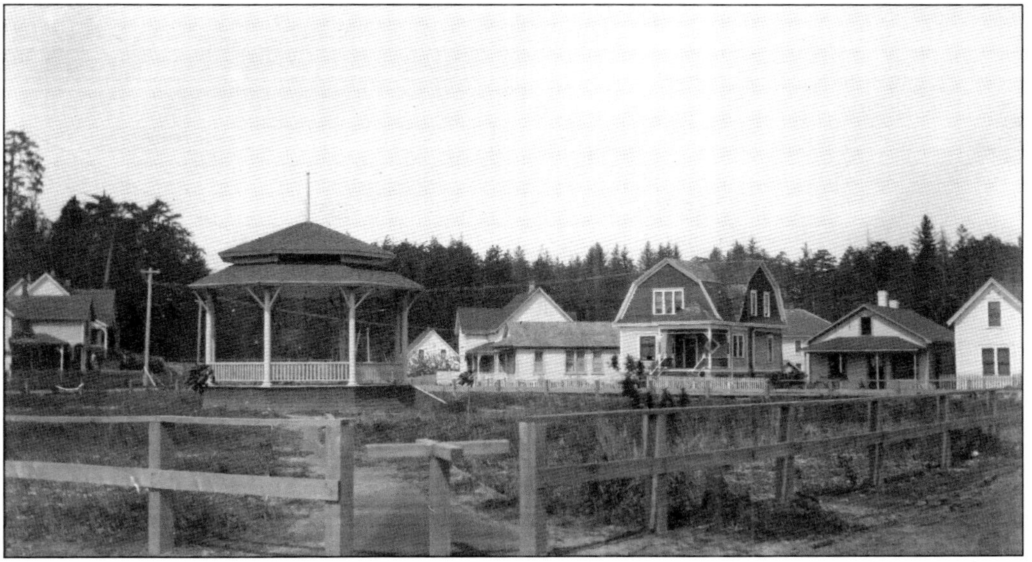

This early view of Lincoln Square shows the bandstand. At the 1905 Arbor Day celebration here, schoolchildren planted trees, Cassie Simpson donated trees and shrubs, and the blue uniformed North Bend Concert Band played. Several of the homes shown here remain. (CHMM 995-D158.)

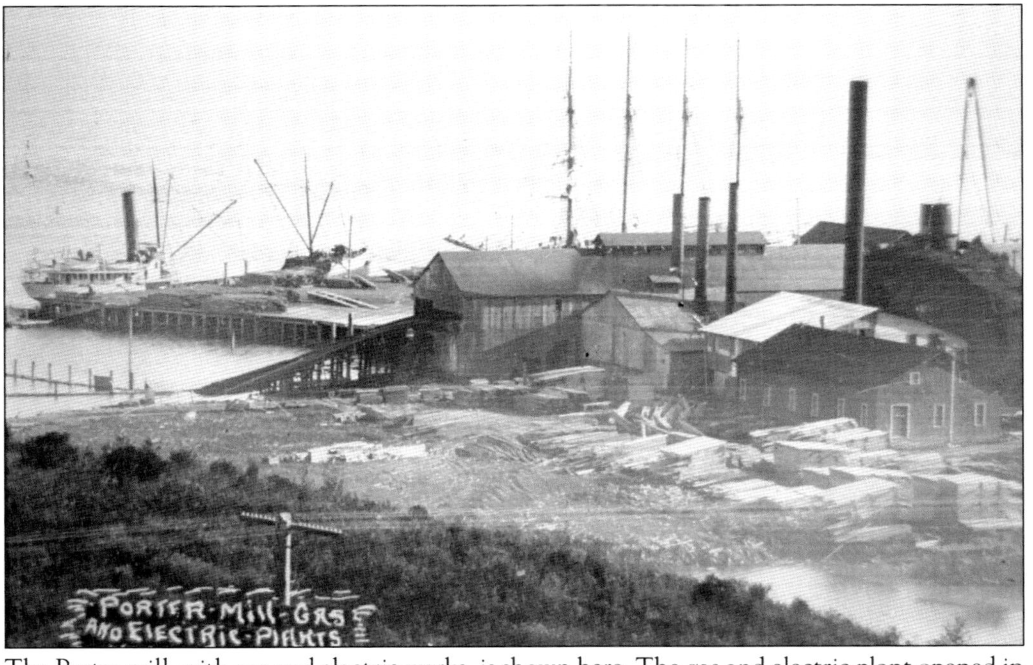

The Porter mill, with gas and electric works, is shown here. The gas and electric plant opened in 1908. A heating and scrubbing process converted crude oil into gas with hydrogen sulfur added for smell, before distribution into North Bend's and Marshfield's mains. Electricity for both towns was generated here and also at the C. A. Smith factory on Isthmus Slough. Gas service ended in 1938. (CHMM 009-16.1418A.)

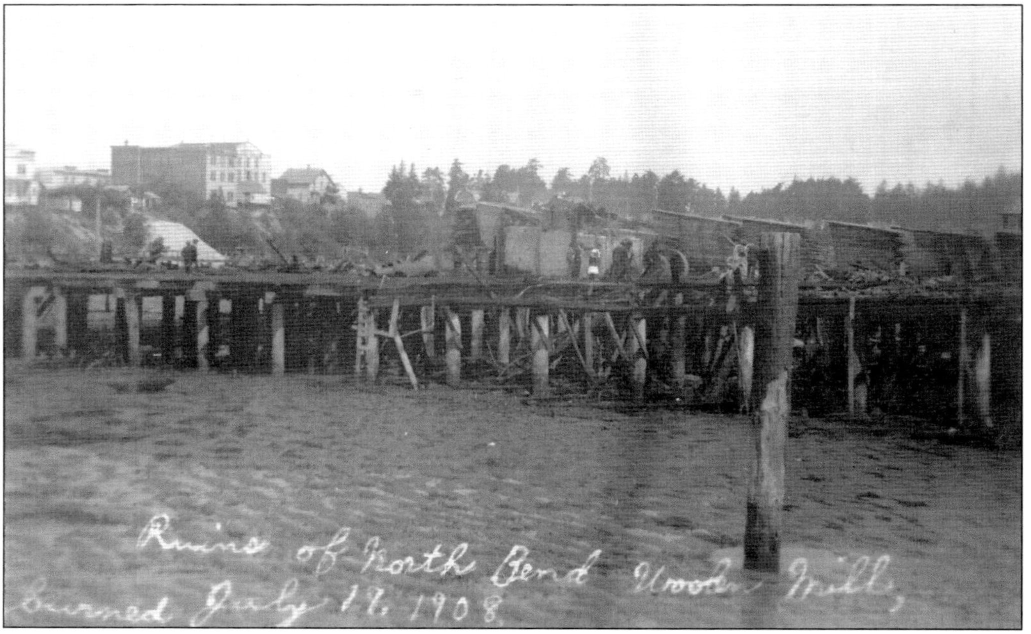

This photograph shows the charred remains of the Woolen Mill, which burned in July 1908. The Hotel North Bend and the Annex stand in the background. The next year another waterfront building, the city warehouse, was destroyed by fire. Arson was suspected in both cases, but never proven. (CHMM 010-2.2.)

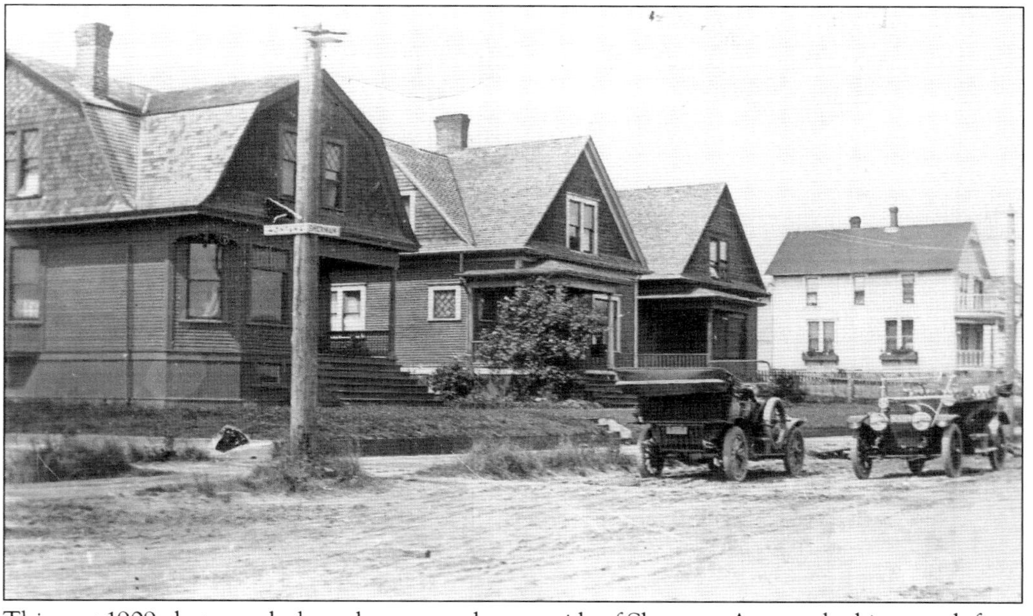

This post-1909 photograph shows houses on the west side of Sherman Avenue, looking north from the Montana intersection. In 1906, Charles Winsor, manager of the Bank of Oregon, owned the closest home. Next is that of M. E. Everitt, town druggist. Then comes the abode of Dr. and Mrs. Rowen Gale, and finally the house of Henry Hoeck, contractor, who owned the first automobile in North Bend. (CHMM 993-11.)

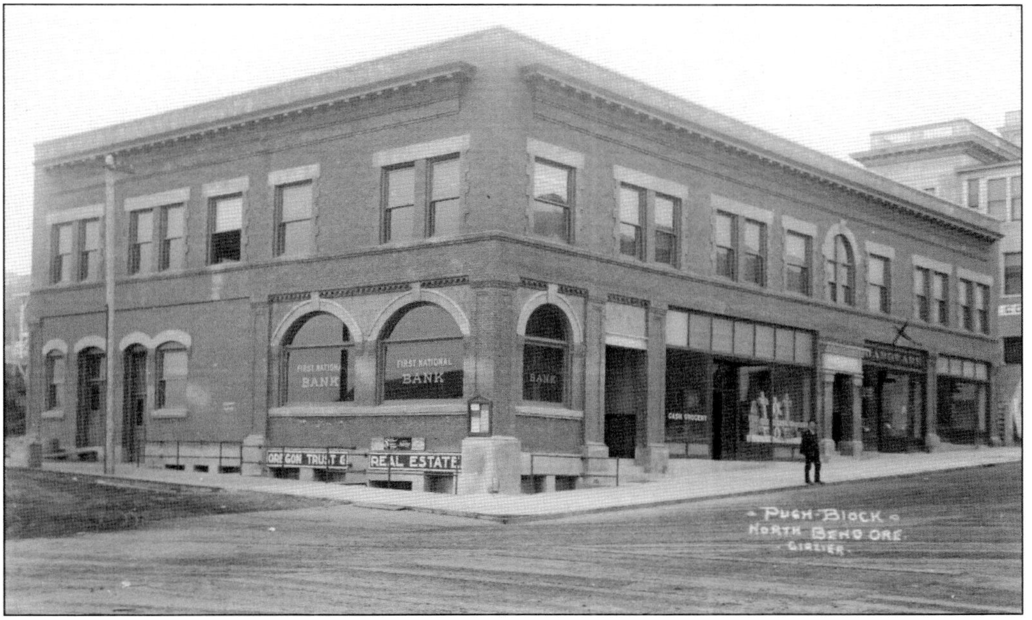

Virgil Pugh's $20,000 "brick block" was constructed in 1909. The First National Bank took space in early 1910. Other occupants were a cash grocery, Hazer Hardware, and the post office. Upstairs offices were rented to lawyers like Fred Hollister, and transfers from the Bank of Oregon building A. H. Derbyshire and C. E. Maybee. Pugh, bankrupt in 1911, lost about $20,000 in L. D. Kinney's Coos Bay Rapid Transit scheme. (CHMM 982-191.21.)

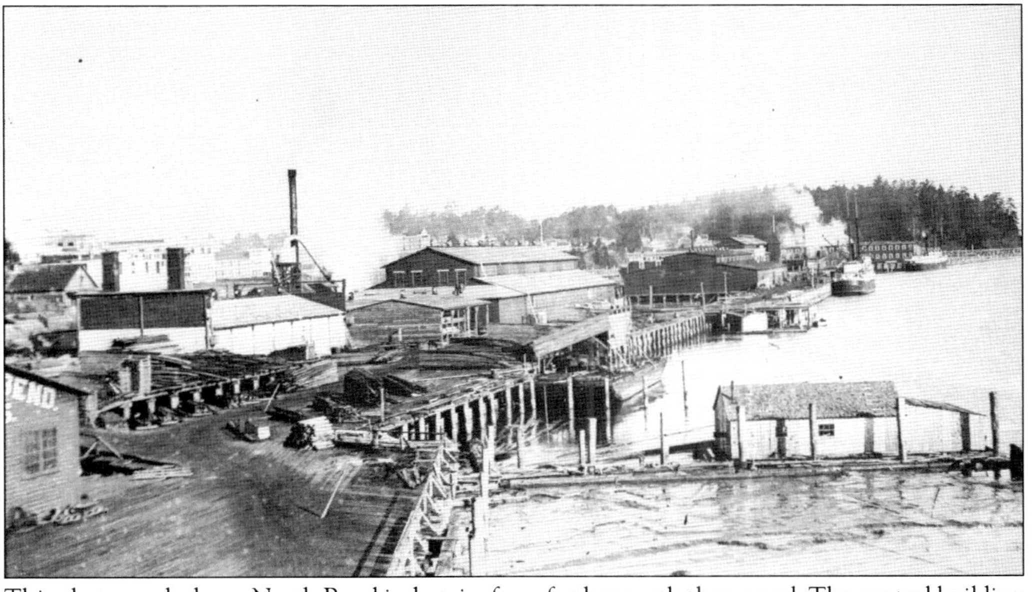

This photograph shows North Bend industries from farther south than usual. The central building on the waterfront is the sash and door factory, the next large building to the right is the city warehouse, and the last building visible (on the dock to the right) is the furniture and veneer factory. (CHMM 009-16.457.)

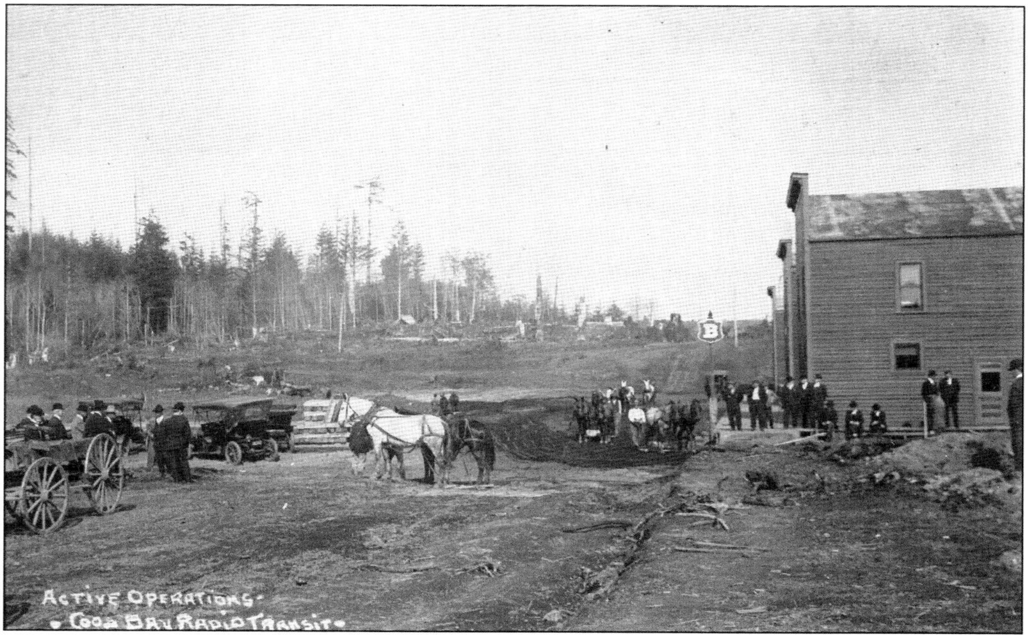

L. D. Kinney's grand plan for the Coos Bay Rapid Transit Company, a streetcar line connecting North Bend with Marshfield, was the rage of 1910. Unfortunately, the plan never got further than a horse drawn wagon with a nickel fare and a boat on the bay. Bankruptcy ensued, and Kinney eventually ended life at the state insane asylum. The "B" sign in this photograph stands for Plat B. (CHMM 992-8-0923.)

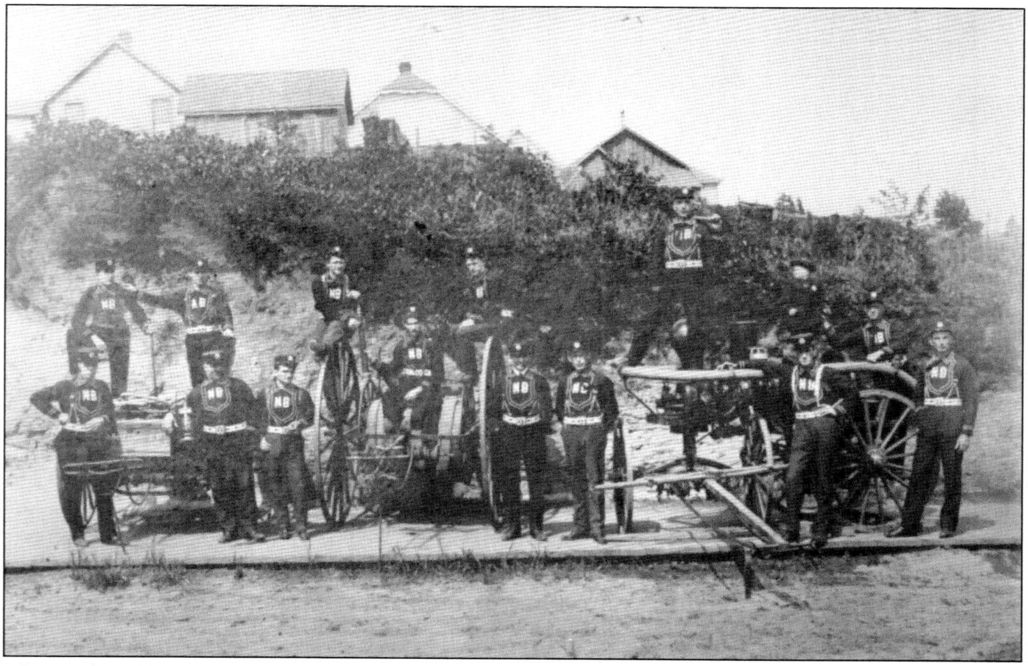

This is the oldest known picture of North Bend's firemen. They are equipped with hand propelled hose reels. Their caps and vests have "NB" on them. (CHMM 007-33.28.)

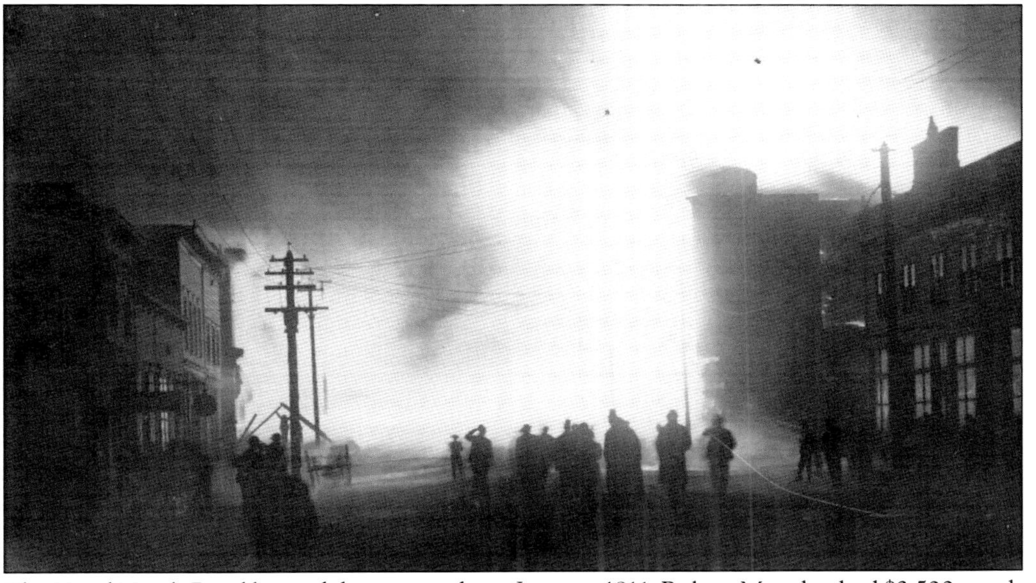

The Hotel North Bend burned during a night in January 1911. Robert Marsden had $3,500 worth of insurance on it. The Simpson Lumber Company owned the Annex and had no insurance. The city's salt water mains produced no pressure and the Marshfield Water Company mains were also useless. Arson was suspected. (Graham Family.)

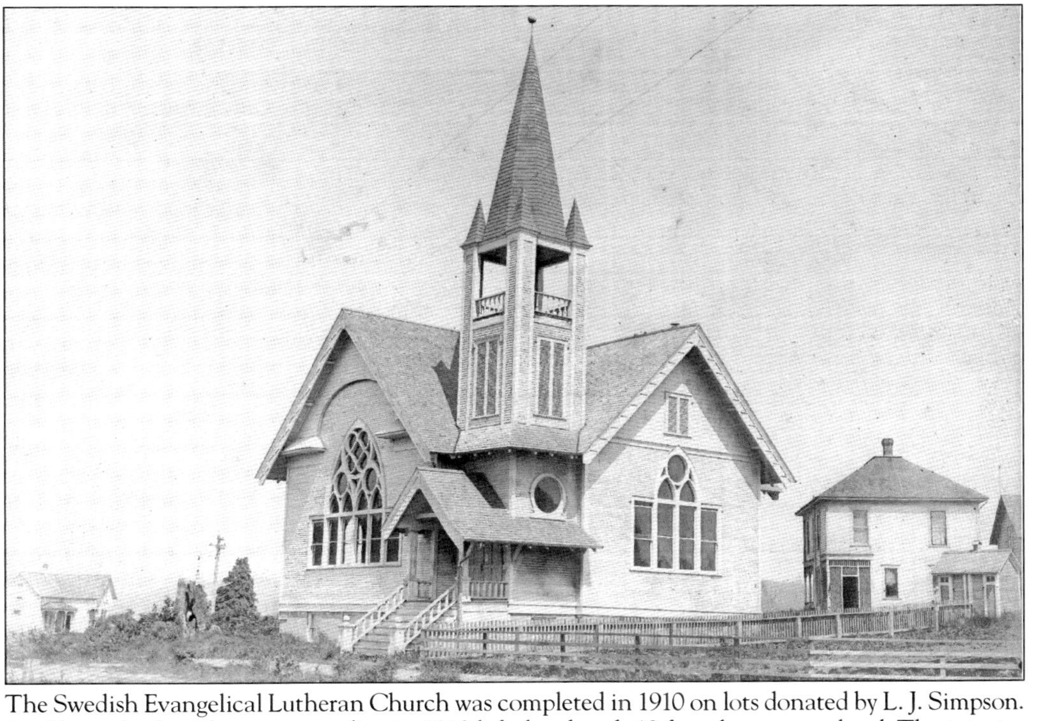

The Swedish Evangelical Lutheran Church was completed in 1910 on lots donated by L. J. Simpson. It still stands, though street regrading in 1913 left the church 10 feet above street level. The interior has high arched ceilings but the original pulpit, high above the congregation, has been removed. As the tall bell tower deteriorated, part of it was removed. (CHMM 007.33.132.)

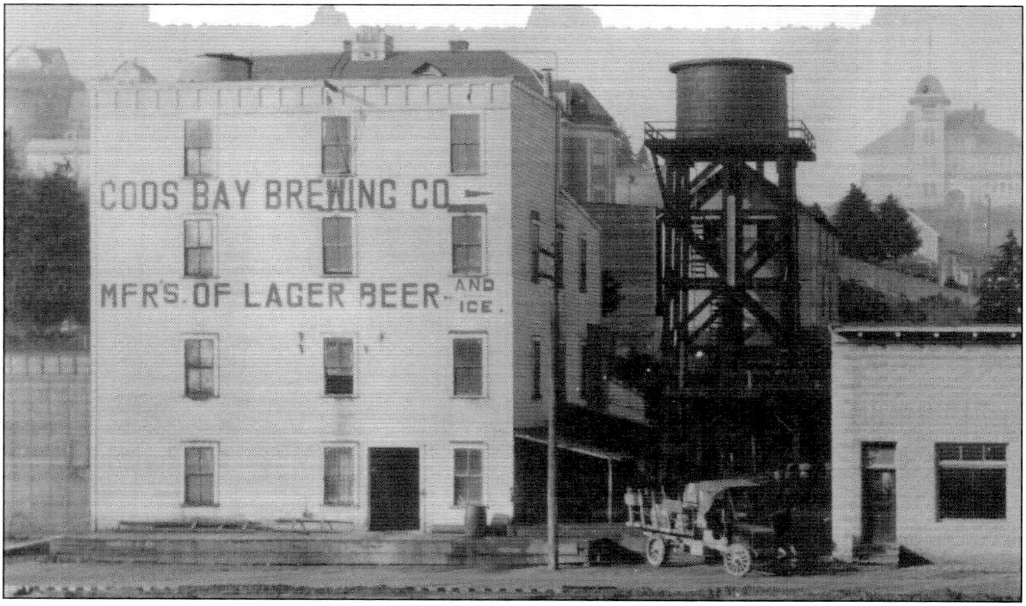

The Coos Bay Brewing Company, located on Stanton Avenue, was established in October 1907. Owner Charlie Thom produced Coos Bay and Pacific Pride beer as well as ice for the saloons. The large water tower ensured a steady supply, as Flanagan and Bennett's Marshfield Water Company provided unreliable service. In 1911, Thom also built a concrete bottling works, seen just right of the Atterbury delivery truck. (CHMM 972-62A.)

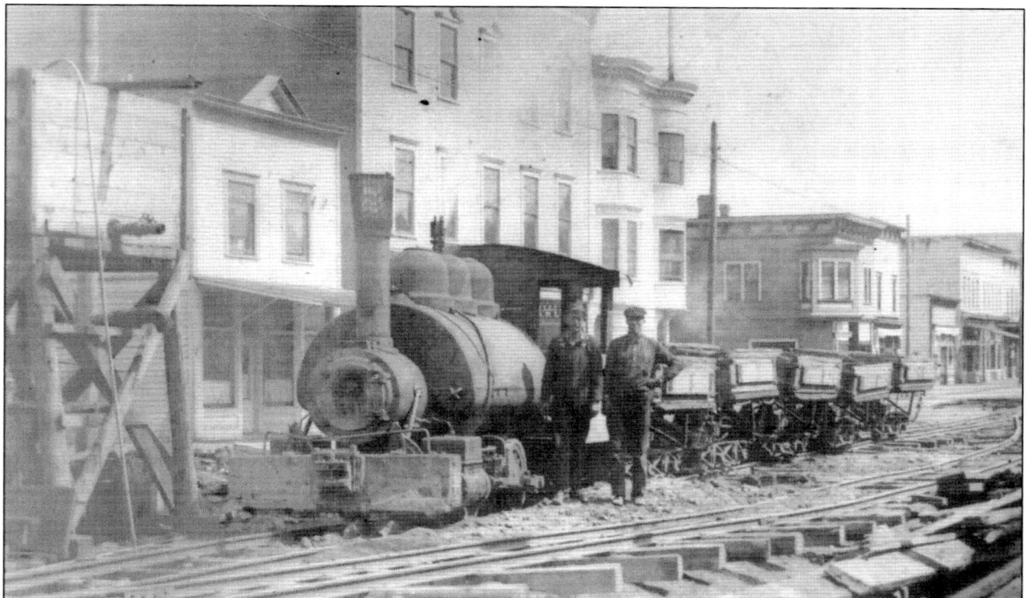

In 1913, North Bend contracted with the Marshfield firm of Perham and Gidley to grade and level Union, McPherson, Meade, Monroe, and the northern part of Sherman. Engineer Roy Bogue drove this narrow gauge locomotive with dump cars. His fireman is unidentified. The photograph was taken in front of Eckhoff Hall. (CHMM 974-75.)

Five

Growing Up

Louis Simpson fostered town life from a community band, theater, library, and baseball, to land for churches and charitable and patriotic fundraising. Big celebrations of developmental events were his trademark.

Celebrations date to company town days. People enjoyed themselves on the Fourth of July when a Civil War cannon was fired (until it exploded in 1901). Louis Simpson sponsored the Grove's (today's Ferry Road Park) 1902 fete that had fireworks, food, and drink for area guests. Ship launchings were often marked with band accompaniments, holidays, and civic events. Citizens even formed a "Do It While Living Club" to honor city notables, rather than wait for funeral orations.

The City of North Bend's great early celebrations involved the coming of the Willamette Pacific railroad (a Southern Pacific subsidiary). The awarding of the franchise caused jubilation. When the engineers planning the big railroad bridge across the bay were in town, it was an excuse for a supportive parade. Actual construction was cause for a festive 1913 event when the "knockers' hammer" was buried. Completion of the railroad swing bridge occasioned the largest celebration on the bay to date.

The October 7, 8, and 9, 1915, Big Bridge Carnival, suggested by Vern Gorst, occasioned a civic parade led by queen of the carnival Goldie Riggs and her court, with marching bands and fraternal and school groups. Speakers from the area and from the Southern Pacific orated. Boxing and wrestling matches, dances, auto races, and water sports led up to a masked carnival ball that closed the event.

When the first train finally arrived from Eugene in 1916, a three-day August festival brought thousands from around the state to North Bend and Marshfield. Again there were parades, dances, and speeches. The "marriage" of Miss Coos County to Mr. Eugene Lane capped the event. Even the British prison ship *Success* was in port, its wax figures and grizzly prison paraphernalia on display.

The start of World War I sparked patriotic displays as well as "four-minute" speeches by prominent citizens on war topics and in support of government savings bond drives.

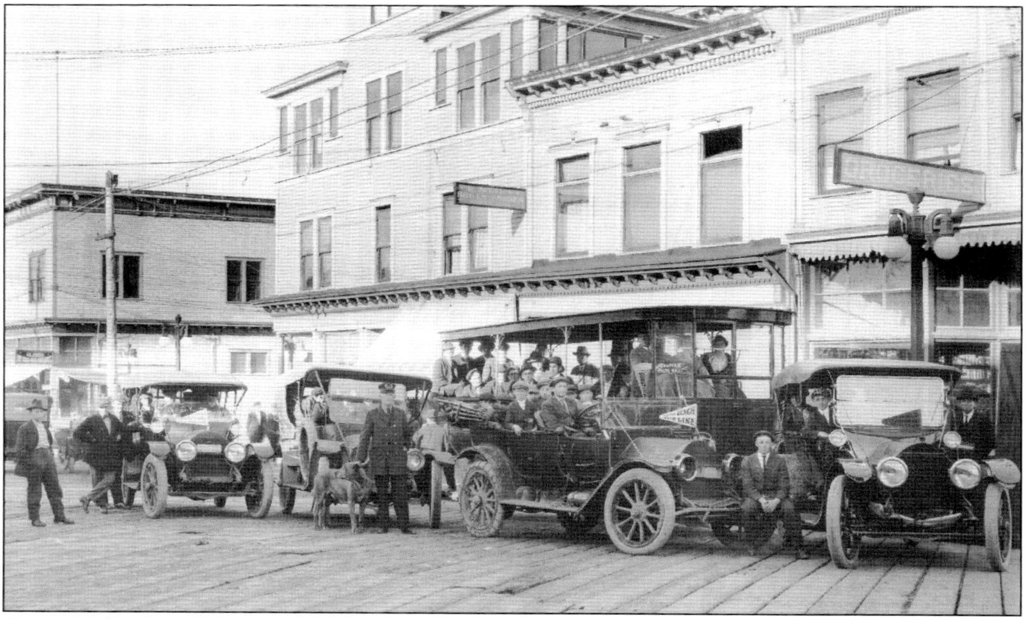

Gorst and King autos are displayed at the Winsor building on Sherman Avenue in 1912. Four autos with pennants show the routes—"Ocean Beach" and "Marshfield North Bend." The bus has a driver's megaphone. Note the planked street and the "Ocean Beach" auto's chains to get through sand and mud. Original fares matched the boat passenger fee between North Bend and Marshfield, 25 cents one way. (CHMM 992-D74.)

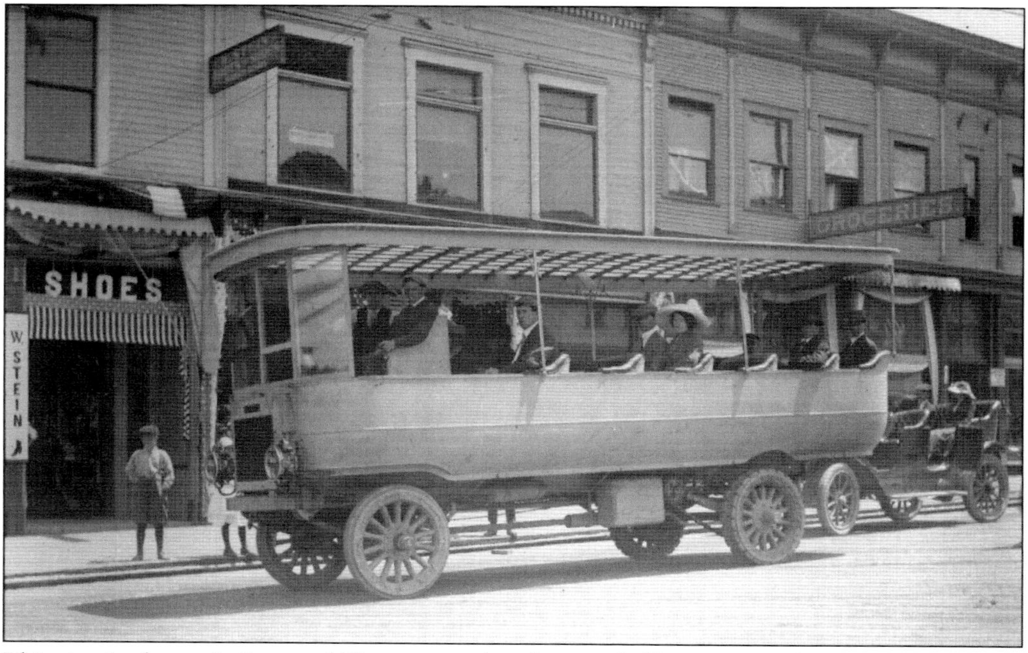

This view is of an early Gorst and King open-air bus that traveled between North Bend and Marshfield on the planked waterfront road. The photograph was taken near the Winsor building in front of W. Stein shoes on Sherman Avenue. The Coos Bay Grocery is behind the bus. (CHMM 992-8-0931.)

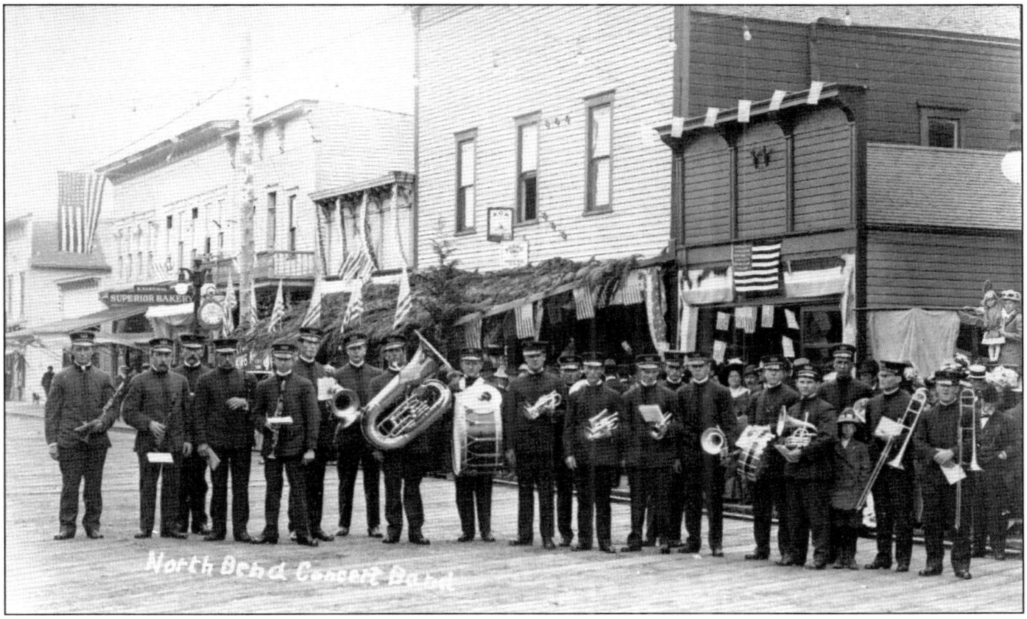

The North Bend Concert Band is shown about 1912 in the 1900 block of Sherman Avenue. The image shows Taylor Hall, where WOW and the Arago Chapter of the Independent Order of Odd Fellows met. The sign for E. Kardinal's Superior Bakery is farther up the block. (CHMM 992-8-0909.)

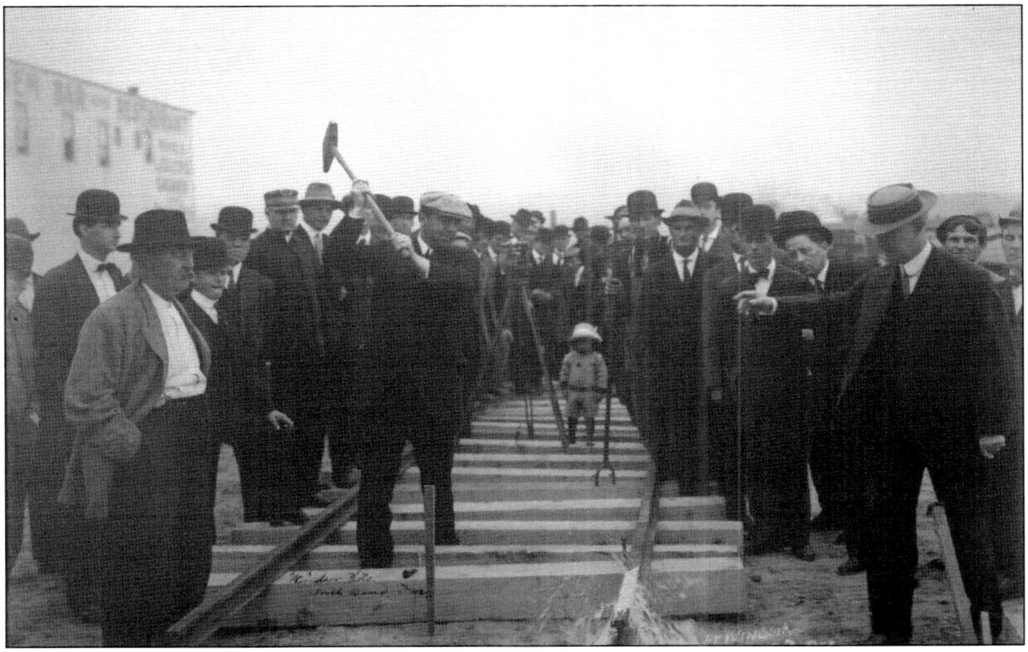

In May 1912, North Bend's council approved a franchise for the Southern Pacific railroad. L. J. Simpson is seen driving the ritual first spike while the railroad's C. J. Millis (a teetotaler) christens the rails with a Coos Bay Cream bottle. After this symbolic event there was a hiatus of nearly a year before serious construction began. (CHMM 992-8-0904.)

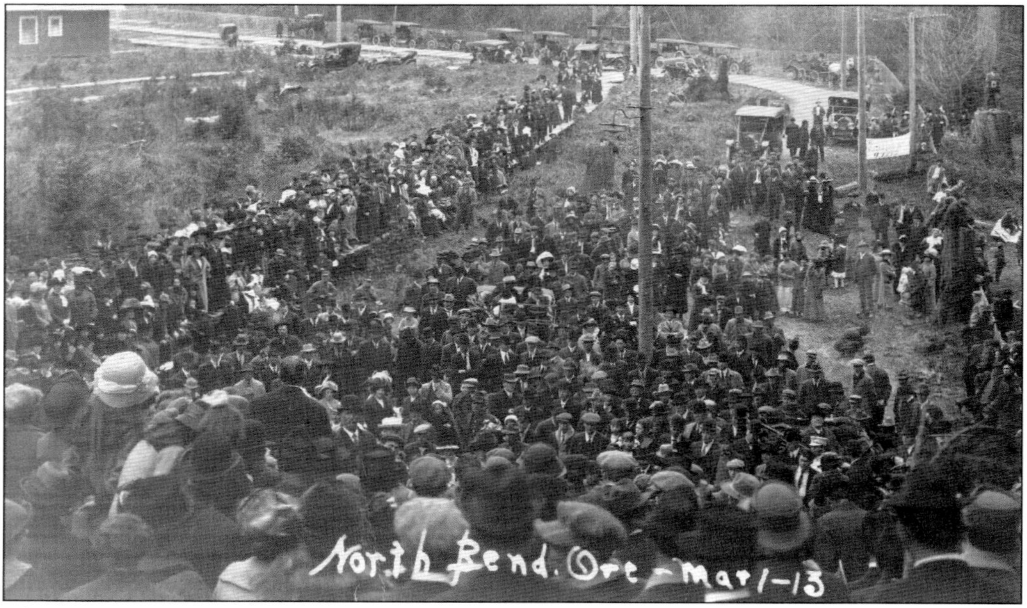

This is a view of the crowd, estimated at 2,000, in today's Simpson Park for the March 1, 1913, celebration of the Southern Pacific's initial construction. W. R. Simpson, North Bend's oldest resident, and Edgar Simpson, Asa Simpson's son, felled the first tree for the railroad right of way. Simpson Lumber furnished sandwiches, clams, and lemonade for the event. Charlie Thom's brewery provided beer. (CHMM 982-190.36.)

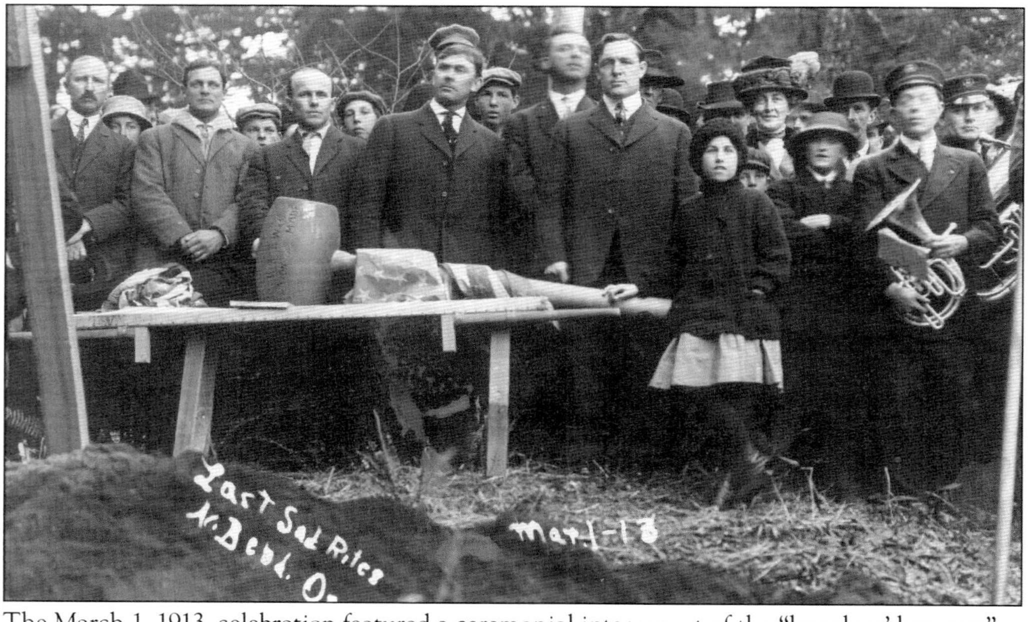

The March 1, 1913, celebration featured a ceremonial internment of the "knockers' hammer"—burying the critics' complaint that a railroad would never come. The North Bend Iron Works cast the 135-pound hammer, Joe Bennett of Marshfield delivered a mock sermon, and H. C. Diers of North Bend covered the hammer with dirt. Later the hammer was dug up and secretly reburied, not found again until 1930s highway construction. (Chris Bryne.)

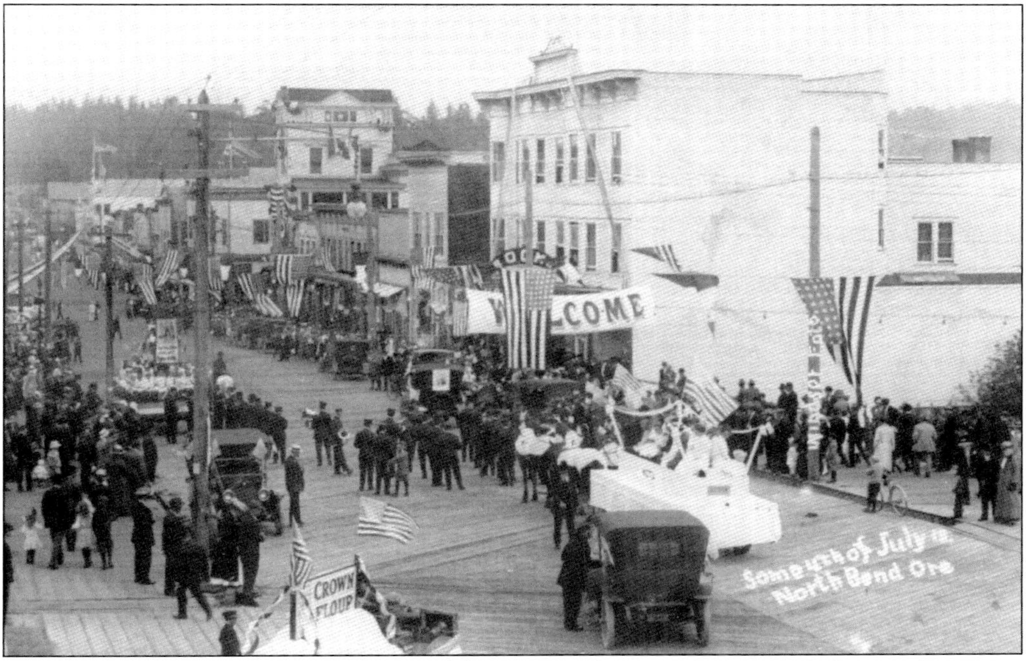

This photograph shows the July 4, 1913, celebration on Sherman Avenue with the parade moving north from Washington. Note the planked streets, the Palace Hotel across the way, and the Winsor building at Sherman and Virginia. The Crown Flour float is about to join the parade, following the Women's Christian Temperance Union vehicle. (CHMM 007-25.218.)

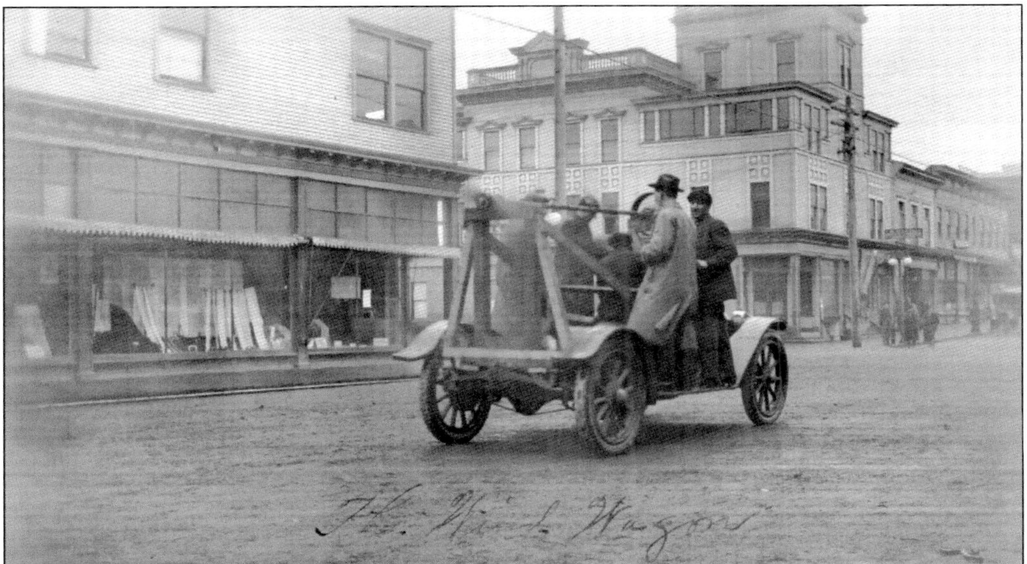

The Wind Wagon, Vern Gorst's 1913 experiment mounting an airplane propeller on a vehicle, used wind propulsion. Milas Richardson, Gorst and King's partner and head mechanic, ran a flat belt off the automobile flywheel to the propeller. Dangerous, with the propeller blade close to passengers, and without adequate power on hills, the wind wagon failed—working only on level ground. (Sami Abboud and CHMM 966-75b.)

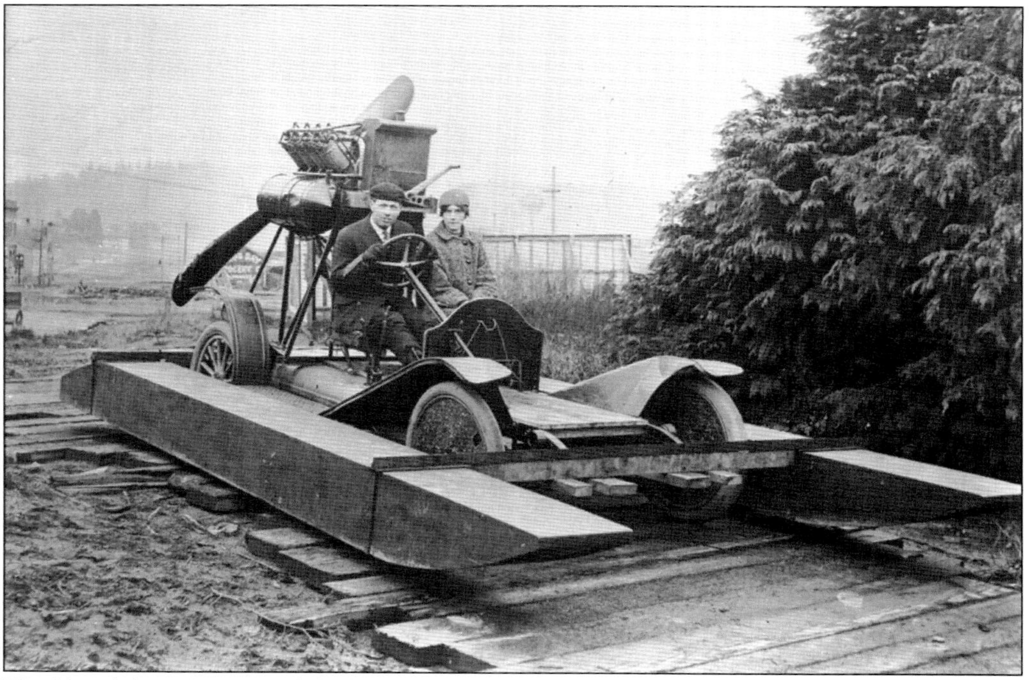

The "Amphibian," a Hupmobile chassis mounted on pontoons, was another Gorst experiment. The machine, intended for land or water, had a Curtiss airplane motor and propeller. Reportedly it could do over 50 miles per hour on the beach, but only 15 miles per hour in the water. (Steven Grief.)

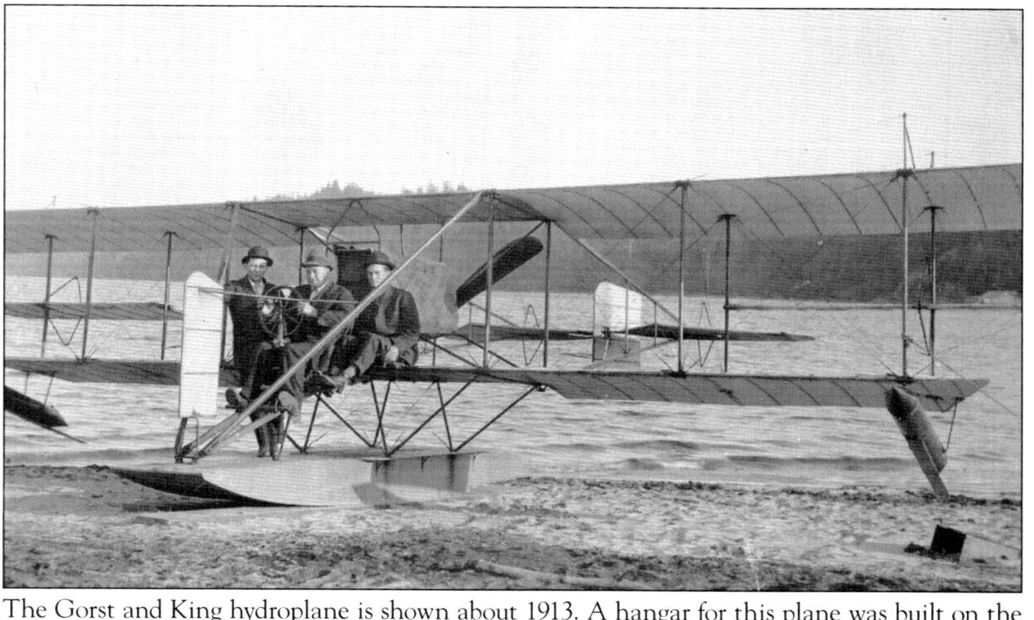

The Gorst and King hydroplane is shown about 1913. A hangar for this plane was built on the bay at Washington Avenue. Ed Steele flew the hydroplane up the coast from Coos Bay to Toledo, Oregon. During the trip a wing struck either on water or a piling, damaging the frame. King refused to spend money for repairs, so it was sold "as is" in Toledo. (CHMM 992-8-1160.)

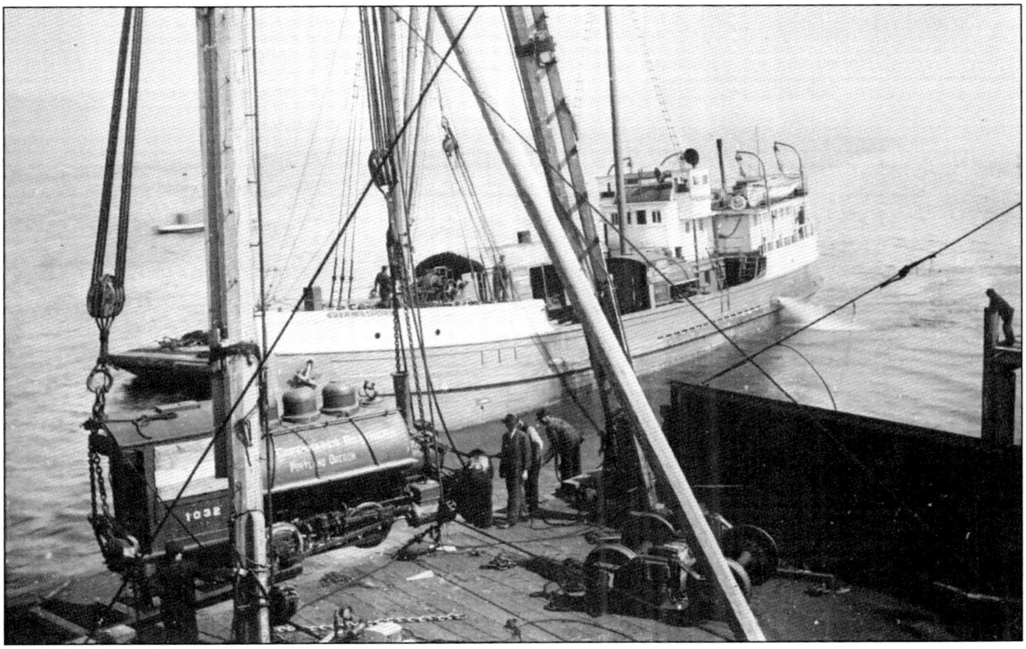

The gas steamer *Tillamook* unloads railroad construction equipment on North Bend's dock for the Southern Pacific's project. Local excitement ran high as, at last, "rail would meet sail" and perhaps real estate sales promises of prosperity for all who purchased land would materialize. (CHMM 992-8-0270.)

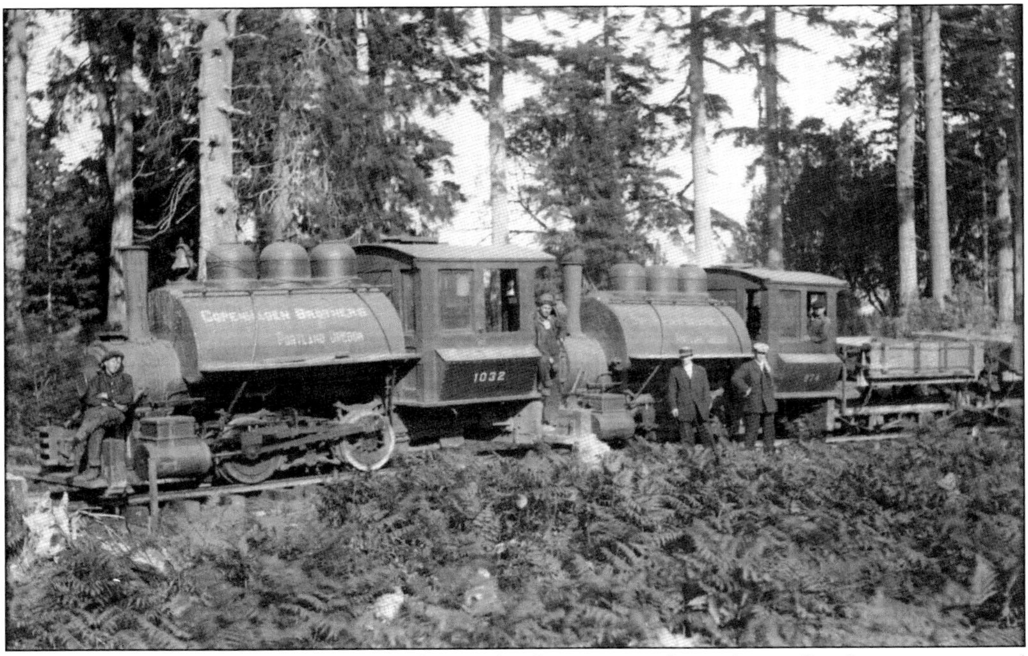

Railroad construction equipment from the Portland contractor Copenhagen Brothers was engaged to build the Willamette Pacific railroad. Later Southern Pacific dropped the Willamette Pacific title and called its branch the "Coos Bay Line." (CHMM 992-8-0910.)

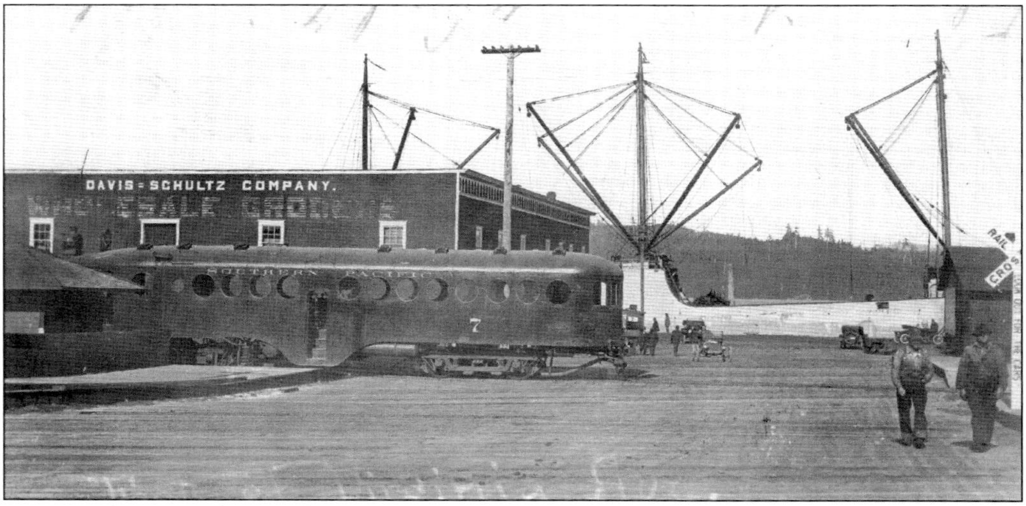

In December 1913, the Southern Pacific sent an 80-passenger, 200 horsepower, rail motorcar for commuter use between North Bend and Marshfield. The fumes from its gasoline engine led to its nickname, "The Skunk." Gorst and King met the railroad fares and offered more frequent service. After two and a half years, Southern Pacific ended this motorcar service.

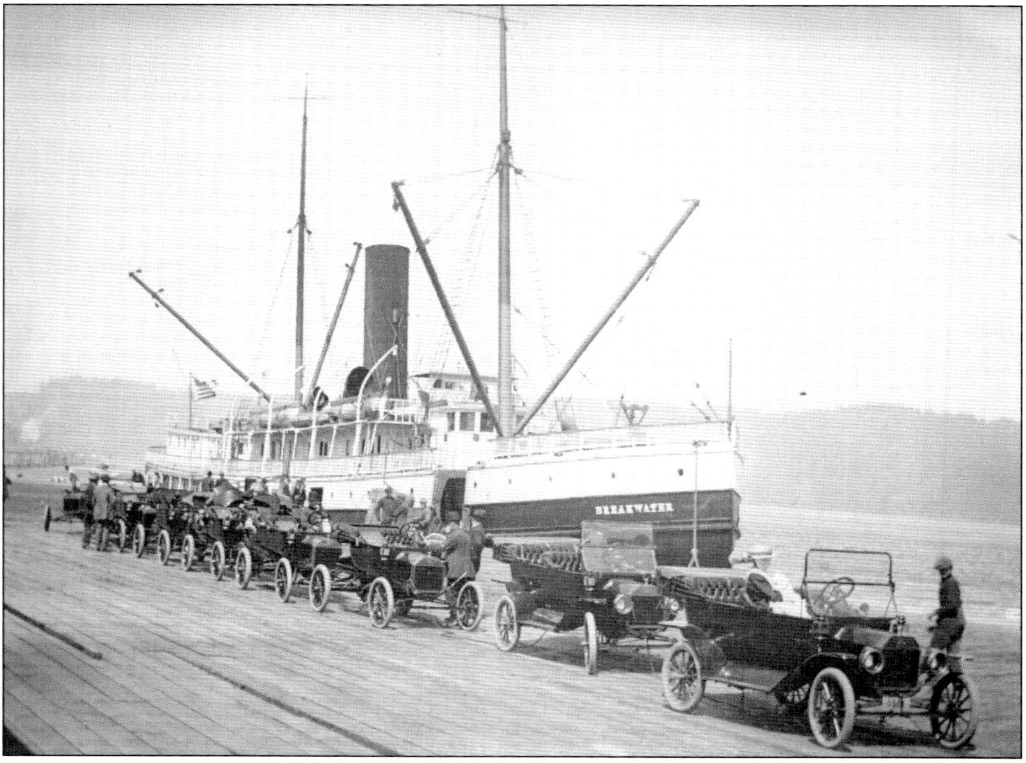

Fords are unloaded from the *Breakwater* to the North Bend dock in transit to Marshfield. (Rates were cheaper than at the private Marshfield docks.) Ford dealers there were George Goodrum, prior to December 1914, and Isaac (Russ) Tower, who on December 29, 1914, became the Ford dealer. Tower Ford—now in Day family hands—continues nearly 100 years later. (CHMM 009-16.456.)

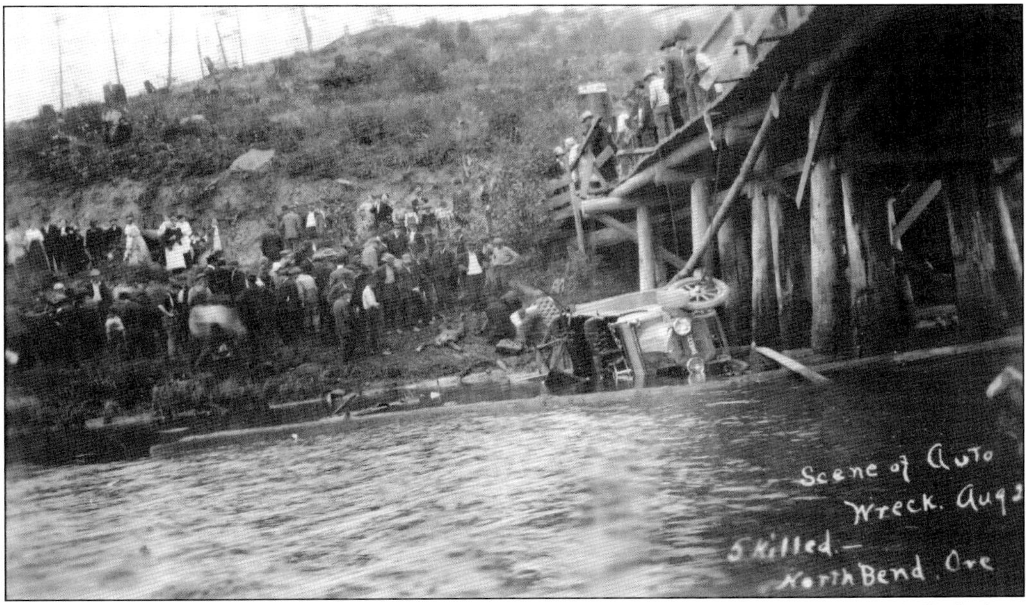

North Bend's worst early auto accident happened on August 20, 1914. Five men were killed when a large Case auto, driven by J. Bulford Davis of Coos River, plunged off the Pony Slough Bridge (Sixteenth Street Bridge) down to tidewater and mud below. Reportedly the driver was going too fast when he swerved to avoid a small boy on the bridge. (CHMM 980-36.14.)

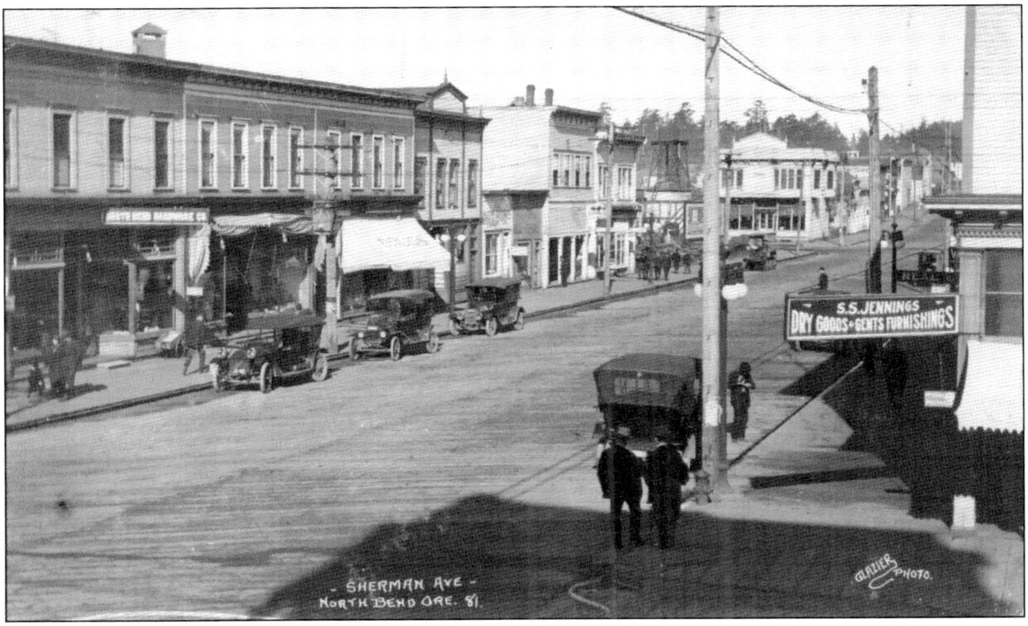

This view, looking north, shows a planked Sherman Avenue. On the right is the S. S. Jennings Dry Goods and Gents Furnishings firm in the Simpson-Myers building. Across the street in the old Bank of Oregon building is the North Bend Hardware Company.

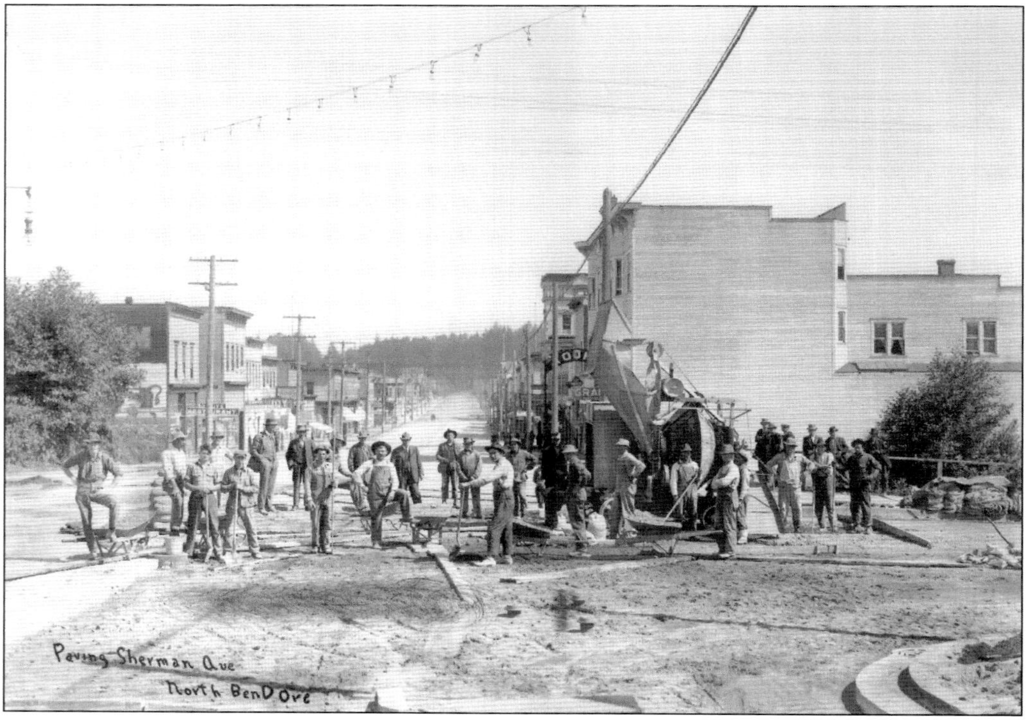

This late-1915 photograph shows a Sherman Avenue paving crew standing at the intersection of Washington Avenue. The Palace Hotel, built in 1908 by John Gunn, stands to the right. An arsonist destroyed the lovely Victorian hotel in 1985. (Patricia Richardson.)

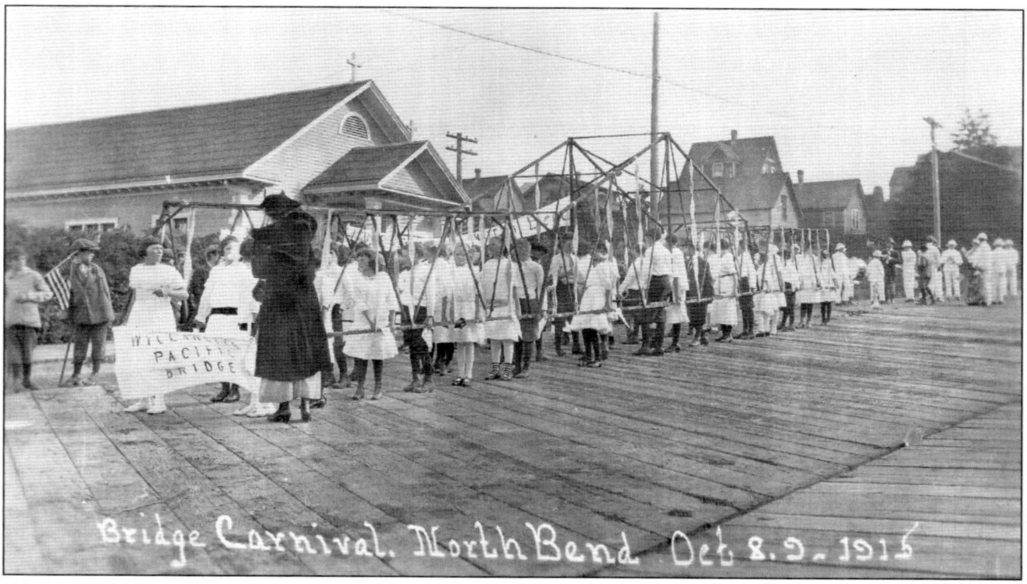

Children with a model of the Willamette Pacific's railroad swing bridge are shown preparing for the October 8 and 9, 1915, Railroad Bridge Carnival parade. The photograph was taken on Sherman hill, with the newly completed (1914) Holy Redeemer Catholic Church in background. (CHMM 975-34p.)

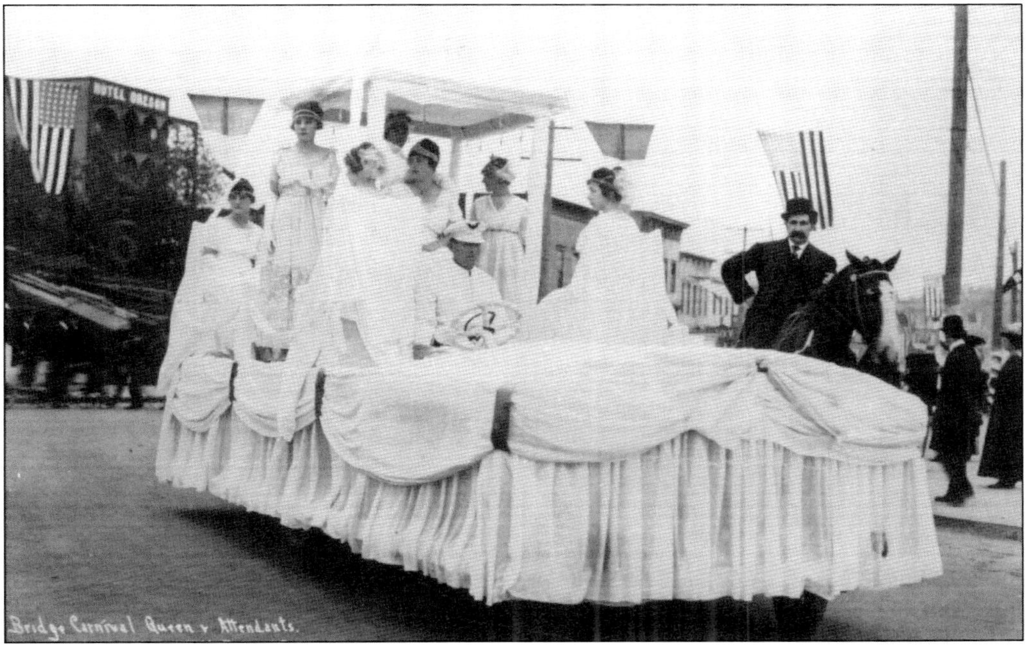

This Railroad Big Bridge Carnival parade float celebrates the completion of the railroad swing bridge in 1915. Queen Goldie Riggs and her attendants are featured on the motorized float. The photograph was taken at the corner of Sherman and Washington Avenues (note the bayside Hotel Oregon sign in the background). (CHMM 007-25.183.)

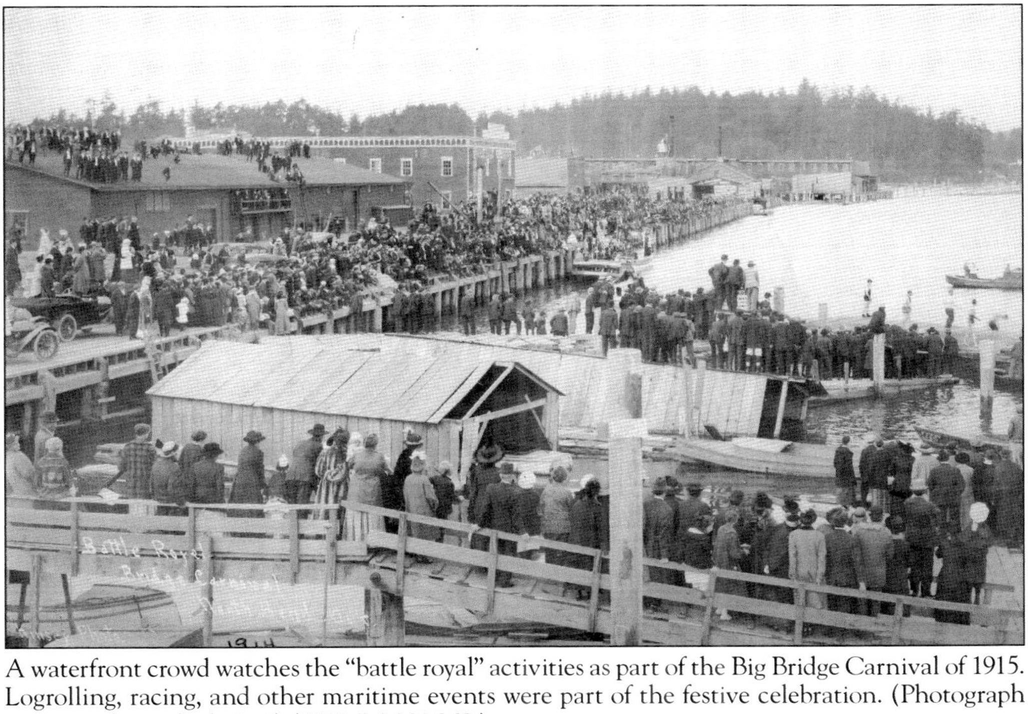

A waterfront crowd watches the "battle royal" activities as part of the Big Bridge Carnival of 1915. Logrolling, racing, and other maritime events were part of the festive celebration. (Photograph erroneously marked 1914.) (CHMM 981-268.)

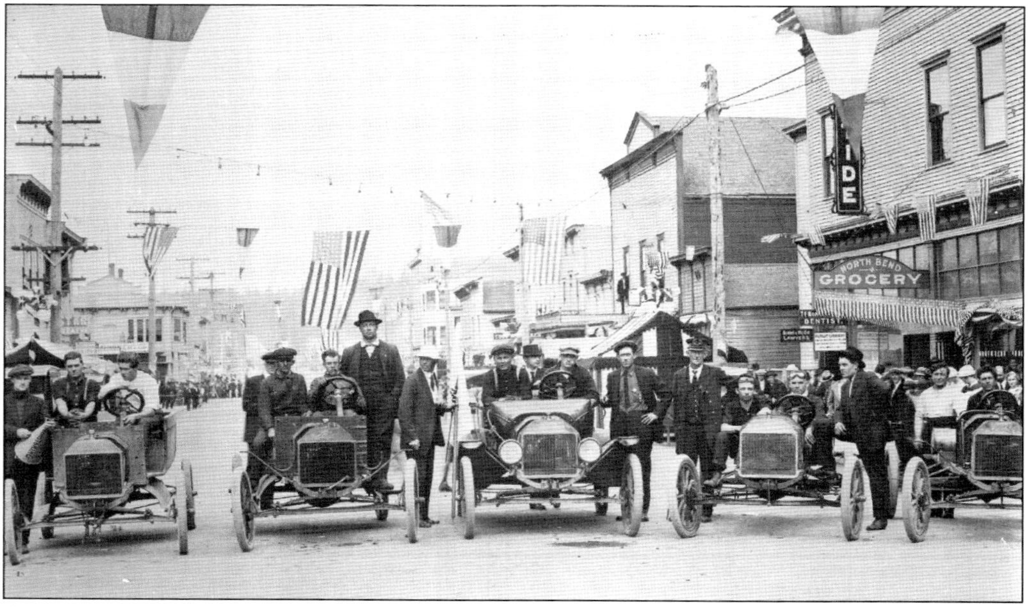

Auto racing was part of the Big Bridge Carnival in October 1915. The race began at Sherman and Virginia. Vern Gorst, near center, holds the white flag. A sign for the *Tide*, a daily newspaper, appears on the Simpson-Myers Building. Several lawyers, a dentist, and the public library also were located there. Across the street the Star Theatre sign is visible. (CHMM 992-8-0914.)

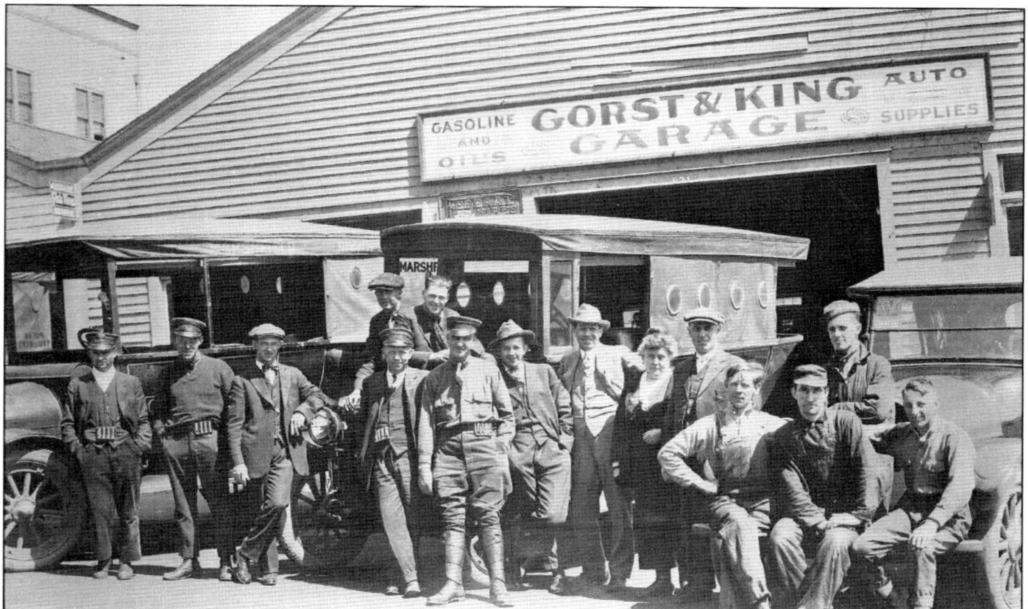

The Terminal Garage, built in 1914 by Edgar Simpson (L. J.'s brother) and C. H. Burrett, was leased in 1915 to Gorst and King. Their busses and autos were serviced here and tire and auto repairs were advertised. Gorst and King sold Chalmer and Reo vehicles. Vern Gorst stands at center with hands on hips. Sarah Brigham, office manager, is right of center, and Charles King is next to her. (CHMM 992-8-0934.)

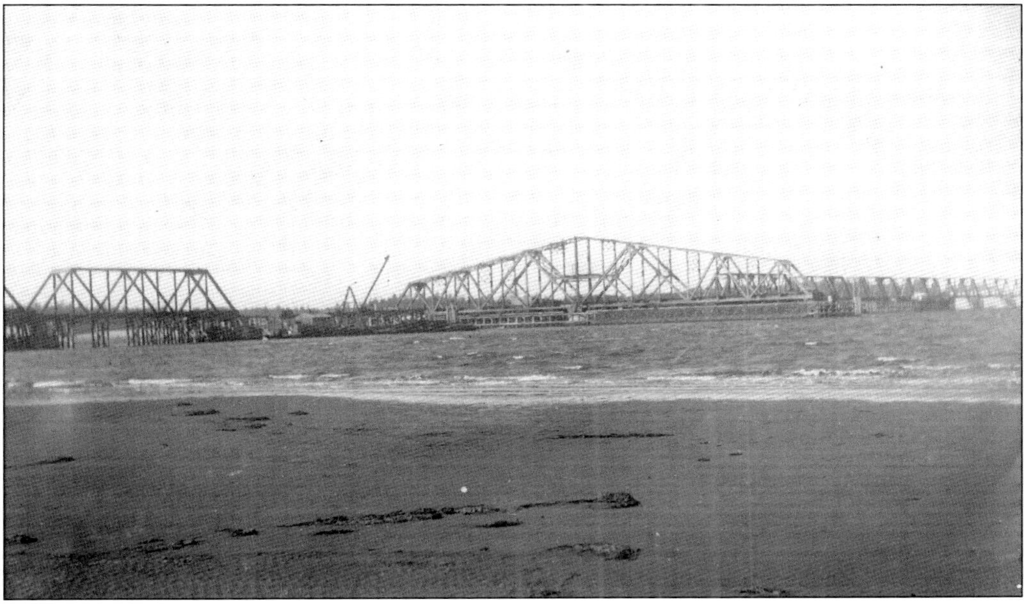

Piles for the construction of the railroad swing bridge over Coos Bay were first driven in July 1915. The bridge cost $1,250,000, used 700 tons of cement, and was 2,168 feet long. Its trestle approaches were nearly a mile long. Several ships hit the bridge. The first was the steamer *Yellowstone* in 1915 followed by the *Martha Buehner* in 1924. (CHMM 996-36.16.)

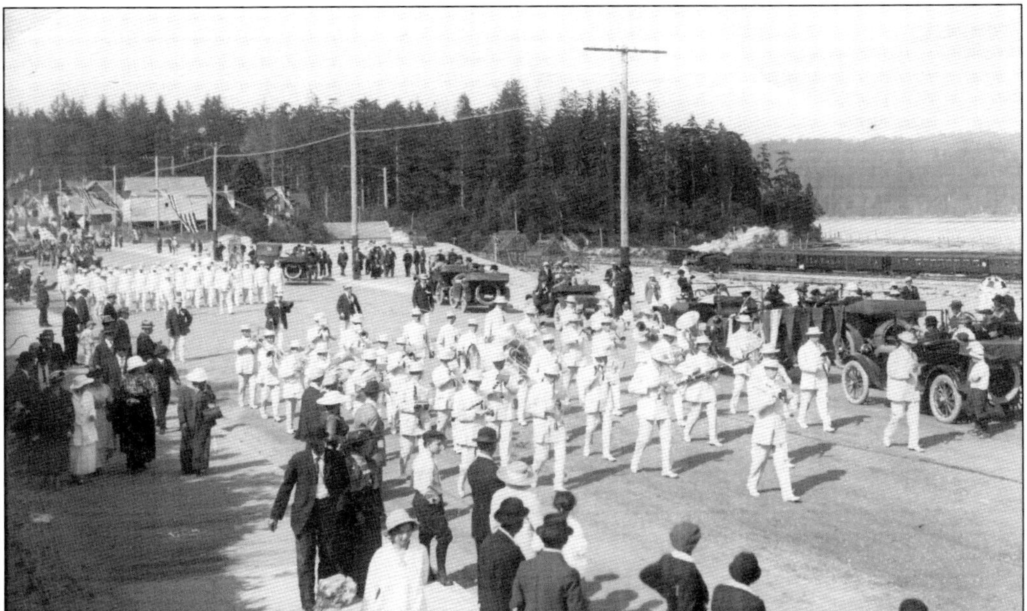

The celebration of the Coos Bay Railway Jubilee was in August 1916. The slogan was "Boost for Coos." Through trains from Eugene to the bay finally arrived. This marching band on north Sherman Avenue was part of the parade. A passenger train is in the background. (CHMM 959-283.)

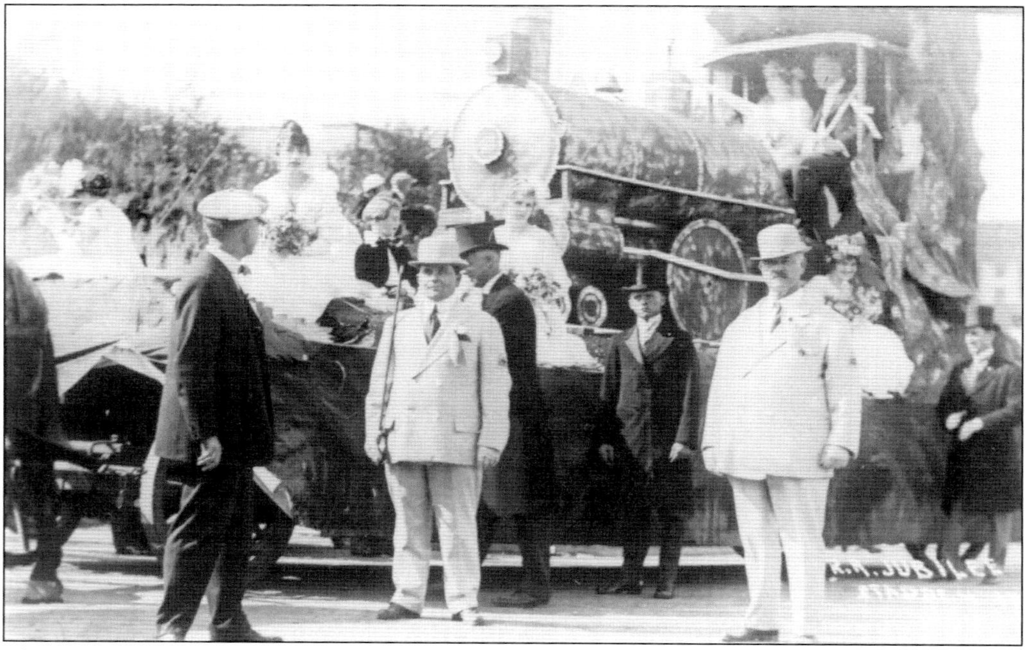

This is a photograph of the main float in the Railway Jubilee parade, 1916. Miss Coos County and Mr. Eugene Lane ride in the engine cab prior to their mock wedding ceremony at the intersection of Virginia and Sherman Avenues. (CHMM 007-25.481.)

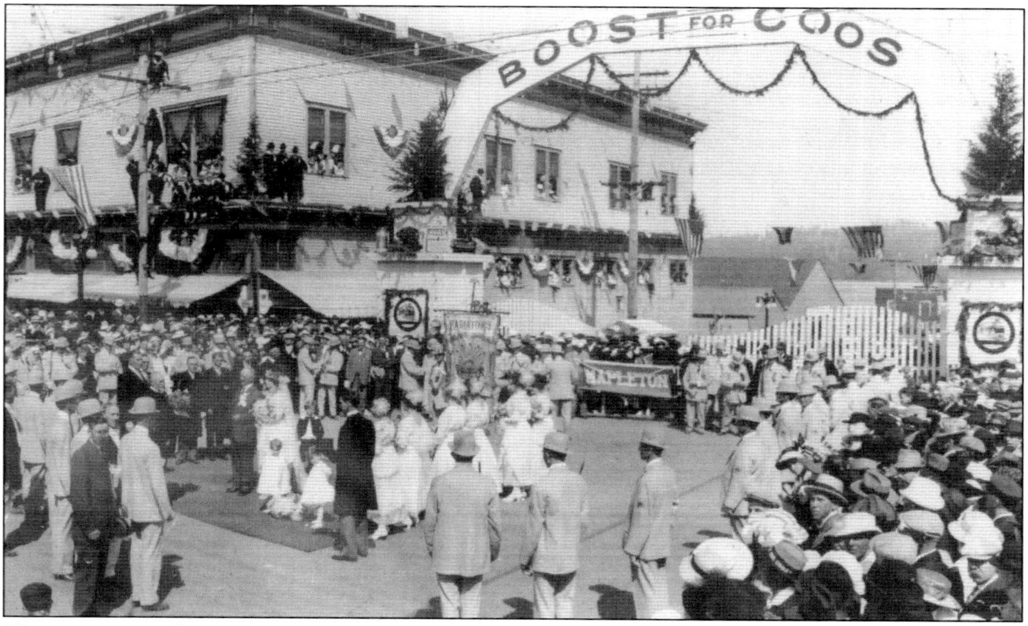

The marriage of Miss Coos County to Mr. Eugene Lane was the highlight of the 1916 Railway Jubilee. Special excursion trains brought men's organizations from San Francisco, Portland, Salem, and Eugene for the event. Pathe Motion Pictures filmed activities. The freshly painted Simpson-Myers building is in the background of this wedding photograph. The sign reads "Boost for Coos" and, on the reverse, "Welcome to North Bend."

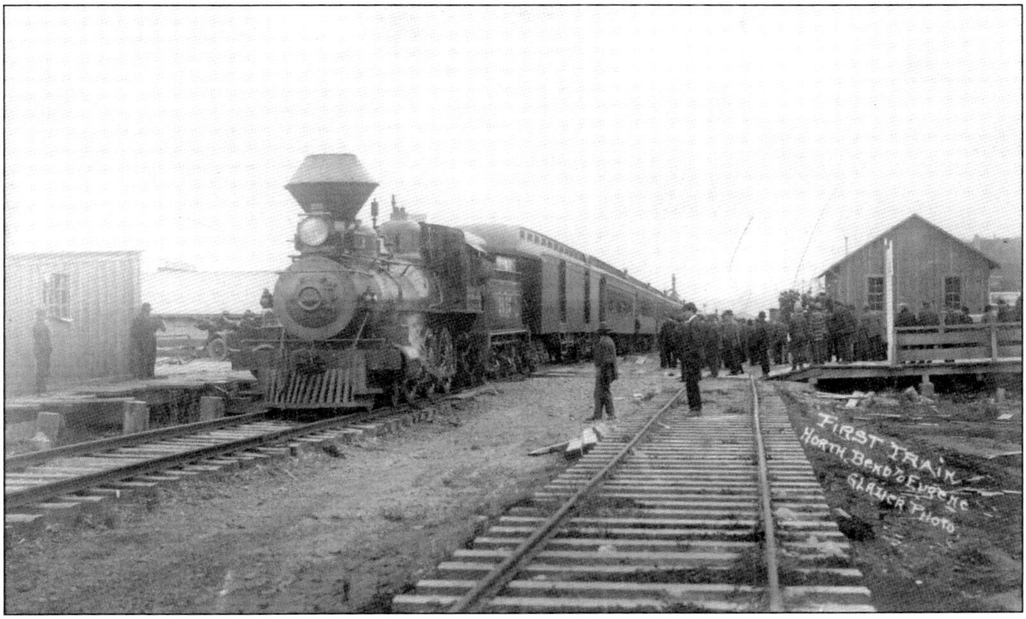

This was the first passenger train to arrive with service to Eugene in 1916. The railway station had not yet been built, but a temporary freight office was in place by the tracks. (CHMM 008-45.55.)

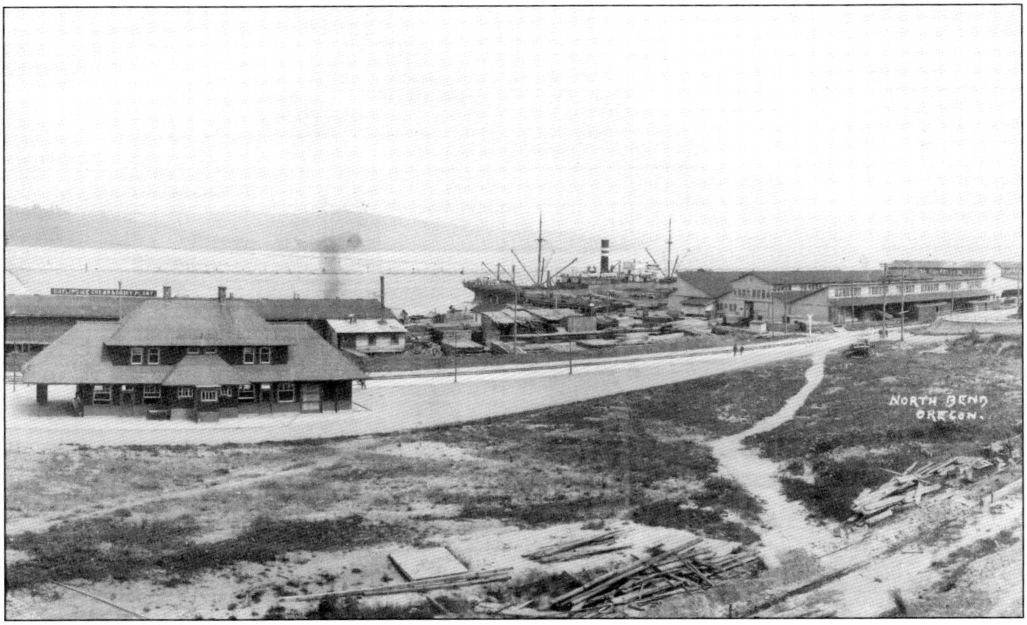

North Bend's passenger station was located just south of Virginia Avenue and west of the tracks. J. E. Steinman built the 32-by-108-foot structure in 1916. It had separate waiting rooms for men and women, plus a baggage room and office. Passenger service ended in 1953. Note the 1923 location of Cutlip's Ice Cream factory on the dock. (CHMM 965-71.8.)

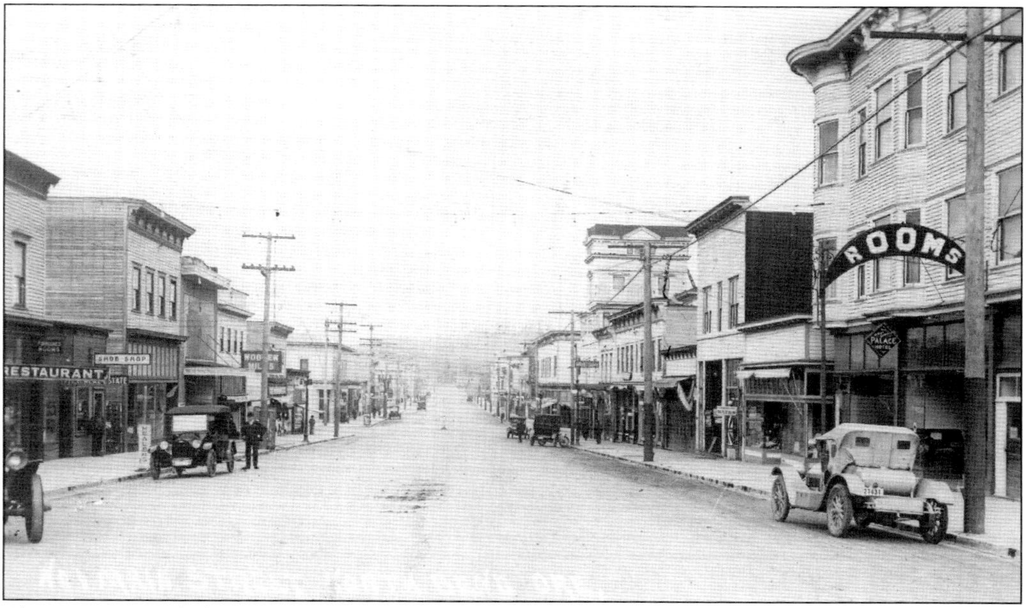

This is a view of Sherman Avenue after 1915. The Palace Hotel is on the right with its square sign advertising "All Night Service." (CHMM 995-16.7d.)

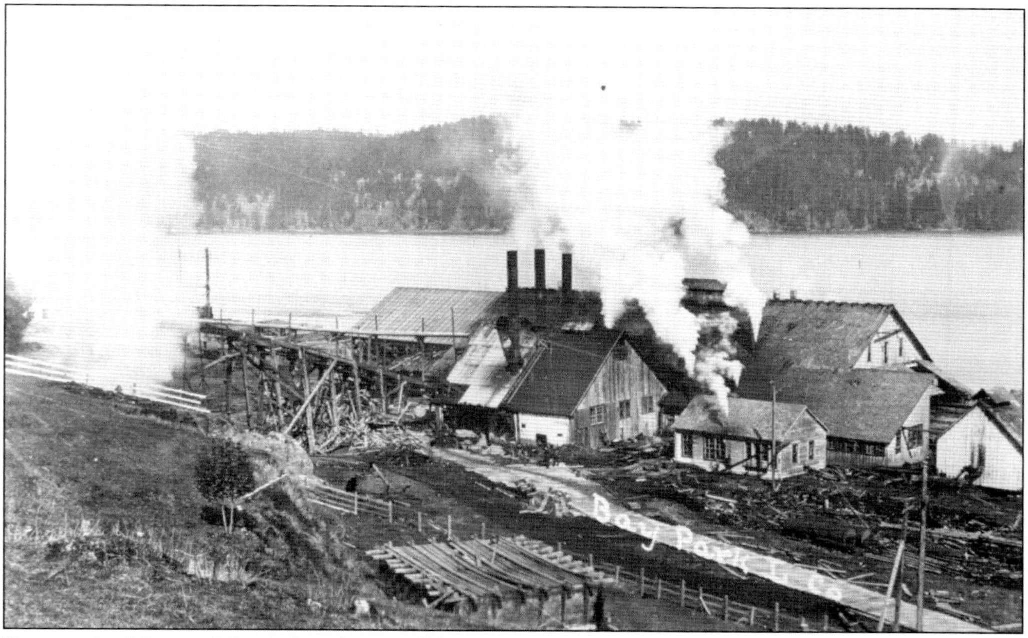

Simpson's old town North Bend sawmill became the Bay Park Lumber Company sawmill. After Asa Simpson's death in January 1915, most of his estate was sold. However, this North Bend property was leased to a team headed by L. J. Simpson. Bay Park Lumber was sold in 1923 to William Vaughan of Coos Bay Logging. Weyerhaeuser bought the property in 1943, but Coos Bay Logging leased it back. (CHMM 009-16.1414.)

Six

The Twenties and Thirties

The city's concern with fire danger, intensified by Marshfield's 1922 Front Street destruction, brought new concrete construction and modern fire equipment. Doctors Philip and Russell Keizer opened a modern hospital. The Independent Order of Odd Fellows built a building, the American Legion raised a hall, Roosevelt Elementary School was erected, L. A. Cutlip opened an ice cream factory, the Liberty Theater moved to a new building, and the Hotel North Bend dominated the landscape. School superintendent Marion S. Taylor headed the bay area's booster group. Dr. J. E. Snyder led the Community Presbyterian Church and advanced civic affairs. Many other active men became local legends. The building boom provided concrete buildings, often designed by either Portland architect John E. Tourtellotte or local Fred Magnussen.

North Bend's 1920s boom ended in 1926 when the old Porter mill, then called Mill A, burned. Men were laid off and storefront sales declined, producing a recession before the national Great Depression. Bennett's fledgling air service connecting to the Willamette valley quit after some months in 1930. Things were so bad in the 1930s that North Bend turned off the streetlights, unable to pay power bills. When the bank closed, the city authorized—unconstitutionally—emergency myrtlewood money.

There was some recovery after 1936 with a new bridge, a new City Hall in 1939, and then a more general rebound—especially for Kruse and Banks' shipyard—as the country moved toward World War II.

While always supportive of North Bend efforts, L. J. Simpson, no longer mayor and living at Shore Acres, took up non-political interests. He and his second wife adopted two children in the mid-1920s and built a new Shore Acres home in 1927–1928. In the late 1920s, he was preoccupied with revitalizing the old Southern Oregon Company's large Empire sawmill. He succeeded in re-opening it only to have the 1929 stock market crash wipe out his progress.

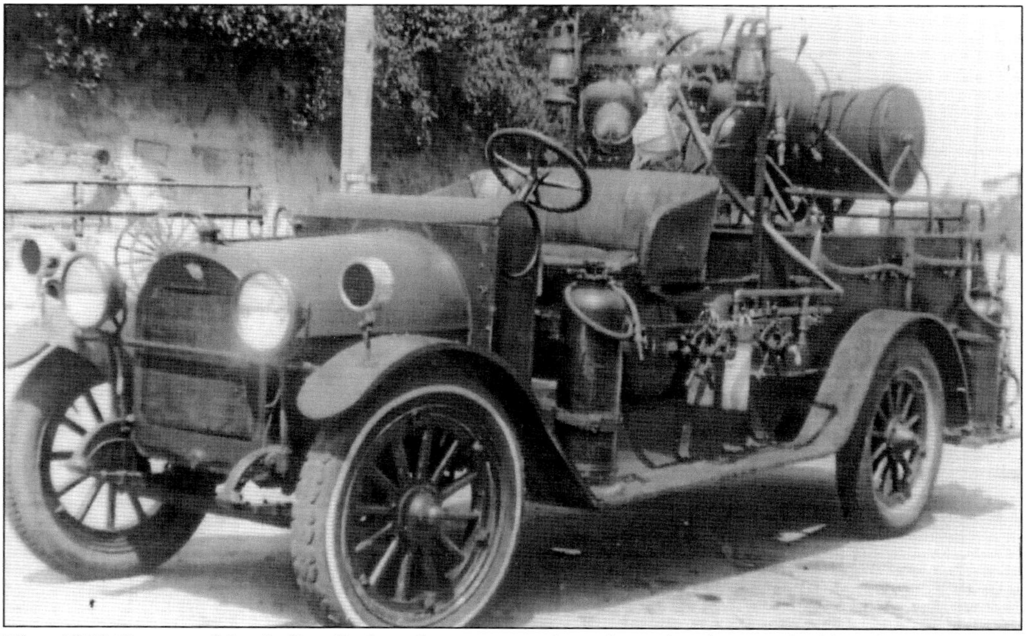

This 1920 Reo was North Bend's first fire engine. A tank under the seat held soda acid, which when mixed with water pressurized a vessel that squirted water. The engine carried 150 gallons of water. Hose reels and rollers are on top. In the background is a non-mechanized hose cart—the old firefighting equipment. (NBFD.)

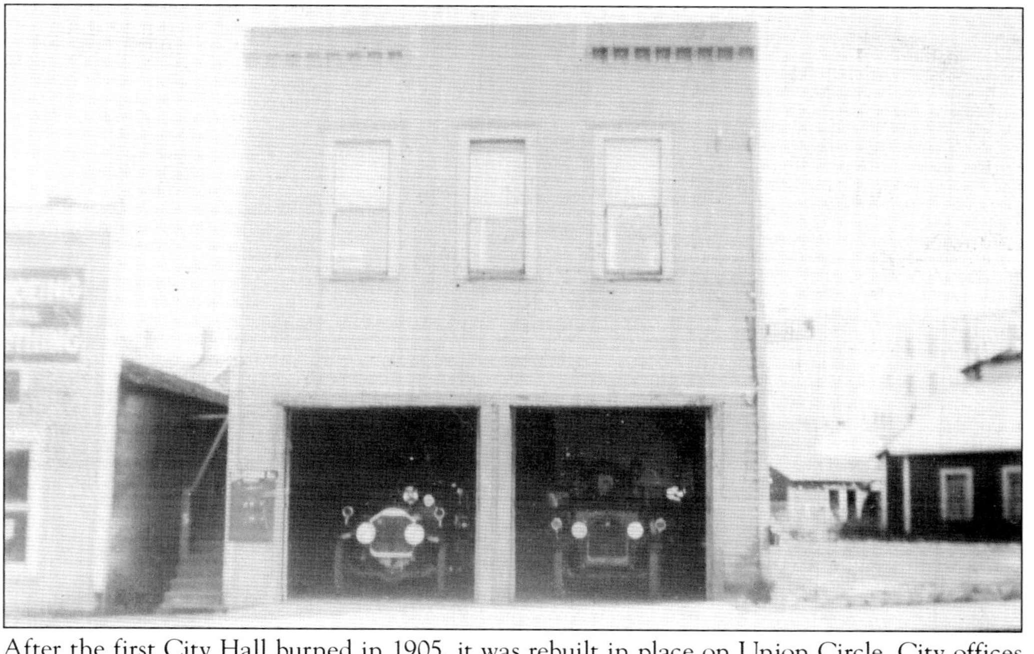

After the first City Hall burned in 1905, it was rebuilt in place on Union Circle. City offices and council chambers were upstairs. This snapshot was taken after the original bell tower was removed. The 1920 Reo is on the left and the 1921 LaFrance next to it. Fire Chief Boynton's home is to the right. (Graham Family.)

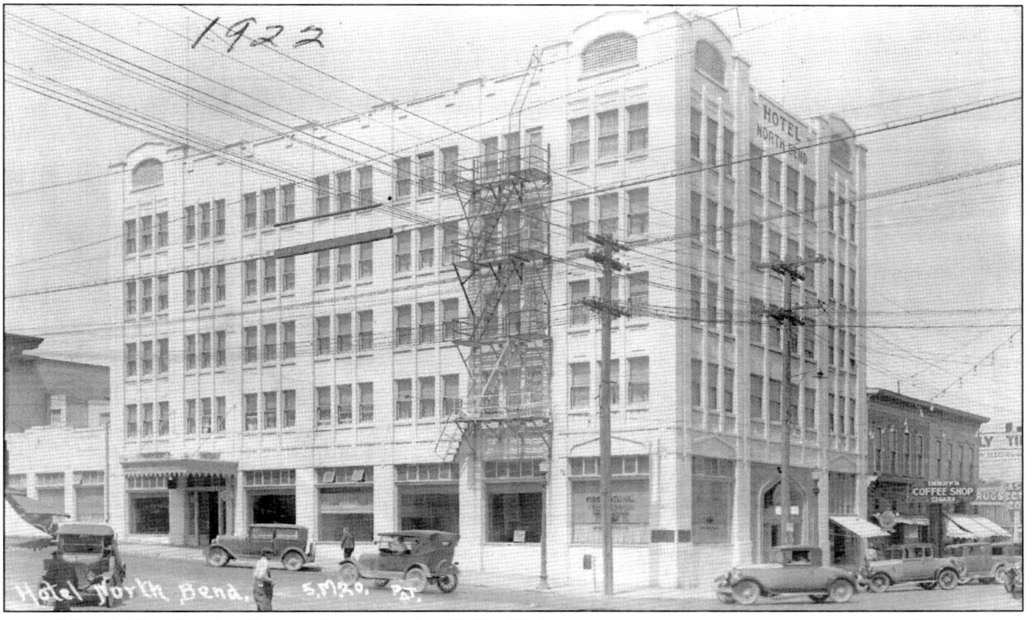

The Hotel North Bend was finished in 1922. This concrete building, with its hotel entrance on Virginia and the First National Bank entrance on Sherman, set the tone for the town. The grand hotel fulfilled a dream L. J. Simpson had since founding North Bend. The building cost $165,000 and had a manager's apartment off the mezzanine. School superintendent M. S. Taylor lived there and managed the hotel during 1925. (CHMM 982-191.13.)

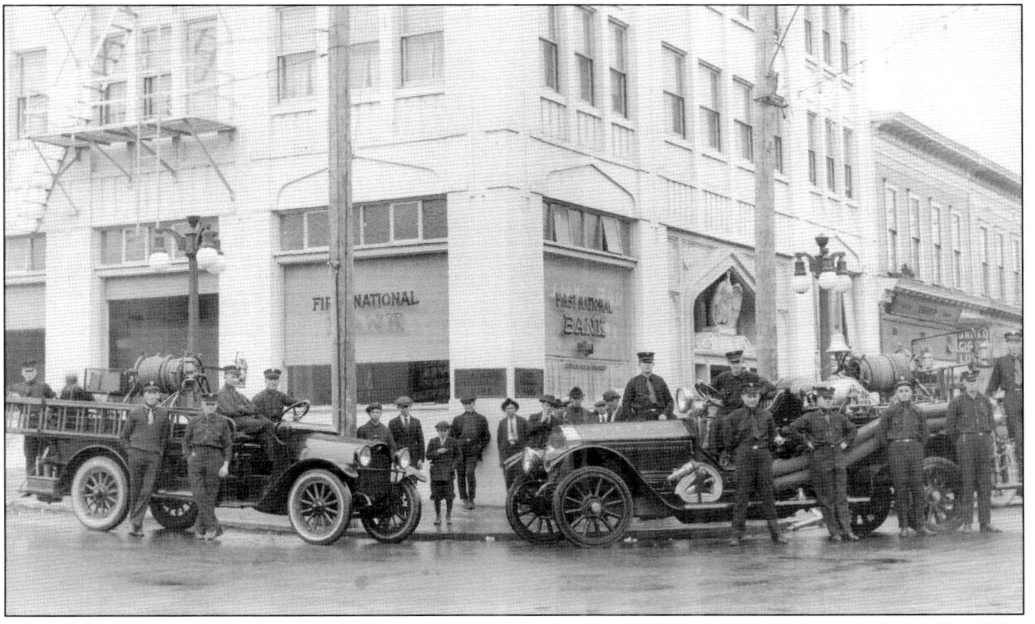

The 1920 Reo is on the left and the city's second engine, a 1921 LaFrance, is on the right. The firemen included Claffer, Anderson, Phillips, Melzer, Loomis, Willton, Shelton, Brainard, Wallace, Gaunt, and Smith. Three-bulbed city streetlights are seen, plus the eagle above the Sherman Avenue entrance to the First National Bank. (NBFD.)

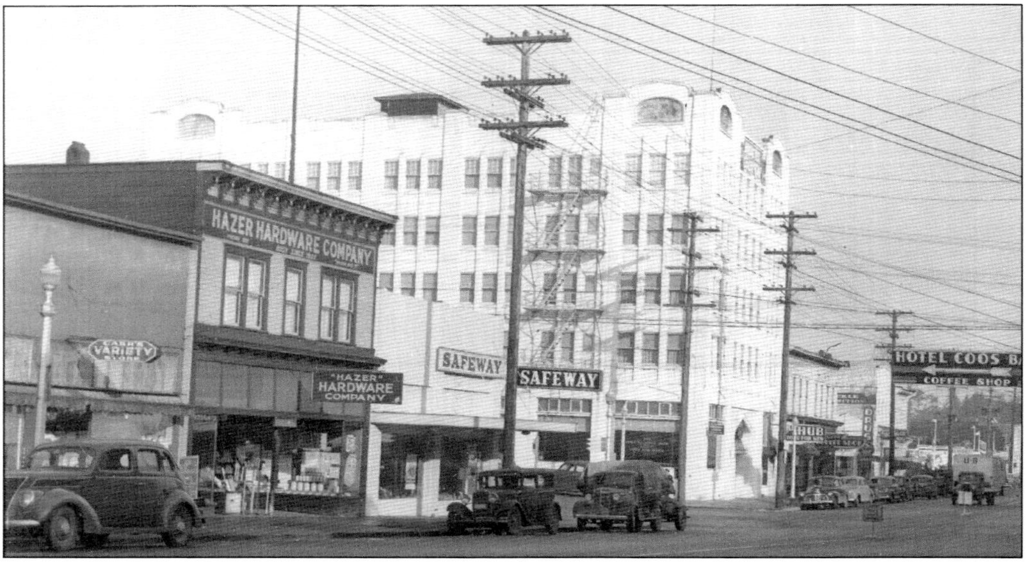

In 1936, the Hotel North Bend was sold for just $50,000 and renamed the Hotel Coos Bay. The owners hung a sign across Sherman Avenue that named the hotel and plugged its coffee shop. A later sign added mention of the short-lived new "Hotel North Bend," which existed after World War II adjacent to the airport. (CHMM 982-191.26.)

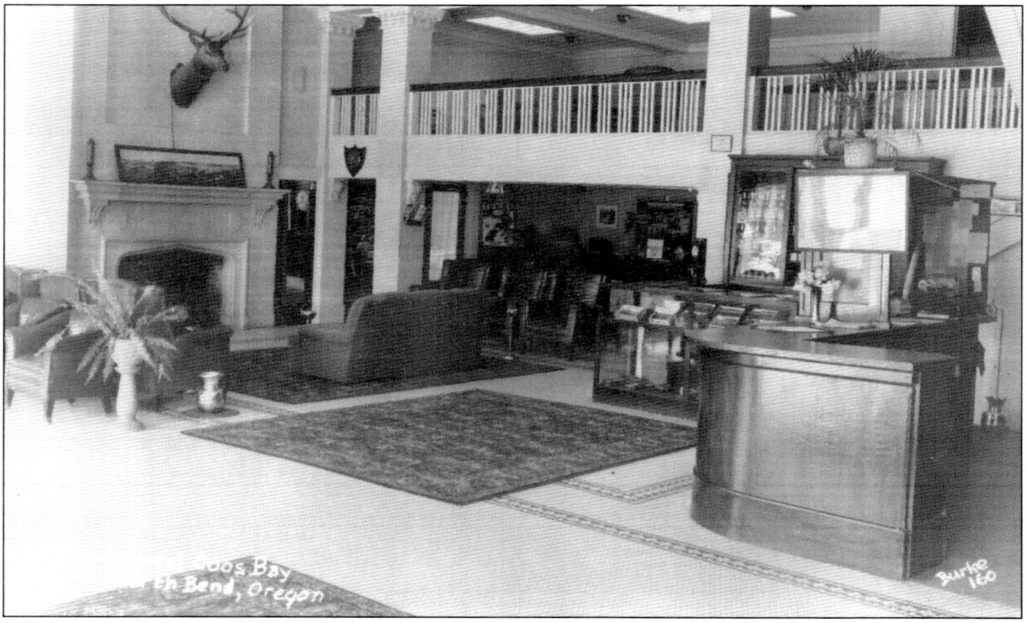

The lobby of the Hotel Coos Bay (formerly Hotel North Bend) as it looked in the late 1930s. The reception desk is at right, then a counter with cigars, and behind it a selection of bottled beverages. The mosaic tile floor, the fireplace, and the mezzanine remain in the building nearly 90 years later. (CHMM 999-D49.)

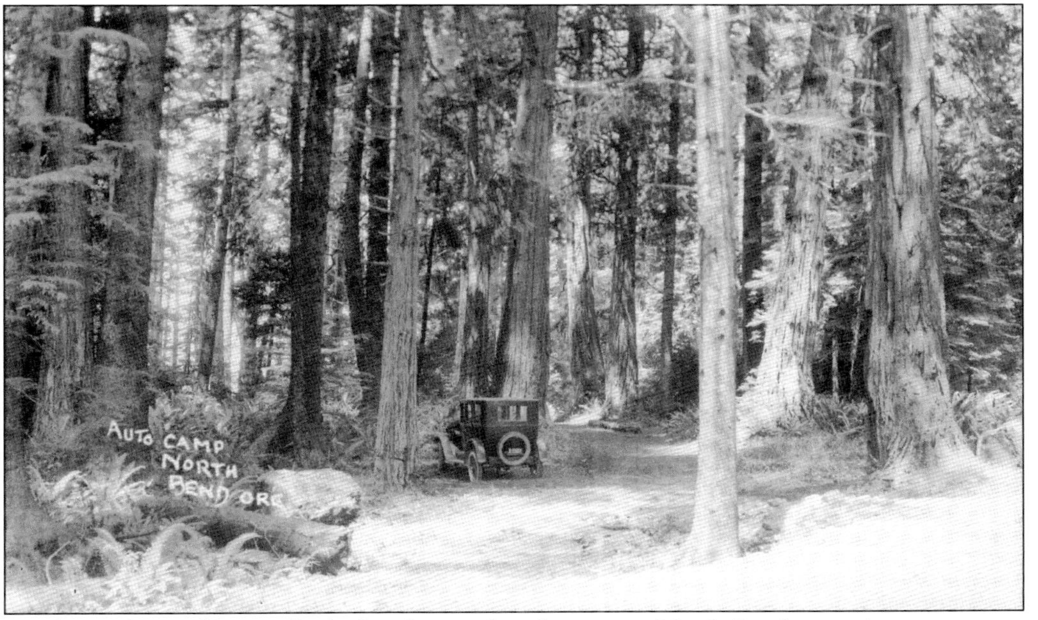

For those who could not afford a hotel or preferred camping, North Bend opened an auto camp in City Park in August 1921. Located in the area now occupied by the North Bend Information Center and the Coos Historical and Maritime Museum, the camp was a rustic stopover for tourists. In 1923, 677 vehicles and 3,200 people stayed there. The auto camp remained until 1948. (CHMM 981-244.6.)

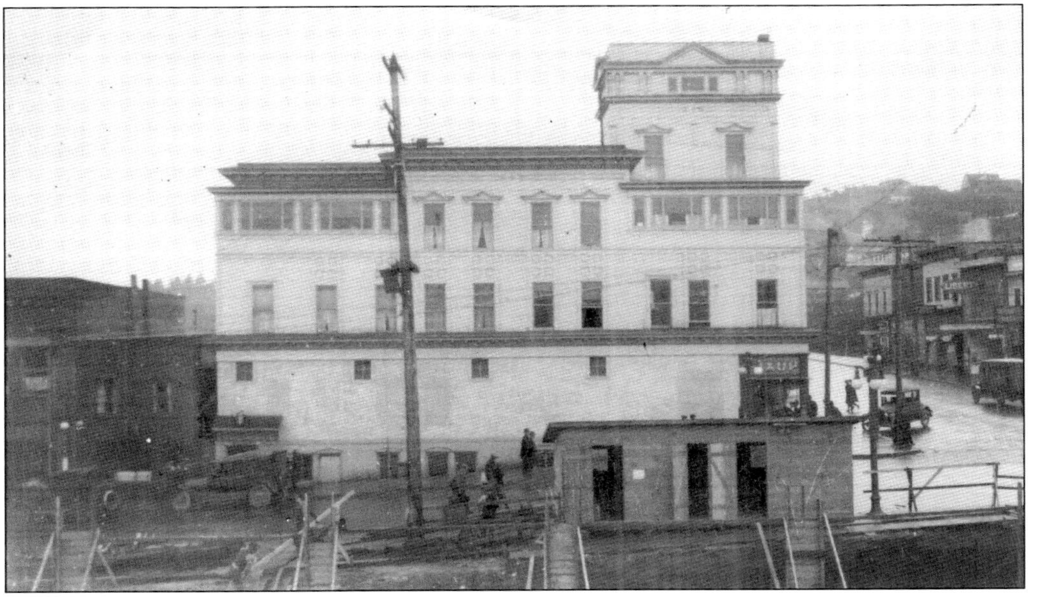

The excavation of the Independent Order of Odd Fellows lot is in the foreground of this photograph. The large building on its Virginia Avenue side is the Winsor building, built about 1904. Its upper floors housed the Commercial Club. Lower floors had professional offices and businesses. Note the Liberty Theater sign across the street, renamed from the Joy. This sign moved with the theater in 1924. (CHMM 981-313-25.)

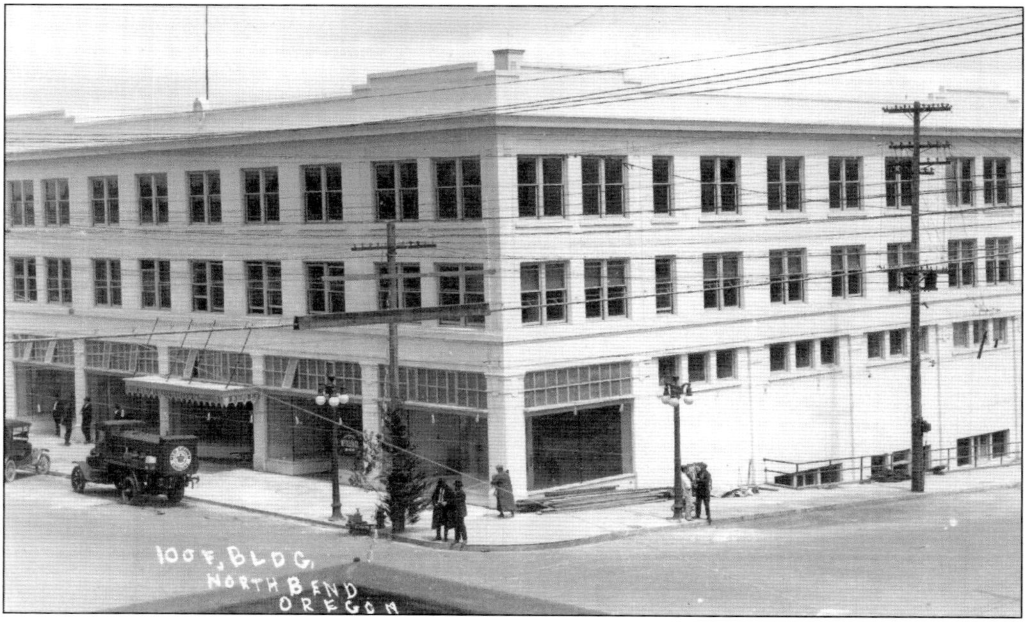

The Independent Order of Odd Fellows building was completed in 1923. This 95-by-100-foot structure had five storefronts on Sherman Avenue, with rental rooms above, and a large meeting room with dance floor and offices on the third floor. Total cost of the building was about $78,000. (CHMM 982-191.12a.)

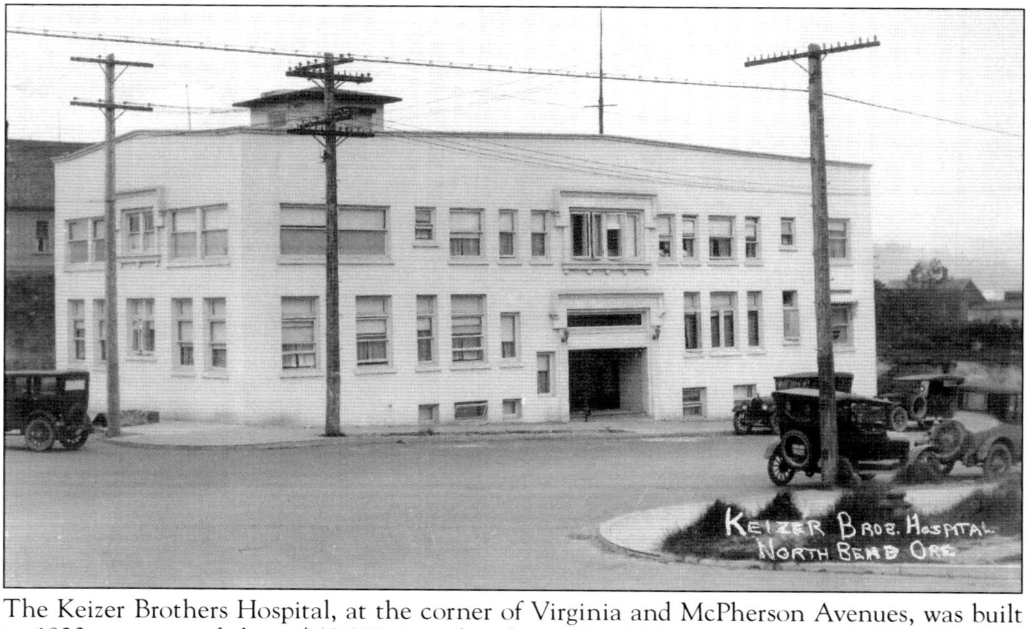

The Keizer Brothers Hospital, at the corner of Virginia and McPherson Avenues, was built in 1923 at a cost of about $60,000. Local architect Fred Magnusson drew the plans for the 50-by-90-foot two-story concrete structure. The need for medical services forced the hospital to announce expansion in 1924 and a new wing, added to the north, doubled hospital space in 1925. (CHMM 968-148.)

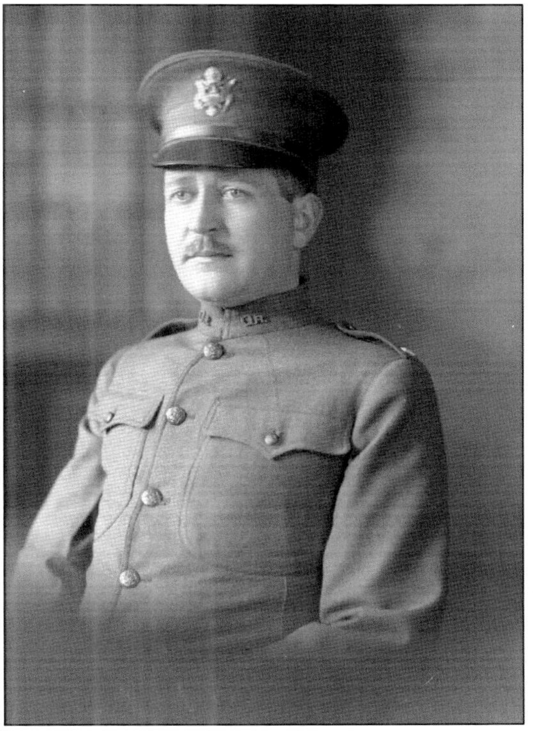

Dr. Phil J. Keizer is shown in his World War I army uniform. Keizer came to North Bend in 1914, opened a medical practice, and joined the military in 1917. His mother received notice in September 1918 that he had died in France, which he had not. After the war, Keizer kept the framed death certificate on his office wall and told patients "Hell, you can see I'm not dead." (CHMM 987-S505.)

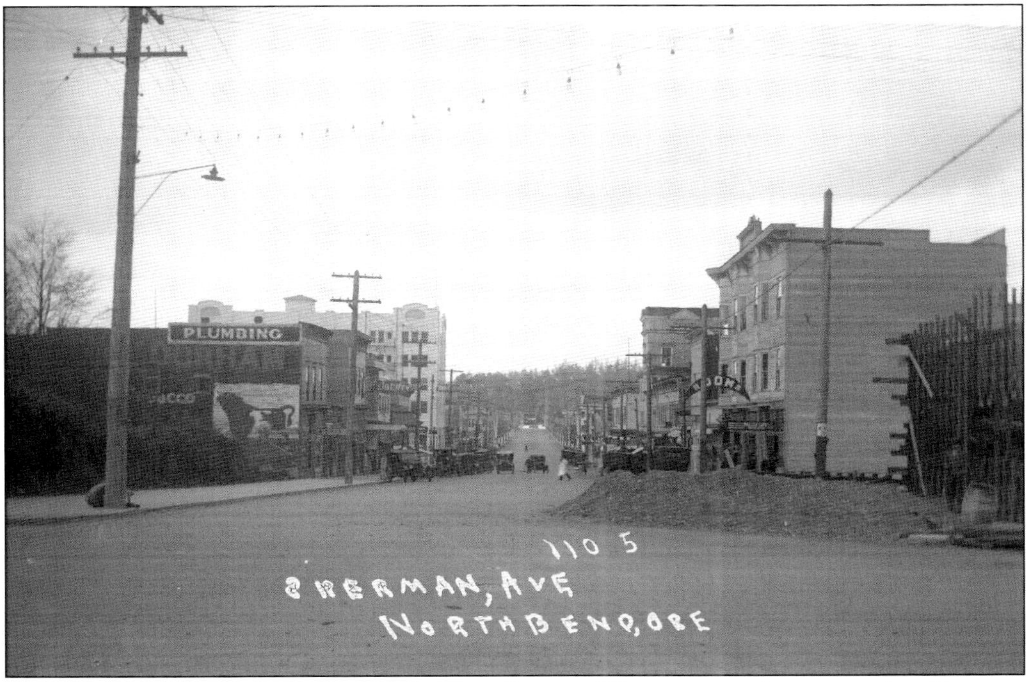

Pictured is the excavation in late 1923 for a new Gorst and King concrete bus terminal on Sherman Avenue near Washington. The Palace Hotel with its "Rooms" sign is directly north of the site. The Palace Café, serving food "family style," was located in the hotel. (CHMM 992-8-3554.)

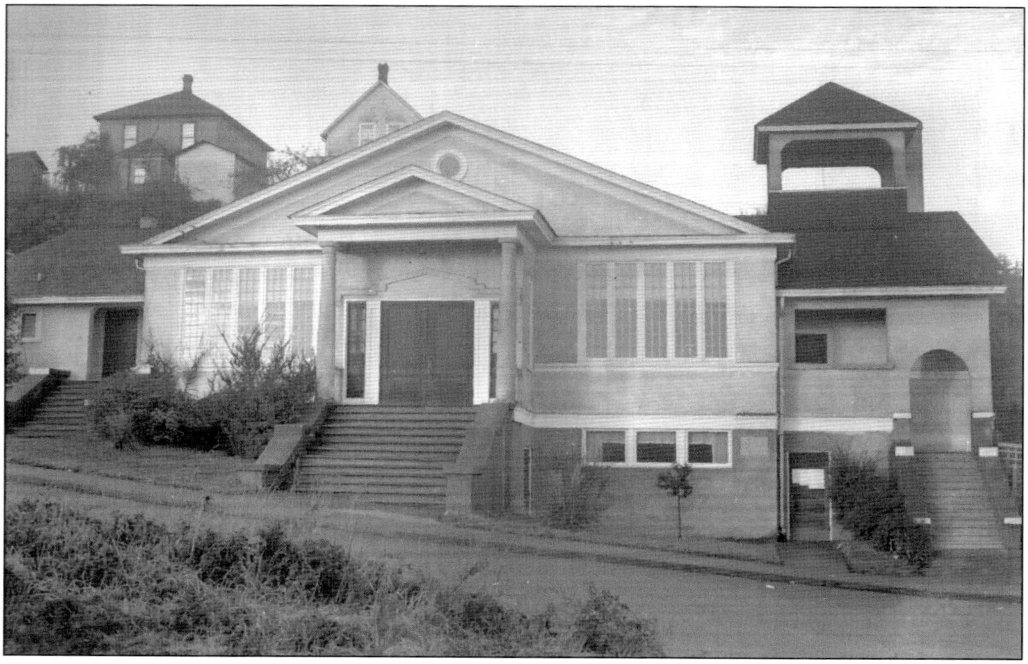

The Presbyterian Community Church, designed by Fred Magnusson, was built in 1924 for $25,000 at the corner of Union and Washington Avenues. The building, championed by Dr. J. E. Snyder, pastor, replaced the wooden church. Unfortunately an error placed the steps, porch, and part of the porch columns in the city right of way, forcing Union Avenue to narrow from Washington to Vermont because of it. The church apologized. (CHMM 989-N9a.)

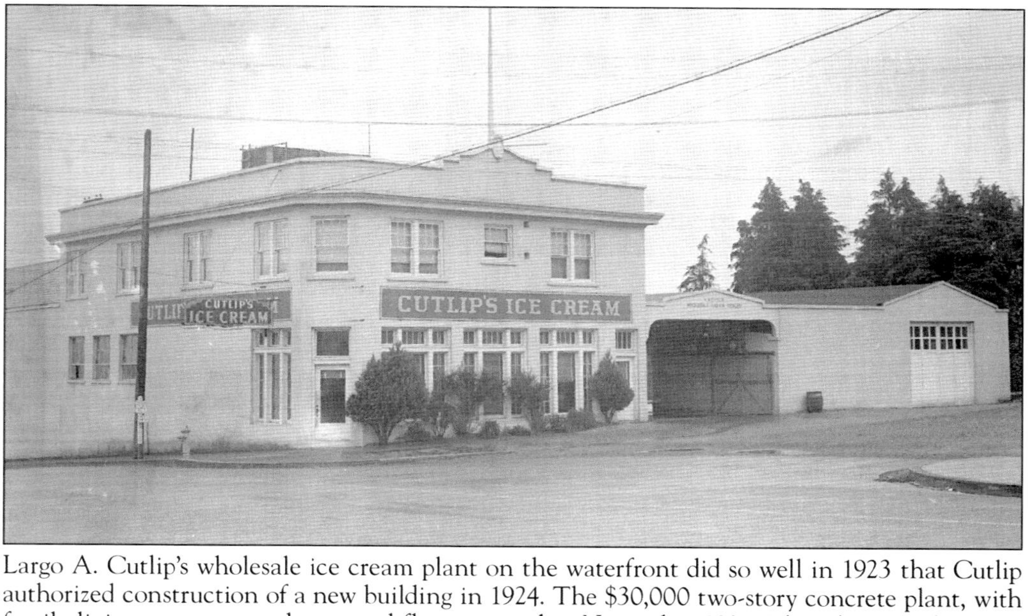

Largo A. Cutlip's wholesale ice cream plant on the waterfront did so well in 1923 that Cutlip authorized construction of a new building in 1924. The $30,000 two-story concrete plant, with family living quarters on the second floor, opened in November 1924. This photograph, taken after 1934, shows the arch with the sign "L. A. Cutlip Wholesale Liquor Dealer," indicating a new post-Prohibition sideline. (CHMM 986-N922.)

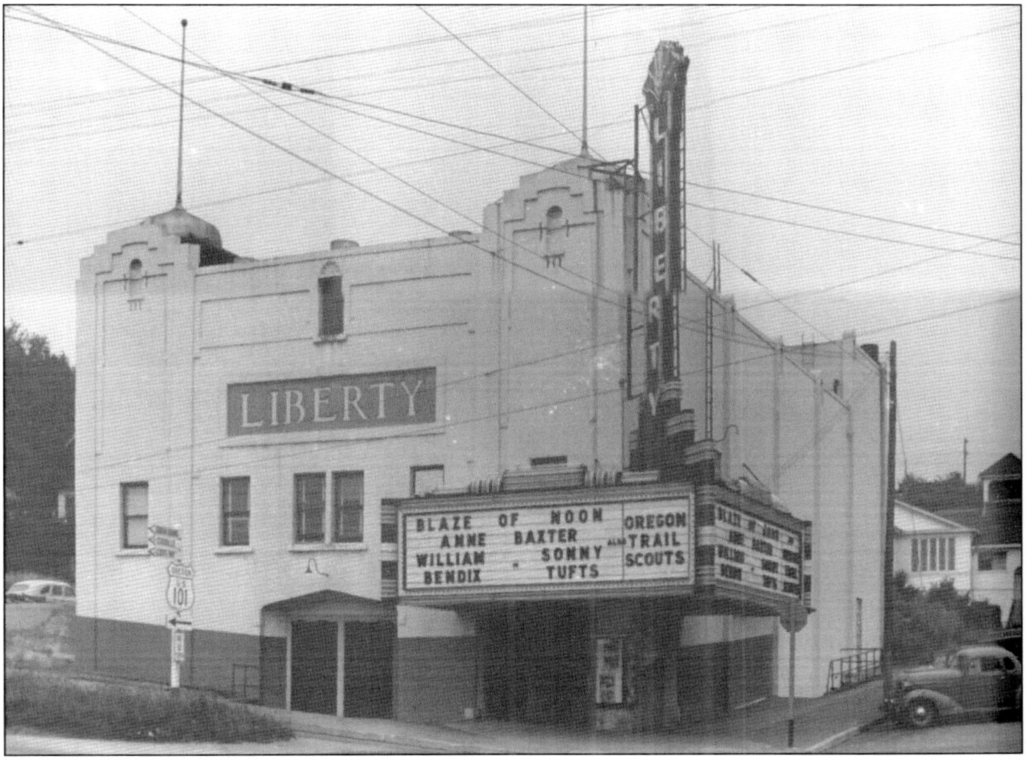

The concrete Liberty Theater, built in 1924 at the corner of Washington and Sherman, was 50 feet wide, 100 feet long, and 50 feet high. Its cost was about $75,000. The theater sat 750, including 54 loge seats. Its Wurlitzer organ was the second largest in Oregon. The original oval Liberty sign was replaced in 1931 by the neon sign shown here. In 1947, the marquee was added. (Little Theater on the Bay.)

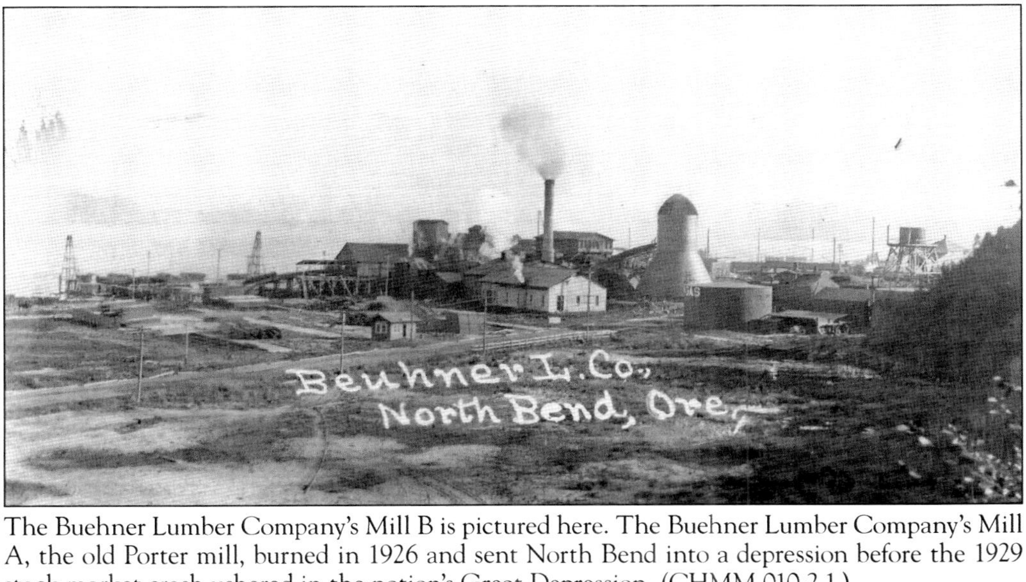

The Buehner Lumber Company's Mill B is pictured here. The Buehner Lumber Company's Mill A, the old Porter mill, burned in 1926 and sent North Bend into a depression before the 1929 stock market crash ushered in the nation's Great Depression. (CHMM 010-2.1.)

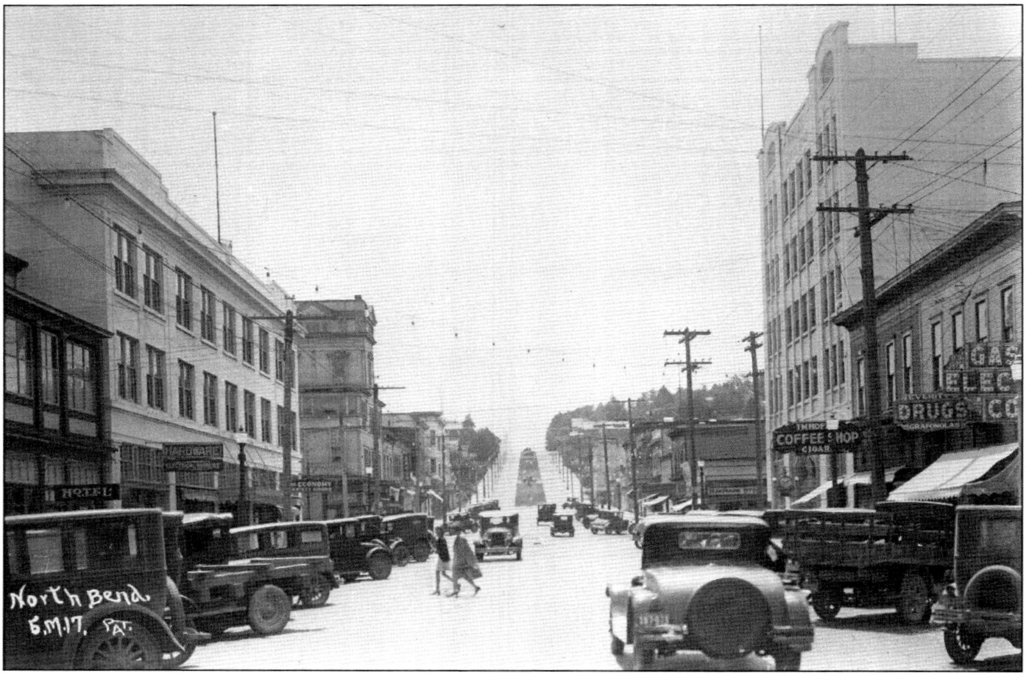

This mid-1920s street scene looks south on Sherman Avenue toward a paved Sherman hill. On the left is a sign for the Martin Hotel. The Independent Order of Odd Fellows building contains a hardware store, the Economy variety store, and J. F. Hackett's furniture store. On the right, the Gas & Electric Company sign sits on the unseen *Coos Bay Harbor* building. The Everitt Drug Store and Imhoff Coffee Shop are also visible. (CHMM 992-8-0946.)

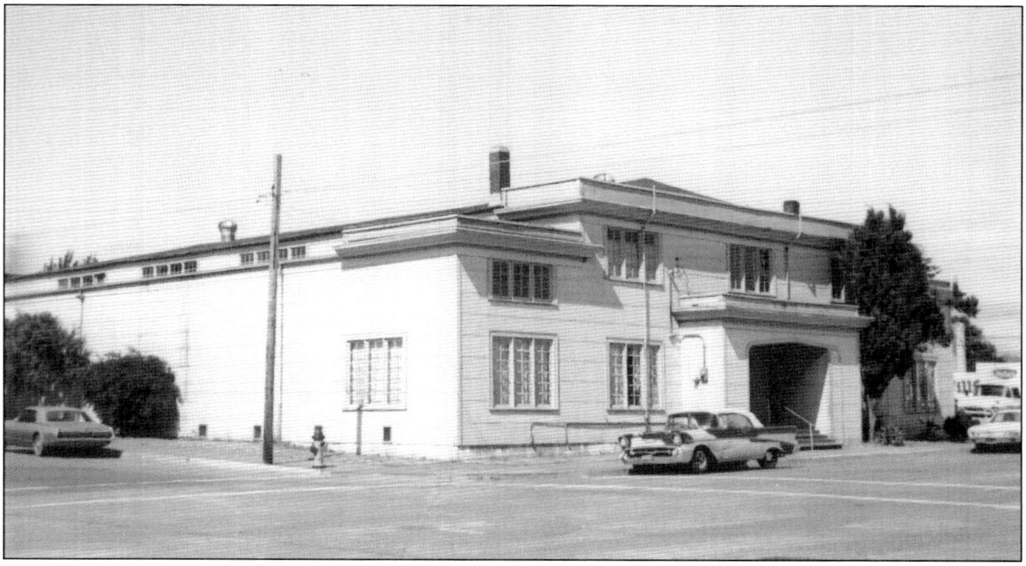

North Bend's community building with a gymnasium floor as well as space for lectures, concerts, and the Chautauqua programs, opened on Montana Avenue in 1926. This structure replaced the pavilion in Simpson Park. Fred Magnusson donated the architectural plans and community groups raised money, provided labor, and made it happen. (CHMM 005-1.43.)

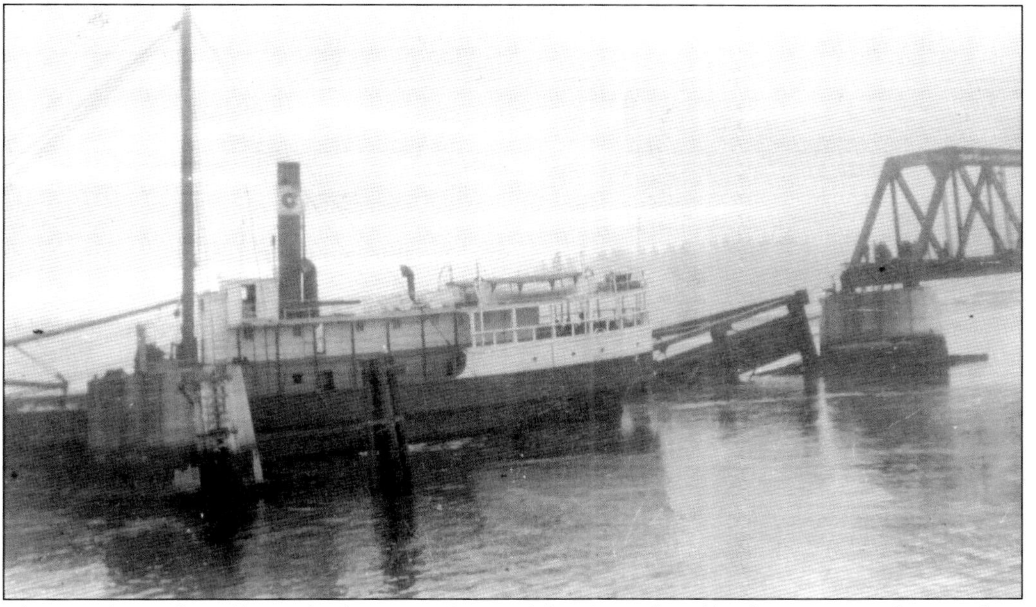

The *Martha Buehner* (formerly the A. M. *Simpson*) hit the railroad bridge in 1924. This accident knocked part of the rail bridge into the bay, forcing the railroad to use the ferry service to get passengers and freight across Coos Bay until the bridge could be repaired.

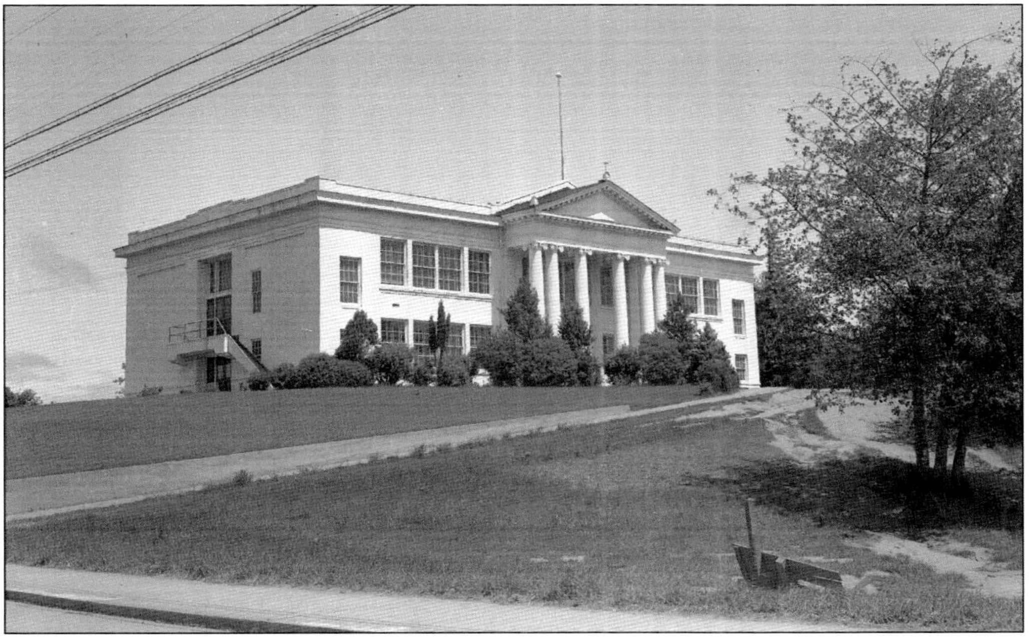

Roosevelt School, named for Theodore Roosevelt, was built in 1924 for $32,000. Hoover and McNeil, who built the Liberty Theater, got the contract. Originally sixth through eighth grades went here; later it became an elementary school. The school closed in 2000 and the Celebration Center now owns the building. L. J. Simpson originally planned his "in town" mansion for the site. (CHMM 991-N81.)

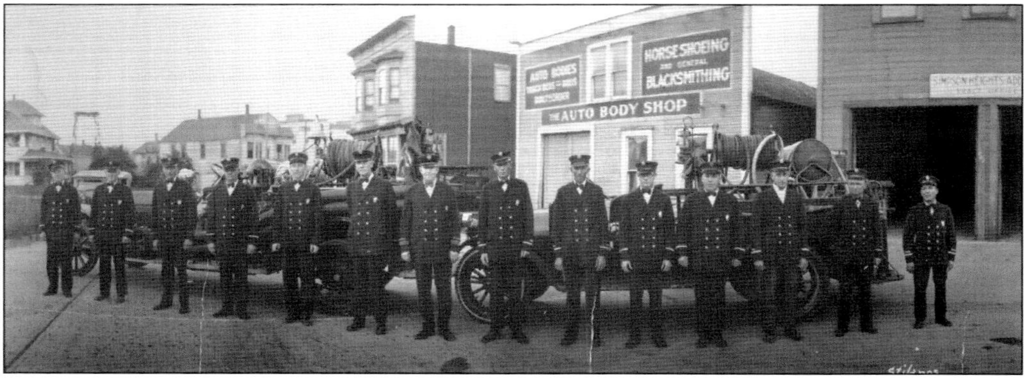

The North Bend Fire Department and its equipment are shown outside City Hall about 1925. Louis Loomis was fire chief. The man on the far left is James Boynton, future chief. The building to the far left stands today as the California Apartments. (CHMM 986-N809.)

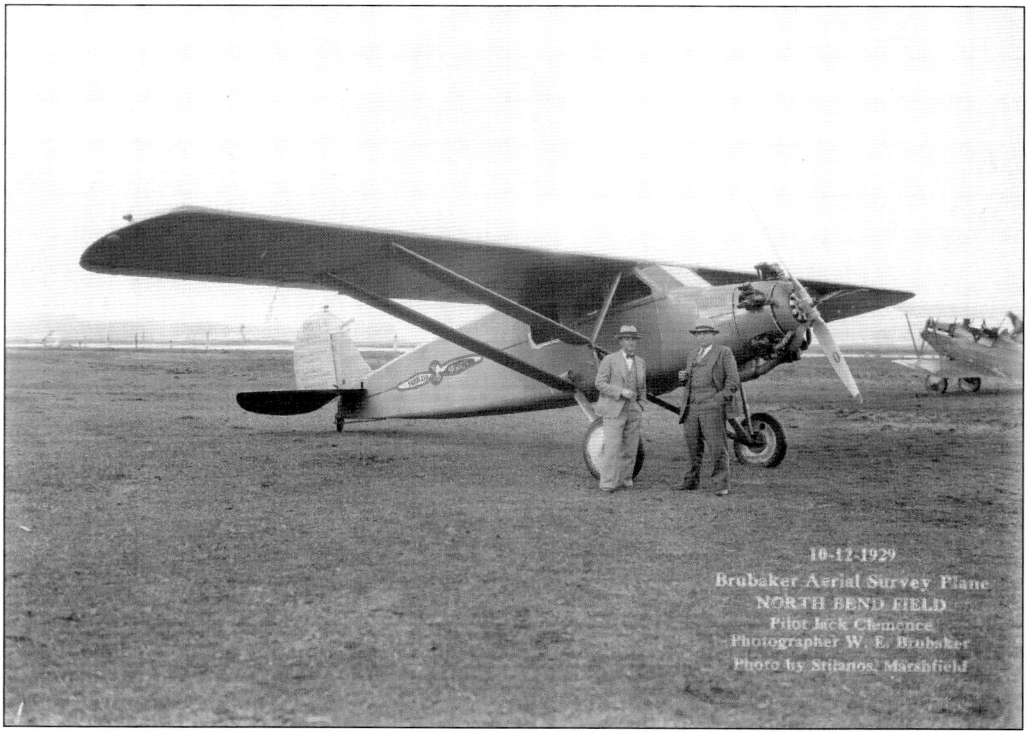

In October 1929 this Portland Airways plane was used to inspect the newly leveled field at Pony Inlet—the future North Bend Airport. At the same time a similar inspection took place at the Eastside airport. In November the recommendation came for Eastside. Nevertheless, North Bend went ahead with its airport and in 1930–1931, Bennett Air Transport scheduled flights here. (NBFD.)

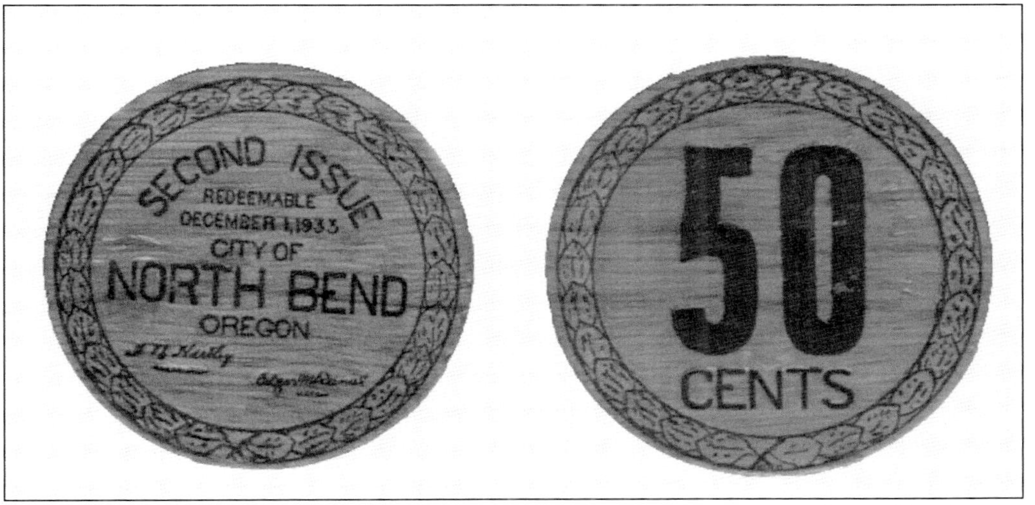

North Bend's bank closed during the Depression. Emergency money was authorized by the city council to help keep commerce going in 1933. Two issues of $1,000 each, in denominations ranging from 25¢ to $10, were printed on myrtlewood blanks—denomination on one side, redemption notice on the other. North Bend alone used myrtlewood for its Depression scrip. (CHMM 488a.)

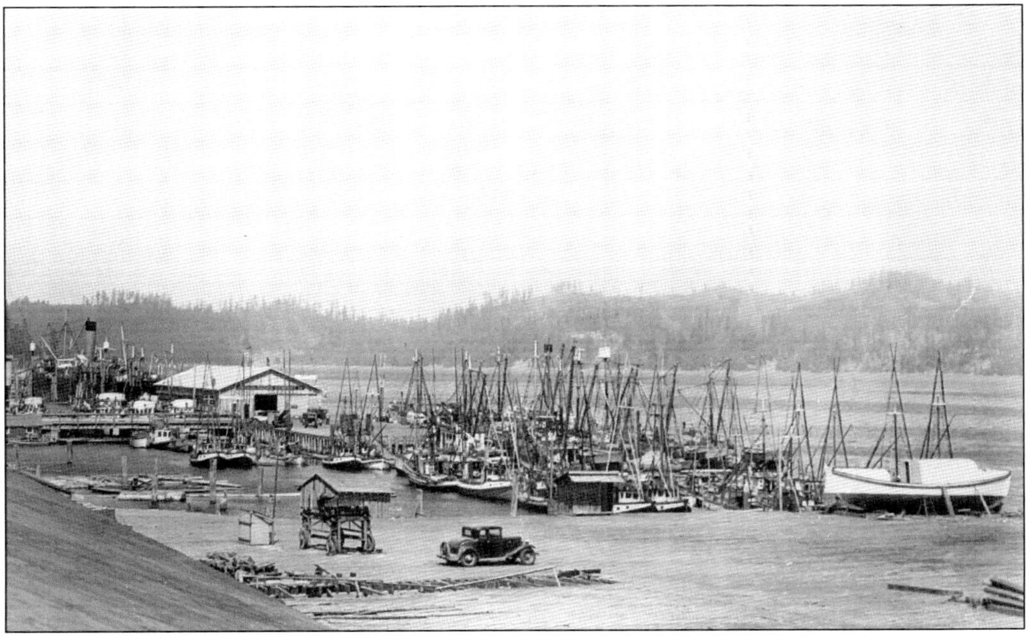

Some of the pilchard fishing fleet is pictured at North Bend's dock. During the 1930s a temporary boom in pilchard fishing increased activity on the waterfront and filled the bay area with fishing vessels. The city wharf, around which the boats cluster, was rebuilt in the mid-1920s to replace the rotted original of 1904–1906. (CHMM 986-N808.)

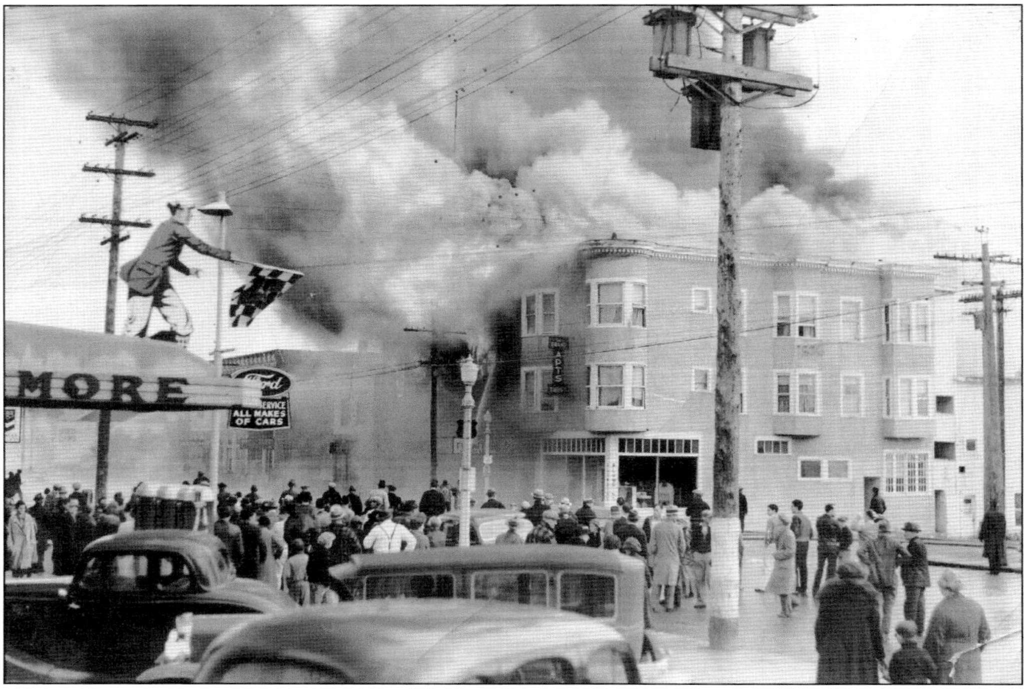

Smoke and water heavily damaged the Grand Apartment building, on the corner of Sherman and California Avenues, in April 1936. The building next door, Gildesheim's Furniture store (old Eckhoff Hall), and the adjacent North Bend Mattress Company store were completely destroyed. The Grand Apartments were refurbished and the building survived until 1960, when it was razed for a parking lot. (NBFD.)

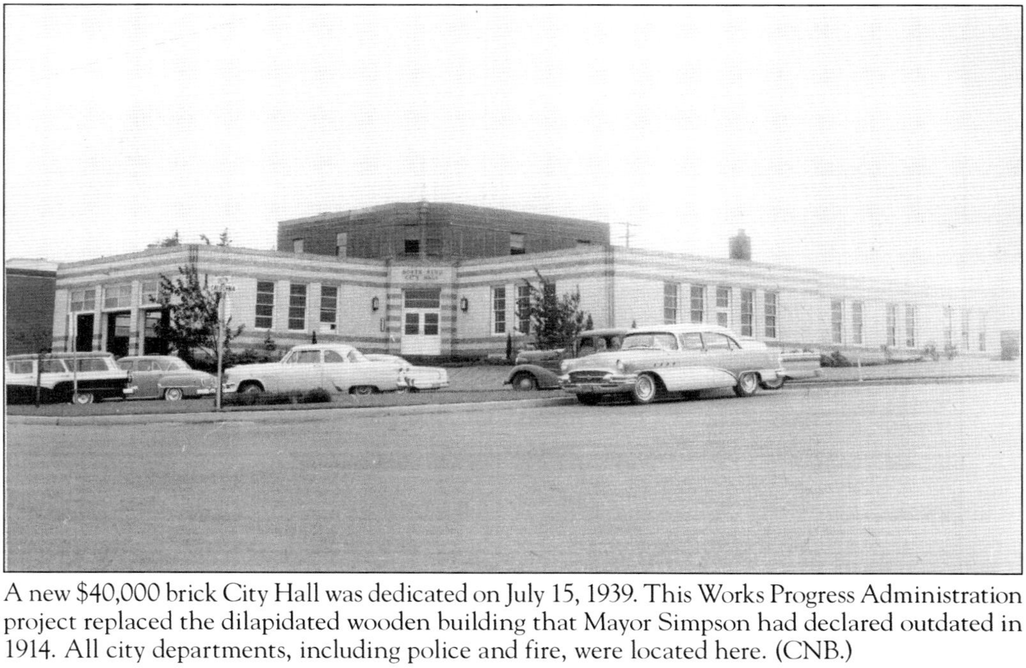

A new $40,000 brick City Hall was dedicated on July 15, 1939. This Works Progress Administration project replaced the dilapidated wooden building that Mayor Simpson had declared outdated in 1914. All city departments, including police and fire, were located here. (CNB.)

Seven

Ferries, Highway, and the Coos Bay Bridge

Increasing auto use led to better roads and the demand for ferry service across Coos Bay. In 1921 Kruse and Banks' shipyard built the ferry *Roosevelt*, (a paddlewheel steamer named for the recent president) to link sections of the Roosevelt Highway—U.S. Highway 101.

North Bend deeded the county a small strip of land, called Roosevelt Road (part of today's Ferry Road) to connect Sherman Avenue with the ferry landing. The *Roosevelt* made her first trip on May 6, 1922.

When the *Martha Buehner* struck the railroad bridge in 1924, knocking an 80-foot section into the bay, the *Roosevelt* was kept unusually busy. Southern Pacific ferried passengers and freight across the bay while the bridge was repaired.

Traffic grew steadily. By 1929 a larger capacity vessel, the diesel screw *Oregon*, replaced the *Roosevelt*. Unfortunately, the *Oregon* was prone to break crankshafts, so the *Roosevelt* was kept on standby. The county, for financial reasons, gave control of the ferry and the road to the state.

Construction of a bridge over Coos Bay began in July 1934. The state told North Bend it would give the road and ferry slip to the city when the bridge was done. The project, a welcome boost during the Depression, cost $2,123,318. The bridge and approaches were 5,888 feet in length, with a 27-foot-wide roadway. There were pedestrian sidewalks on either side of the bridge. Two men lost their lives during construction.

The bridge officially opened on May 2, 1936. While some local groups wished to name the bridge for Asa M. Simpson, the State Highway Commission selected Coos Bay Bridge. (In 1947, the bridge was renamed for its late designer Conde B. McCullough.)

Three days in early June 1936 were set aside for an area-wide celebration. The festivities were dedicated to the late Asa Simpson; his eldest son Louis was the general chairman. Edgar Simpson, another son, brought two rail cars of oxen, wagons, and stagecoaches from California for the parade. Perhaps 20,000 people saw the various activities.

The City of North Bend's logo incorporates the image of the bridge over Coos Bay.

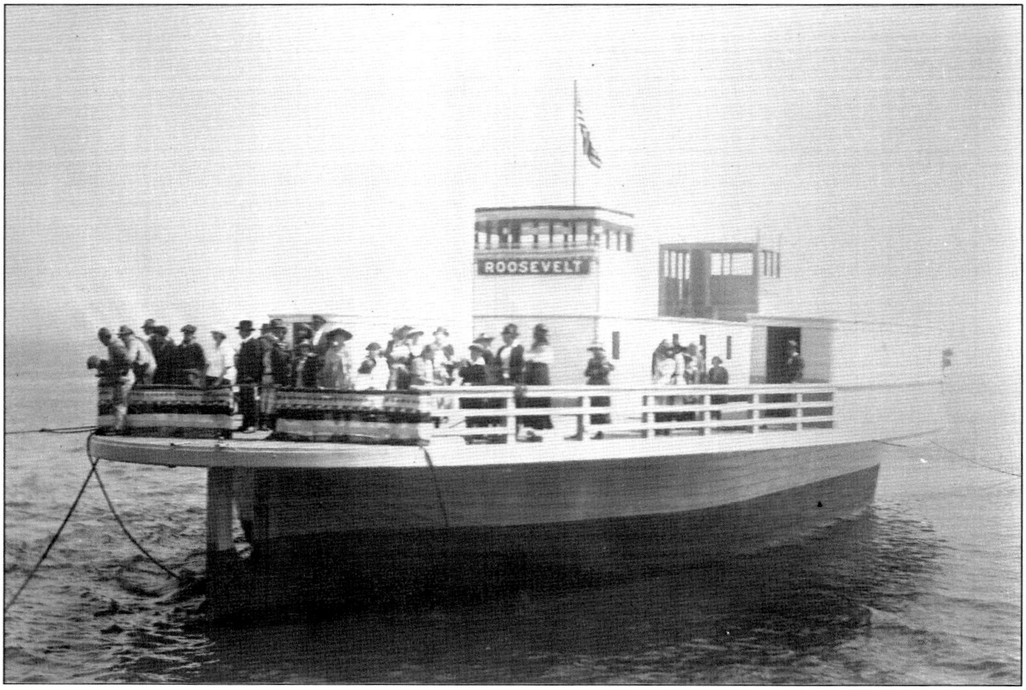

The ferry *Roosevelt* was launched on July 21, 1921, from the Kruse and Banks' shipyard in North Bend. The boxes on her sides are empty as the paddlewheels and the steam machinery have yet to be added. She made her first trip across the bay in May 1922. After the big bridge was built, the *Roosevelt* was sold, stripped, and abandoned in a cove up Isthmus Slough. (CHMM 992-8-0866.)

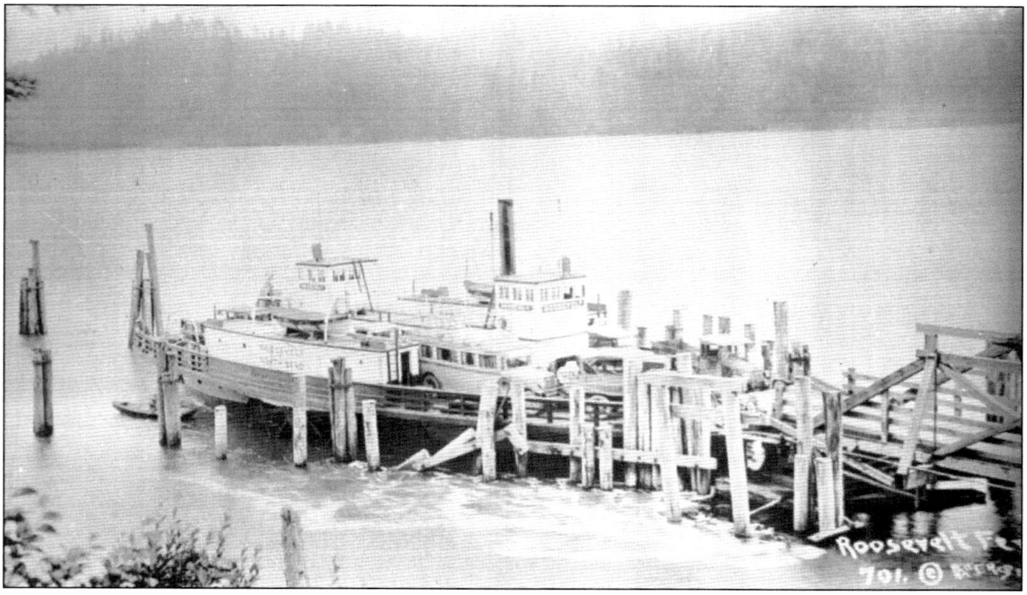

The ferry *Roosevelt* arrives at North Bend. Note the bus on board and the name painted on the box covering the paddlewheel. The ramp mechanism at the end of the landing goes up and down to accommodate tidal changes. (CHMM 009-16.156A.)

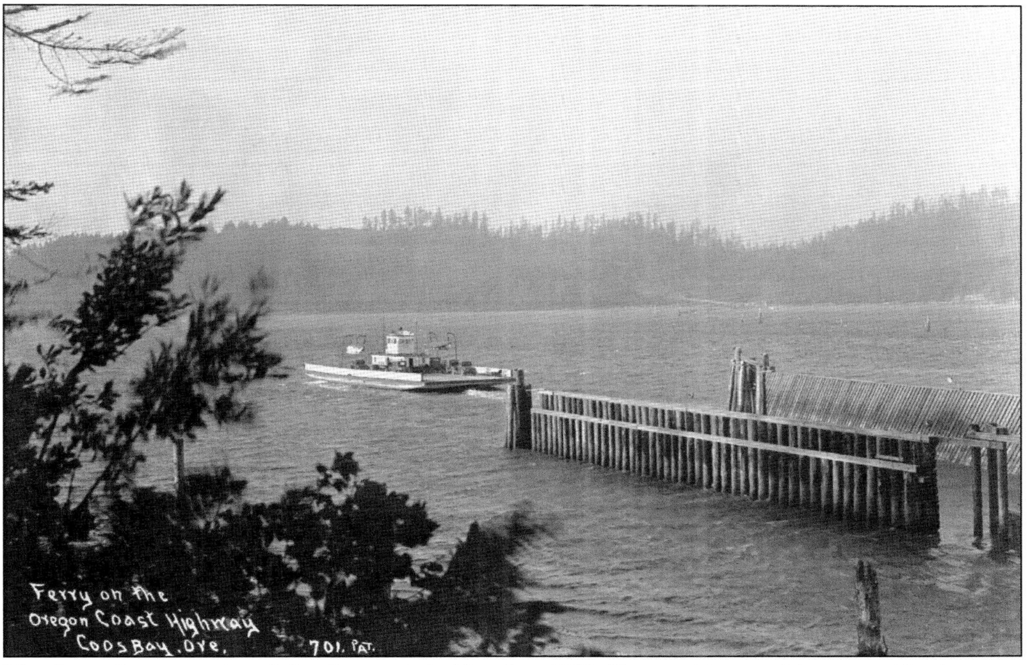

The ferry *Oregon* replaced the *Roosevelt* in October 1929. She could carry 36 cars and had a more powerful six-cylinder Atlas Imperial diesel engine. Unfortunately, she was prone to breaking crankshafts. July 1934 was her busiest month to date, carrying 45,094 autos and 140,432 passengers. (CHMM 992-8-0859.)

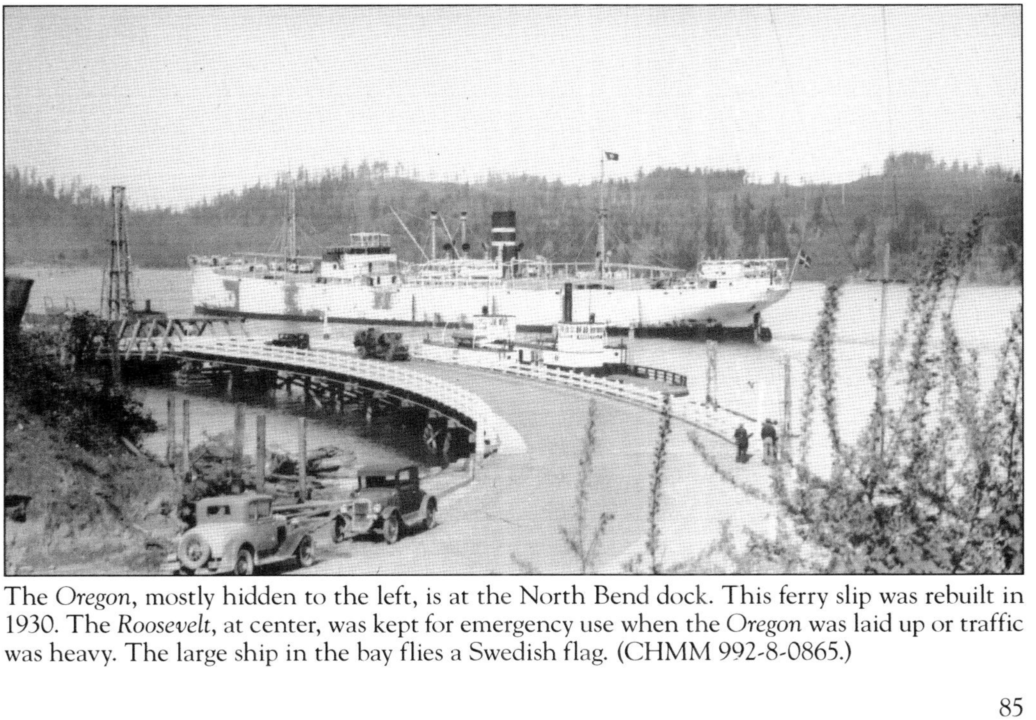

The *Oregon*, mostly hidden to the left, is at the North Bend dock. This ferry slip was rebuilt in 1930. The *Roosevelt*, at center, was kept for emergency use when the *Oregon* was laid up or traffic was heavy. The large ship in the bay flies a Swedish flag. (CHMM 992-8-0865.)

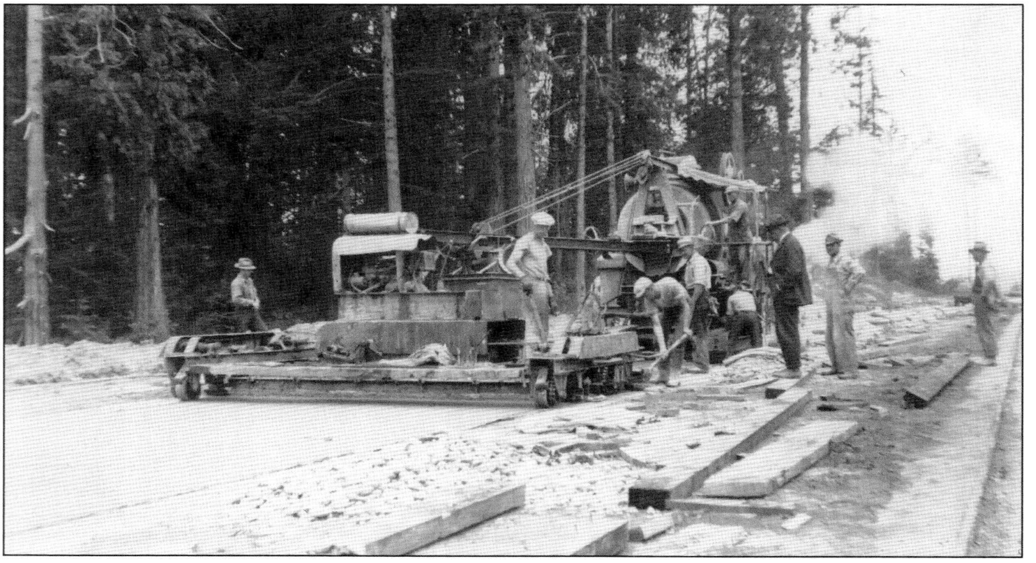

The Roosevelt Highway (U.S. Highway 101) is under construction in the 1930s. The machine in the foreground does road surfacing; the one behind it is a cement mixer. The road was conceived as a military highway to run the length of the U.S. west coast, for defense, should the country be attacked. (CHMM 992-4.5.)

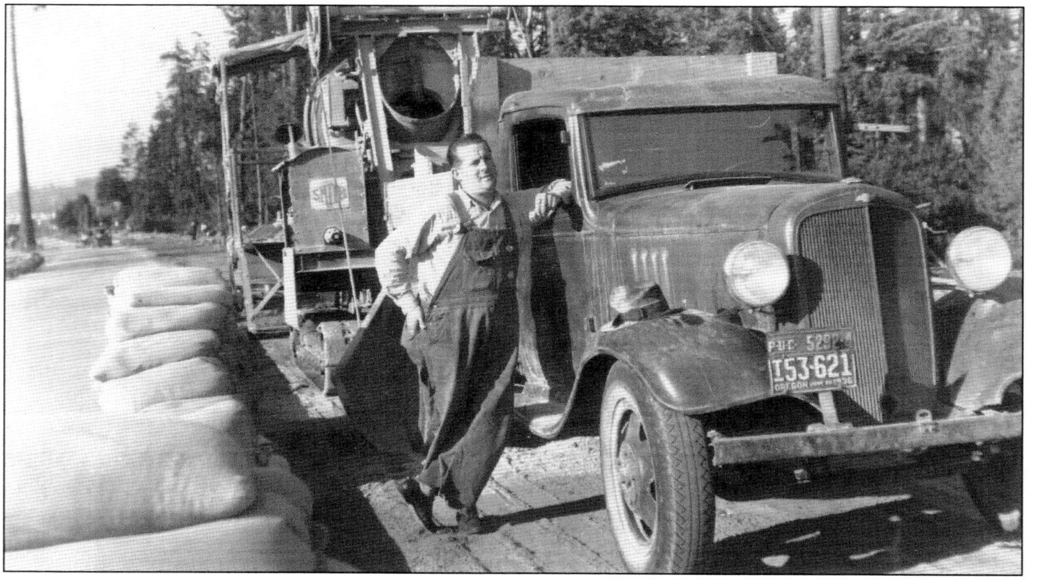

A workman beside a Chevrolet truck is servicing a cement mixer for highway construction. The highway north and south was connected with the construction of the big bridge over Coos Bay. The year on the Oregon license plate is 1936. (CHMM 992-4.10.)

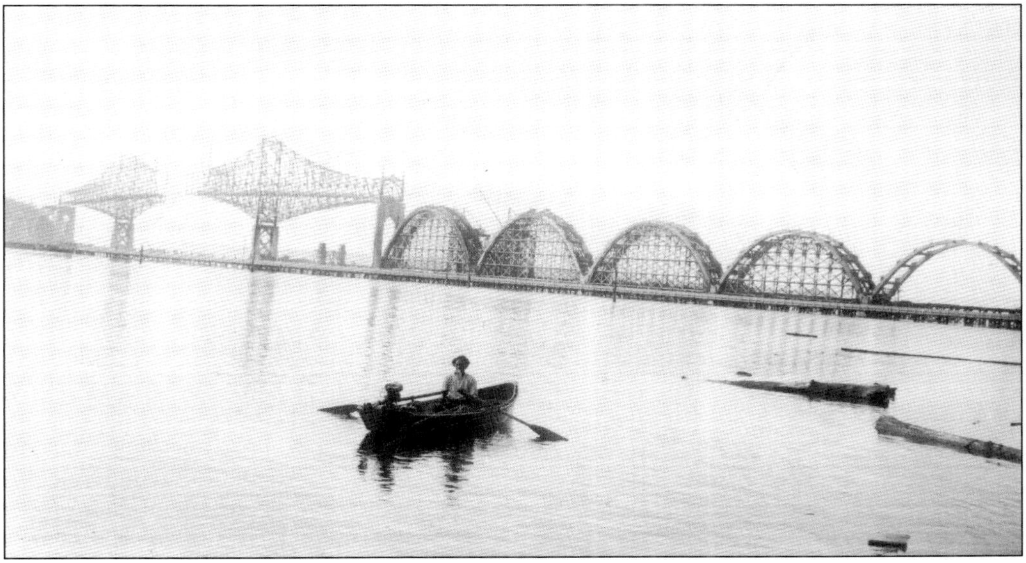

The bridge over Coos Bay is being built around 1935. Construction began in July 1934. The man in his boat lends perspective to the project. Note the temporary pier with roadway along the bridge used to bring construction materials for the concrete support structure to the water site. Coffers, to hold the water back, were constructed so the concrete could be poured. (CHMM 987-8b.)

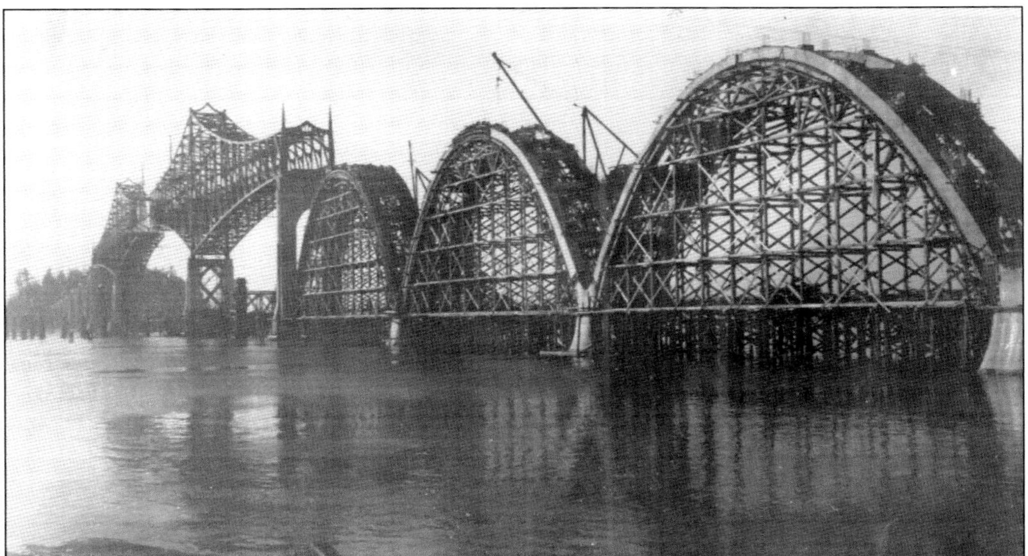

This is a close-up view of the arches supporting the roadway. Northwest Roads Company of Portland built the piers and approaches for $1,529,438. The completed 5,337-foot-long span had a 27-foot-wide roadway, with pedestrian sidewalks on each side. (CHMM 994-D8.2b.)

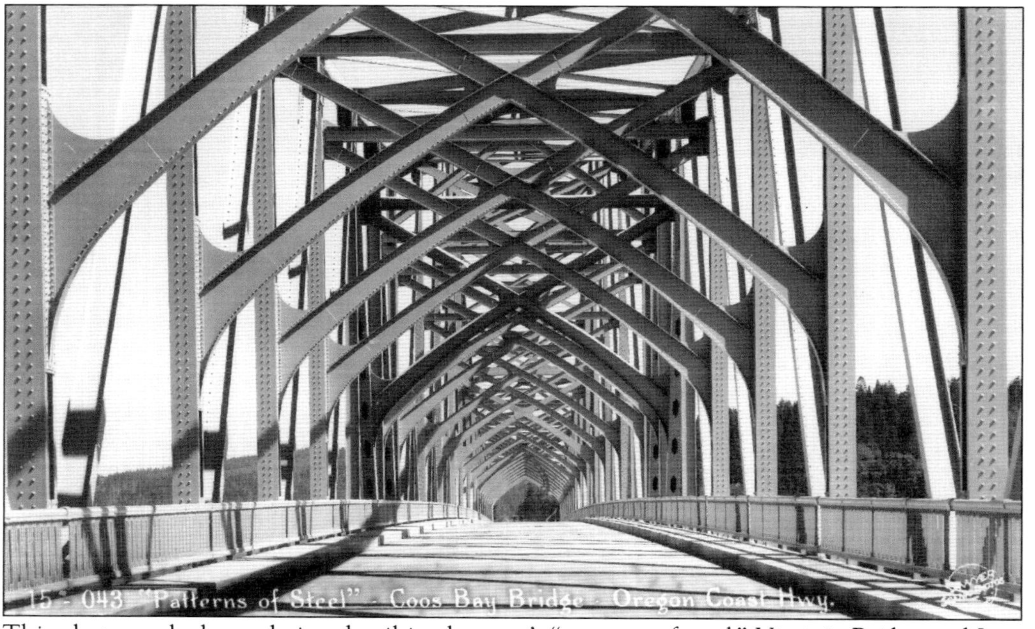

This photograph shows design detail in the span's "patterns of steel." Virginia Bridge and Iron Company of Roanoke, Virginia, provided the steel for the structure. Their bid for the steel was $593,880, making the total cost just over $2,100,000. (CHMM 003-6.3a.)

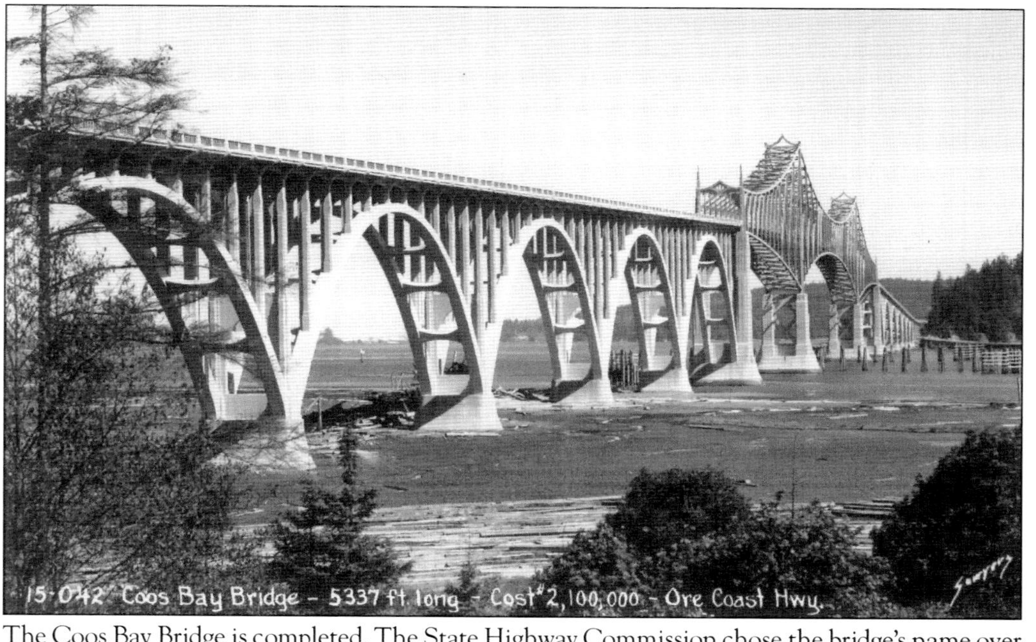

The Coos Bay Bridge is completed. The State Highway Commission chose the bridge's name over the alternative, "A.M. Simpson." In 1947, after the death of designer Conde B. McCullough, the bridge was renamed for him. The city of North Bend uses the bridge in its logo and many people refer to it simply as "the North Bend Bridge." (CHMM 001-6.2.)

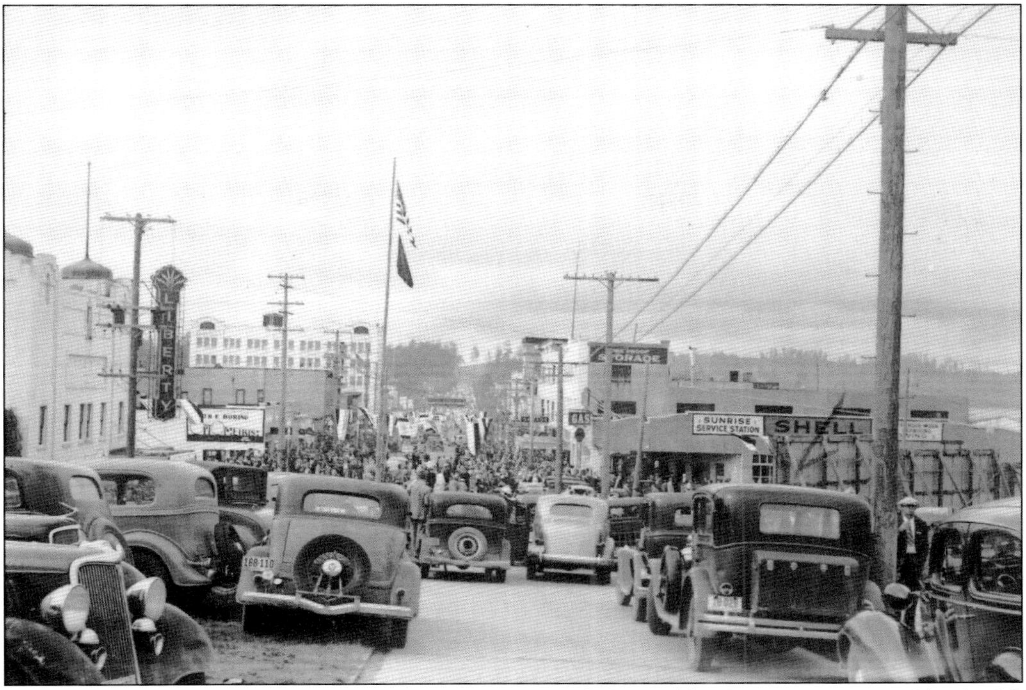

The bridge officially opened on May 2, 1936, and was dedicated by Oregon governor Charles H. Martin. People parked all over Sherman hill to watch the bridge parade. Note the center ground between concrete roadways (only the downhill side is visible). When 1920s paving originally was done, the center ground was used to plant palm trees for North Bend's proposed "city of palms" branding. (CHMM 995-23.141A.)

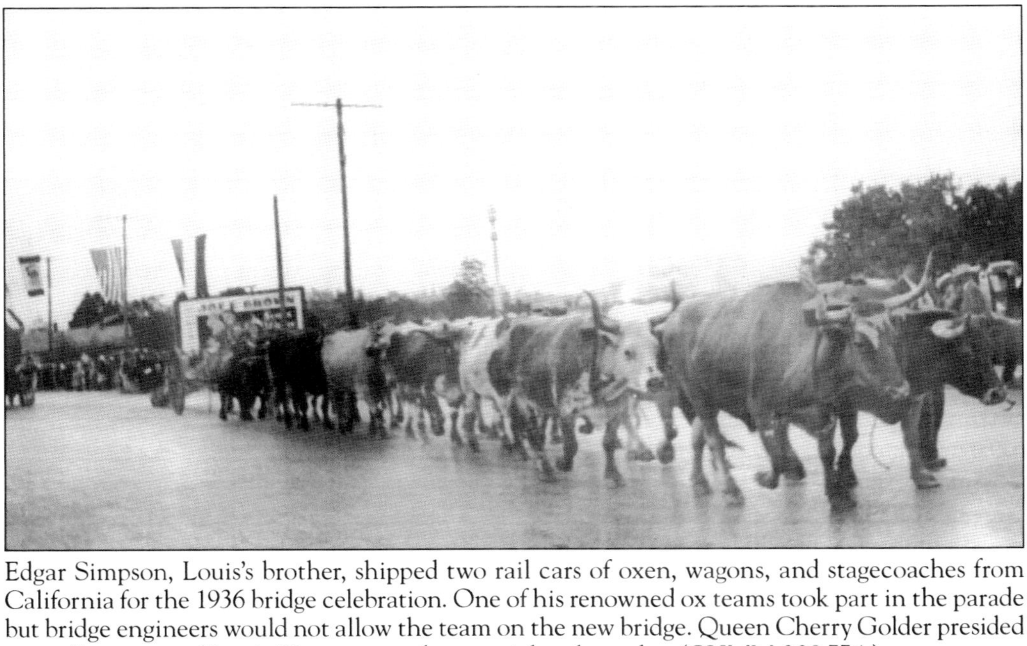

Edgar Simpson, Louis's brother, shipped two rail cars of oxen, wagons, and stagecoaches from California for the 1936 bridge celebration. One of his renowned ox teams took part in the parade but bridge engineers would not allow the team on the new bridge. Queen Cherry Golder presided over all events and Louis Simpson was her special ambassador. (CHMM 008.77.1.)

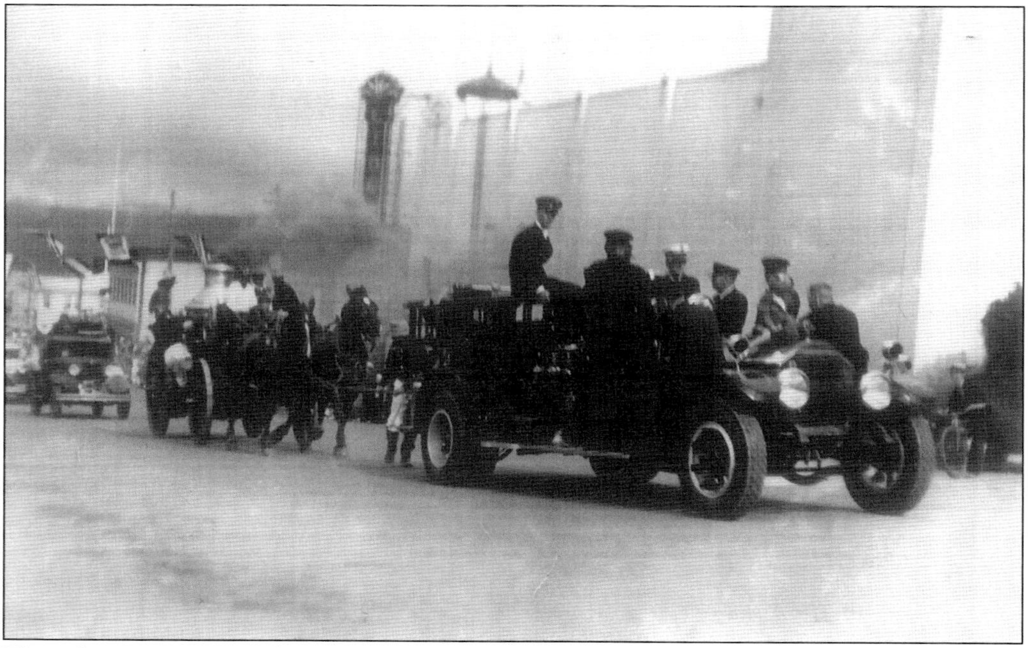

These fire engines on Washington Avenue by the Liberty Theater were the last feature of the 1936 bridge celebration parade. The old Marshfield Nott steam pumper follows the North Bend engine. The little girl holding a dog on the hood of the North Bend engine is Wanda Boynton, the fire chief's daughter. KOOS radio broadcast coverage of the parade and other events. (Graham family.)

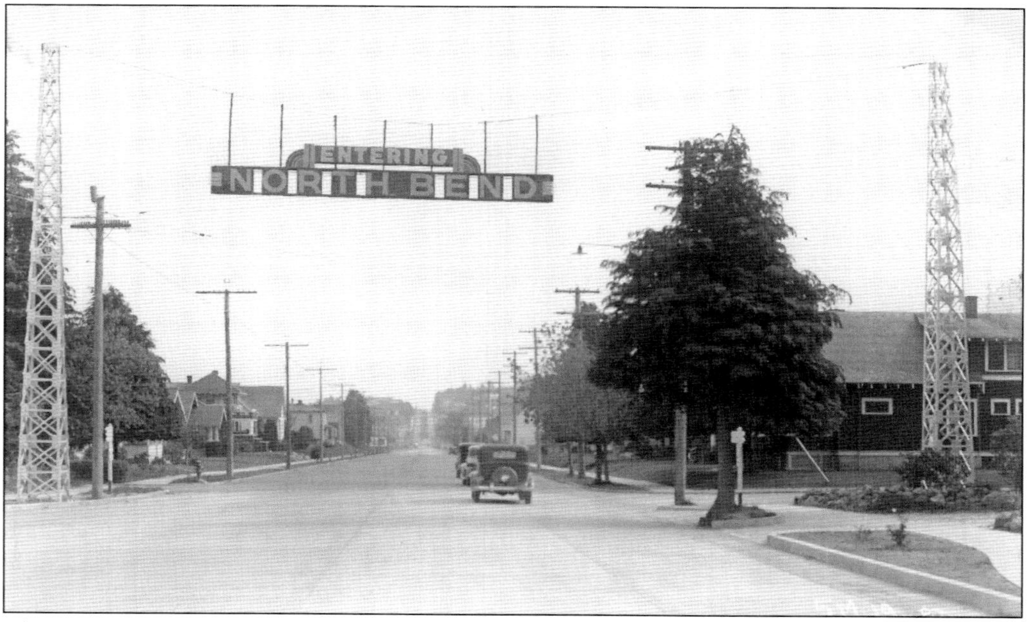

This is North Bend's second overhead welcome sign. The increased traffic after the bridge was completed prompted the city to authorize a welcome sign. The first sign went up in 1936 but came down in February 1937 after high winds damaged it. The sign was replaced in May 1937. The second version has vents for air to pass through. (CHMM 982-190.15b.)

Eight

Kruse and Banks' Shipyard

Knud Valdemar Kruse (1853–1936) worked in San Francisco and Alaska before coming to work for Simpson at North Bend in 1899. When Simpson shipbuilding ceased in 1903, Kruse created a shipyard at the Stave Mill about a mile north of Marshfield. The *Annie E. Smale* was built there in 1903 and the *Hugh Hogan* in 1904.

Robert Banks (1870–1964) met Kruse at the Dickie Brothers' San Francisco shipyard. He built on Humboldt Bay (Eureka, California) and traveled to Alaska before partnering with Kruse in 1905. Their Stave Mill shipyard produced its last vessel, the steam tug *E. P. Ripley*, in 1907. They then built a yard adjacent to Simpson's Porter mill. The steam schooner *Fairhaven*, launched in 1908, was the first vessel from the new yard. Their shipyard had three ways in 1911 and expanded to five during World War I.

The firm's peak employment came during the 1917–1918 war when over 600 people helped to fulfill the United States Shipping Board's emergency fleet contract for Hough and Ferris type wooden hulls. These vessels replaced tonnage lost to German submarines.

After the war, employment declined. About 1924, Mountain States Power purchased some of the southern shipyard for its new plant. In May 1925 there were 85 men at work. In addition to ships, the company did framing for house builders, sash and doors, and some specialty work.

Over its lifetime, the firm produced steam and gas schooners, tugs, barges, scows, the ferry *Roosevelt*, and in 1919 and 1920, the last two tall ships of sail (over 100 gross tons) built on Coos Bay.

On July 30, 1933, a fire at the nearby Western Battery and Separator Company swept through the shipyard. Only the north end (office building, planer shed, machine shop, and wharf) was saved. Essential facilities were replaced.

When Kruse died, his son Fred took over his father's position.

World War II brought orders for eight YMS wooden minesweepers, and four ATR rescue tugs for the U.S. Navy. But the era of large wooden craft had passed.

The firm closed down in 1945 after selling its property to Weyerhaeuser. They had produced over 70 wooden vessels.

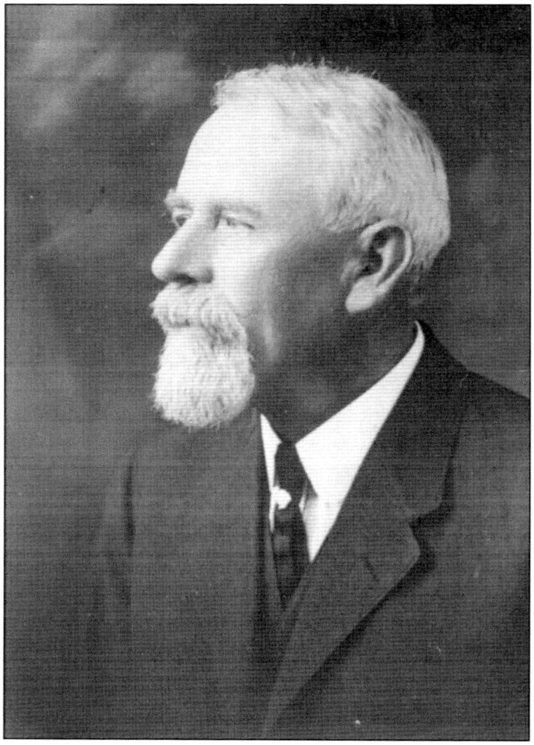

K. V. Kruse was born in Denmark and educated as a marine draftsman in Germany. He came to the United States in 1872. He worked for 20 years as a ship's carpenter on the West Coast. During the Alaskan gold rush he built a stern-wheeler on the Yukon River. He came to North Bend in 1899. (CHMM 007-25.58.)

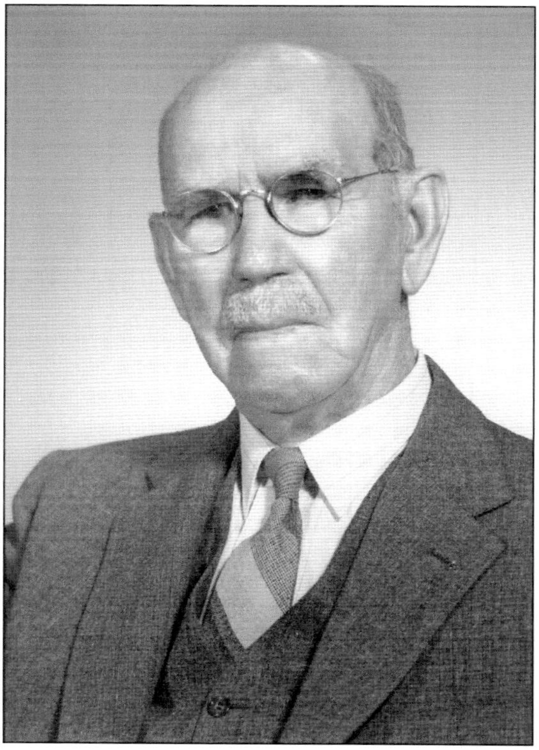

Robert Banks was born on Prince Edward Island, Canada, and learned shipbuilding in Connecticut and Rhode Island. Once on the West Coast, he worked in San Francisco, Eureka, and the Seattle area. He was in Alaska in early 1905 before joining Kruse at the Stave Mill shipyard in late 1905. (CHMM 007-25.51.)

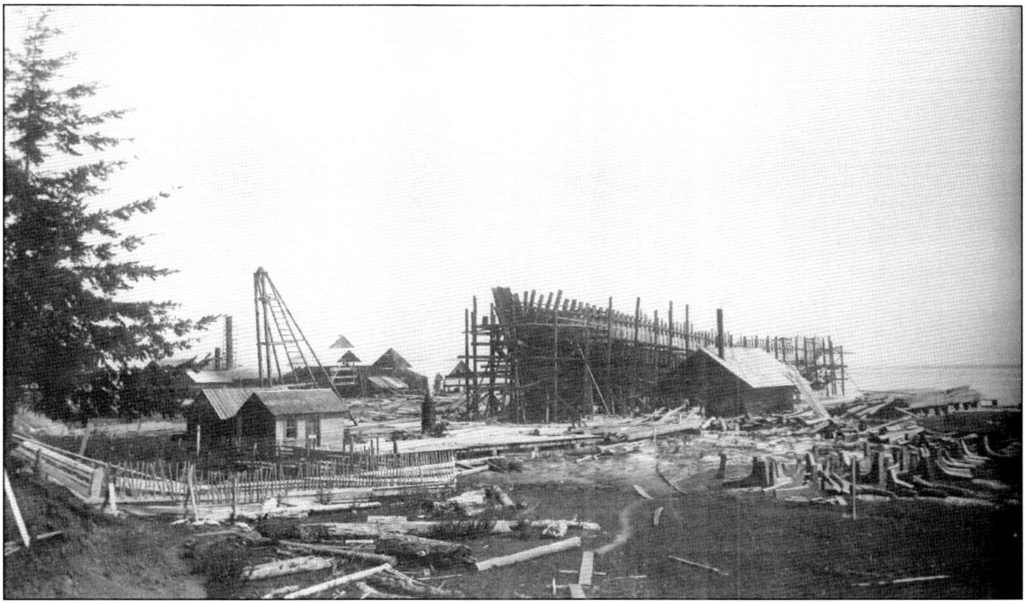

The *Annie E. Smale* is under construction at Kruse's Stave Mill shipyard. Built in 1903, she was a 200-ton four-masted schooner. The Stave Mill location was just south of North Bend in Ferndale (north Marshfield). (CHMM 009-16.53.)

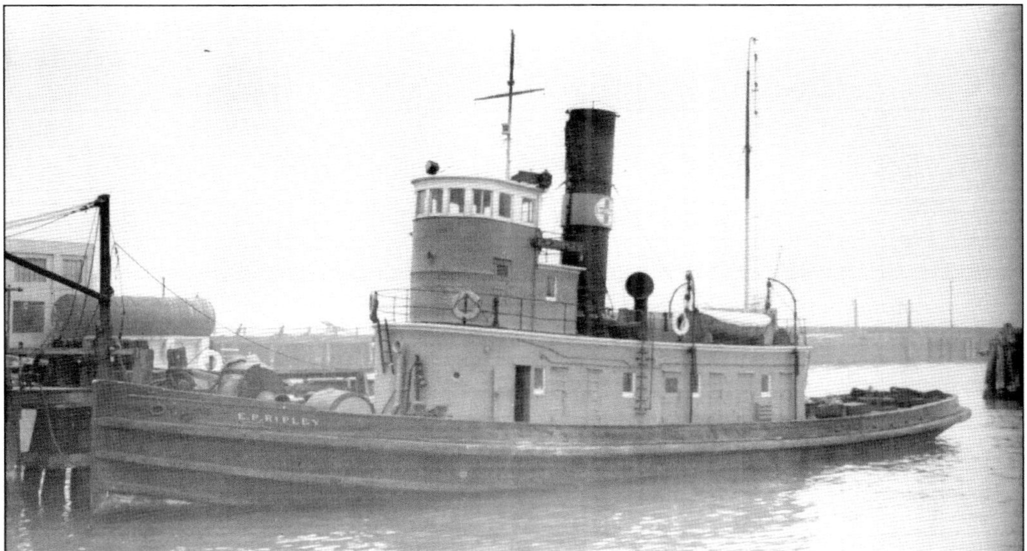

The *E. P. Ripley*, a 115-ton steam screw tug, was built in 1907, the last vessel from the Kruse and Banks' Stave Mill location. She was constructed for the Atchison, Topeka, and Santa Fe Railroad. (CHMM 009-16.64.)

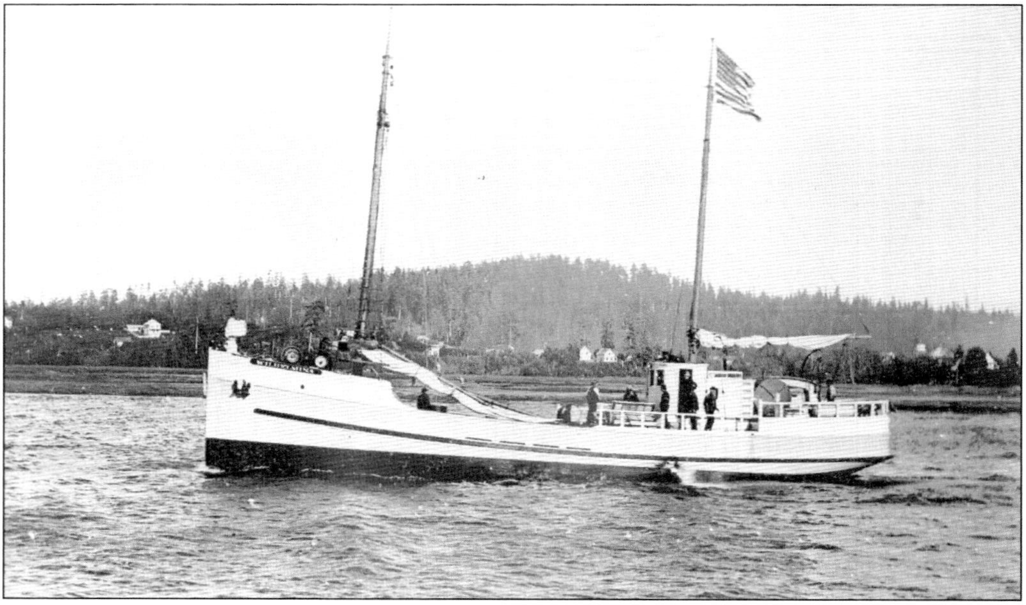

The *Wilhelmina*, an 80-ton oil screw vessel, was built at the Porter shipyard in 1908 for Charles Thom of the North Bend Brewery. The small freighter carried beer and general cargo to coastal Oregon ports. She wrecked on August 22, 1912. (CHMM 009-16.74B.)

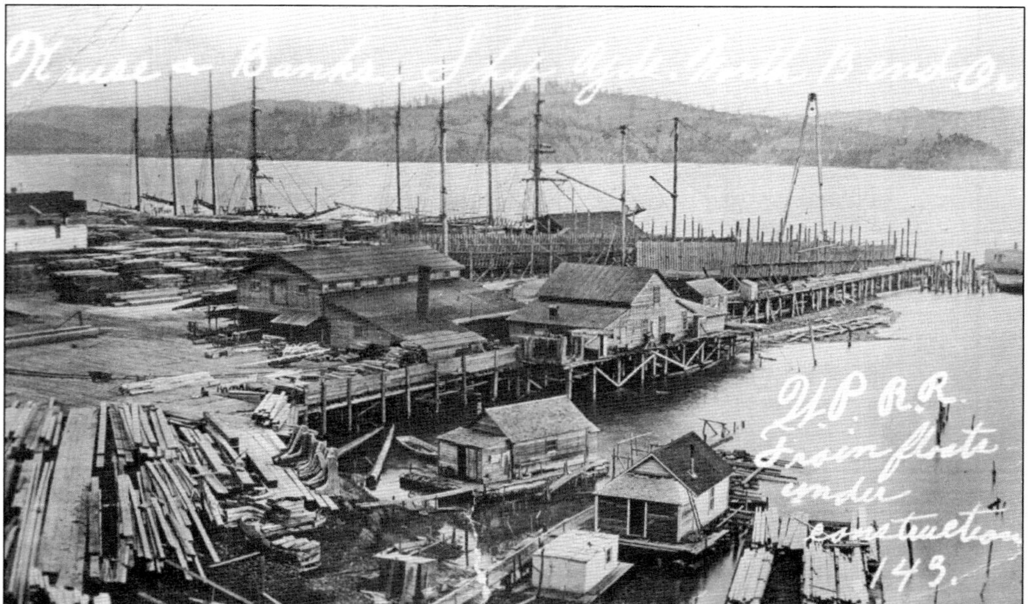

Train barges are shown under construction for the Western Pacific Railroad's proposed line from San Francisco to Salt Lake City. Each barge carried numerous rail cars between San Francisco and Oakland. (CHMM 009-16.1632.)

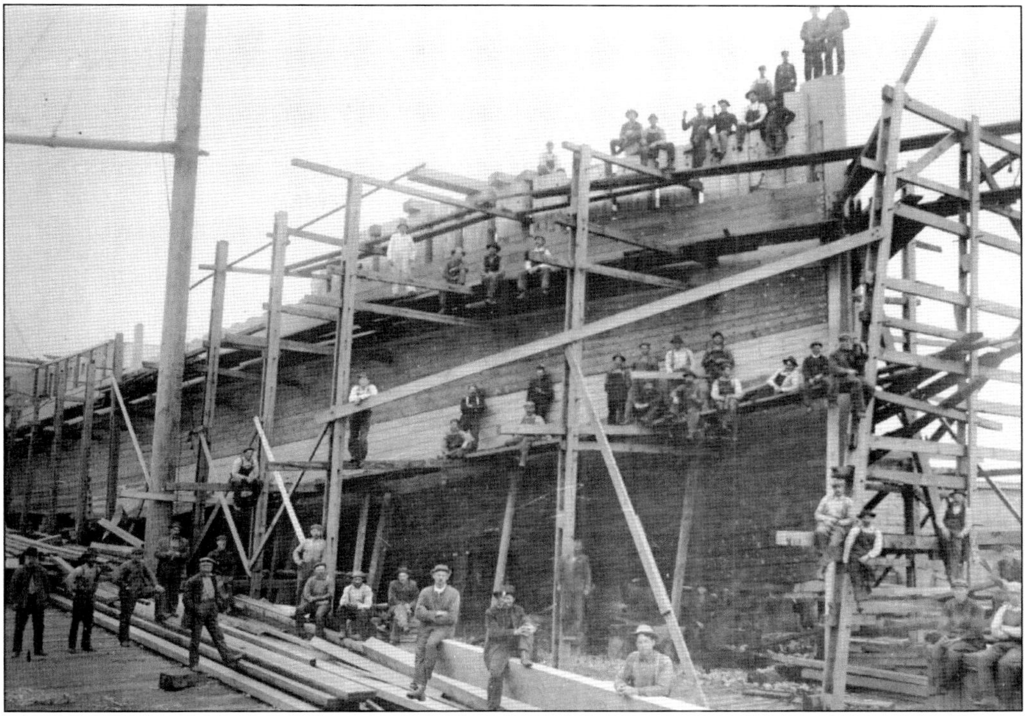

The A.M. *Simpson* is shown under construction in 1911. This 193-ton steam schooner was the last ship built on Coos Bay for the Simpson Lumber Company. (CHMM 009-16.85.)

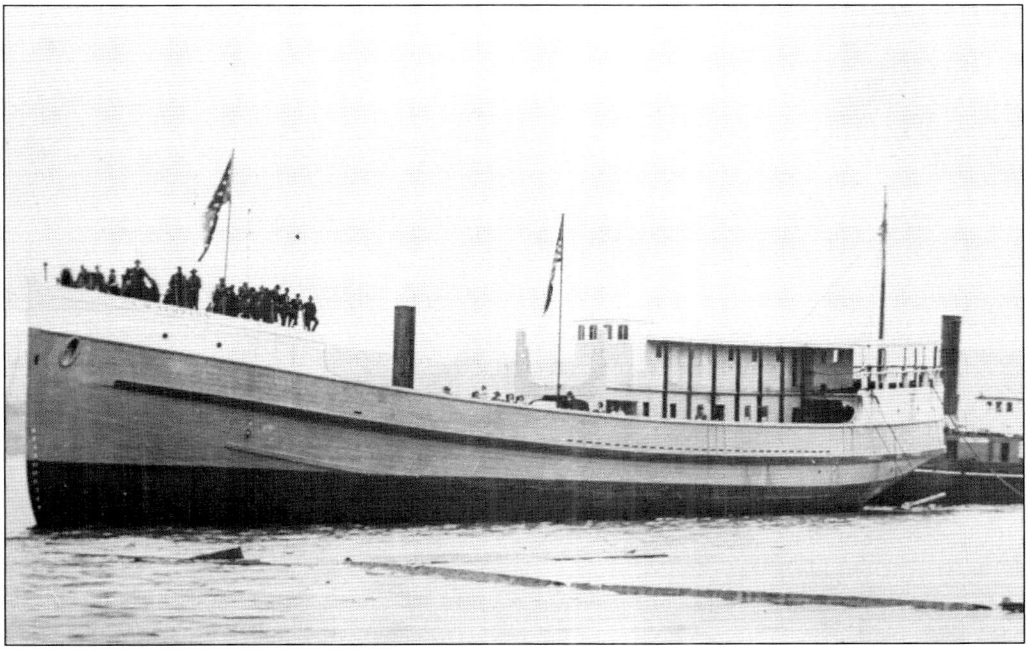

This is the launch of the A. M. *Simpson* in 1912. After Asa Simpson died in 1915, she was sold to the Buehner Lumber Company and renamed the *Martha Buehner*. (CHMM 009-16.1634.)

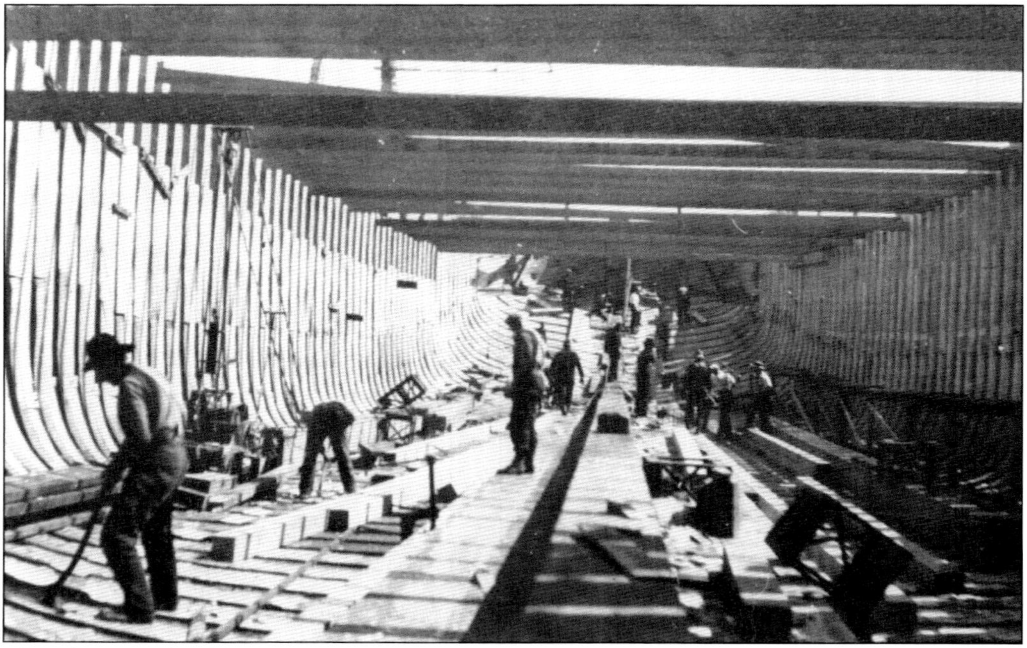

This photograph of ship construction shows the curved wooden "ribs" of the ship rising from its keel, or backbone. (CHMM 009-16.1660.)

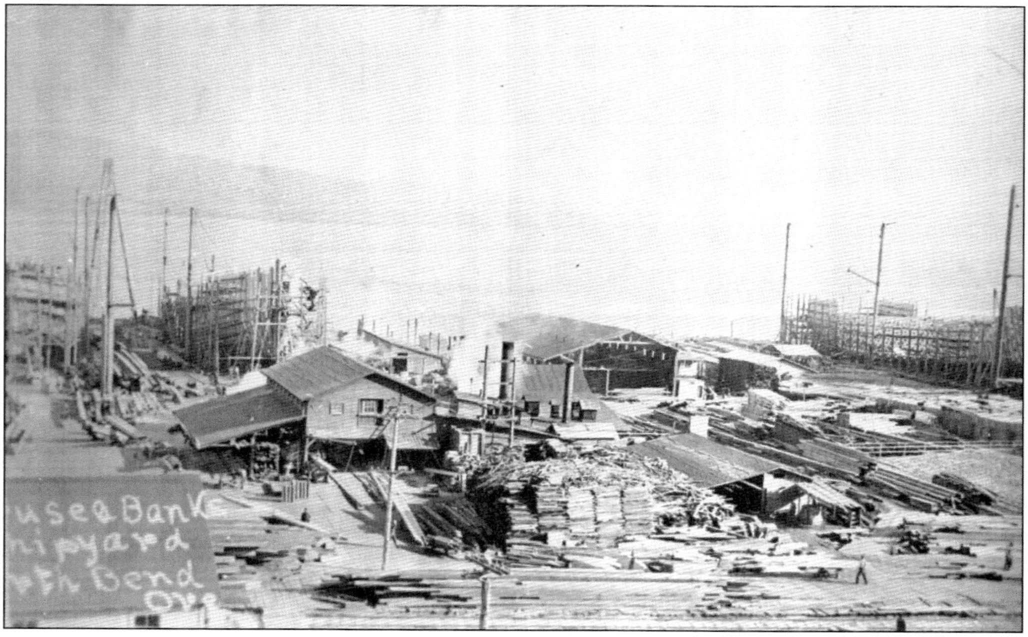

This photograph shows a general view of ships under construction on the ways at Porter. (CHMM 009-16.124.)

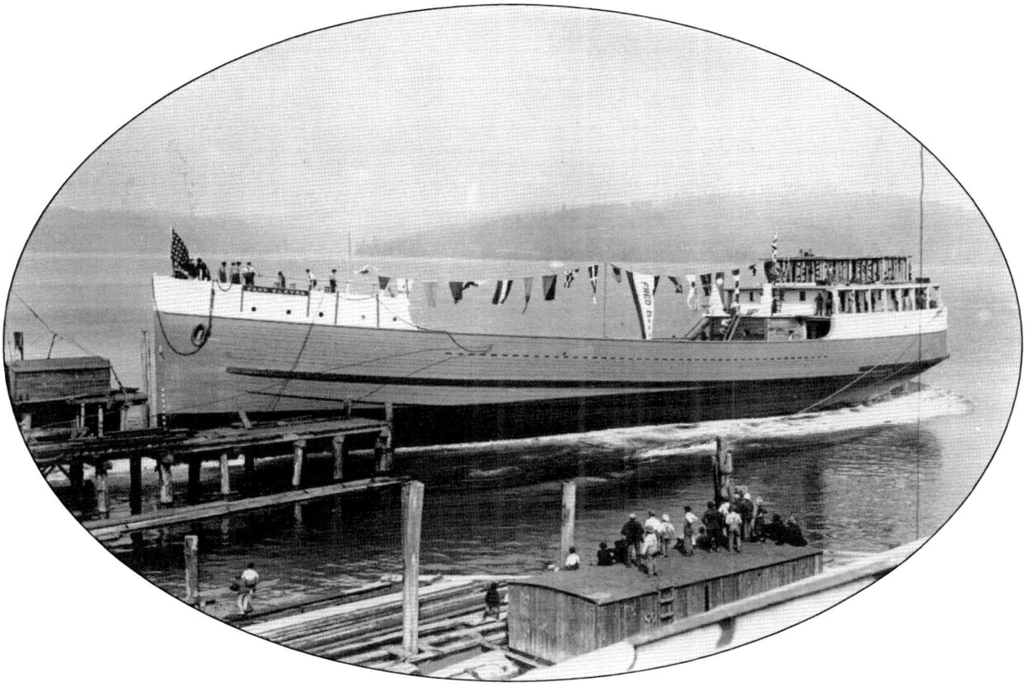

The *Fred Baxter* was launched in 1917. The vessel was constructed for the J. H. Baxter Lumber Company. (CHMM 992-8-2594.)

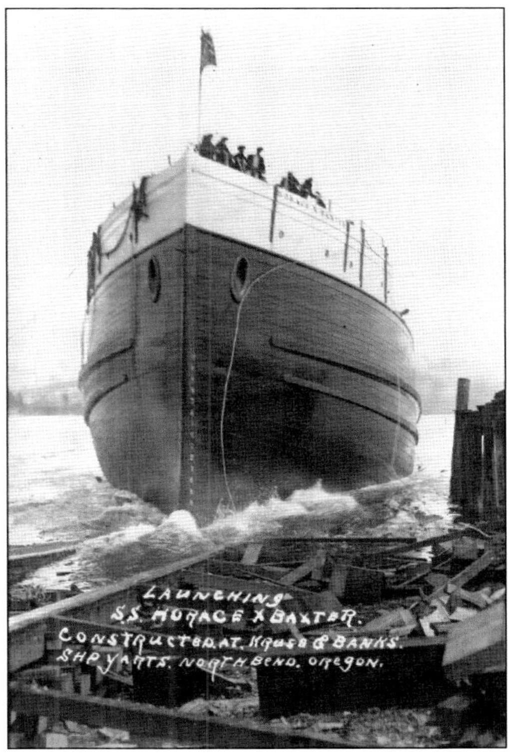

Pictured is the *Horace X. Baxter*, built for the J. H. Baxter Lumber Company and launched in 1917. The 214-ton steamer was later renamed the *Port Orford*. The ship wrecked in 1942. (CHMM 992-8-2595.)

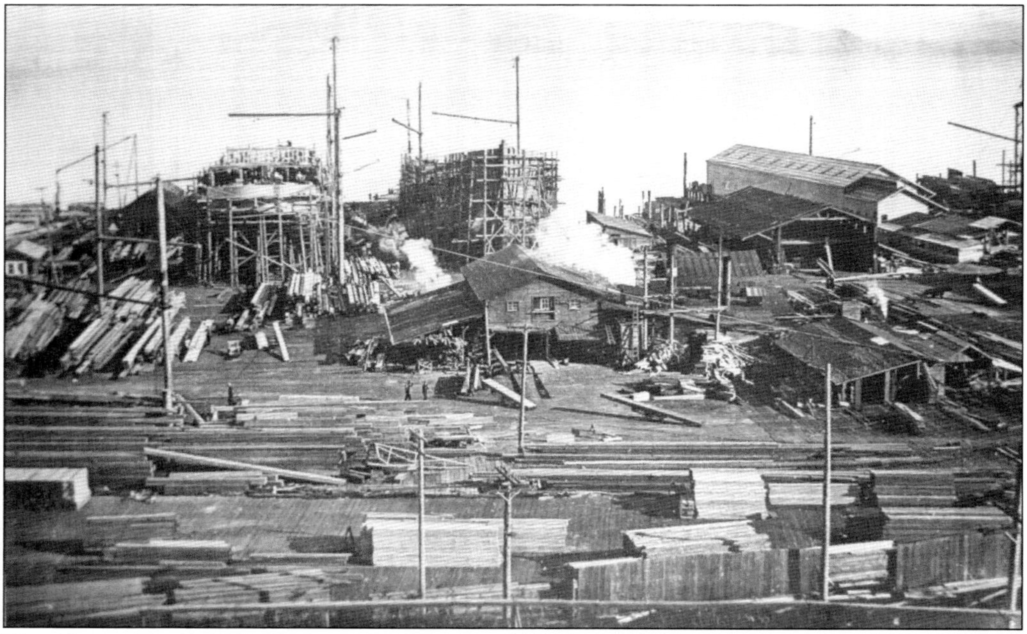

This November 19, 1917 photograph of Kruse and Banks' yard shows the north end of the shipyard with two wartime emergency fleet vessels under construction. Shipyard employment reached its peak during World War I. (CHMM 009-16.129.)

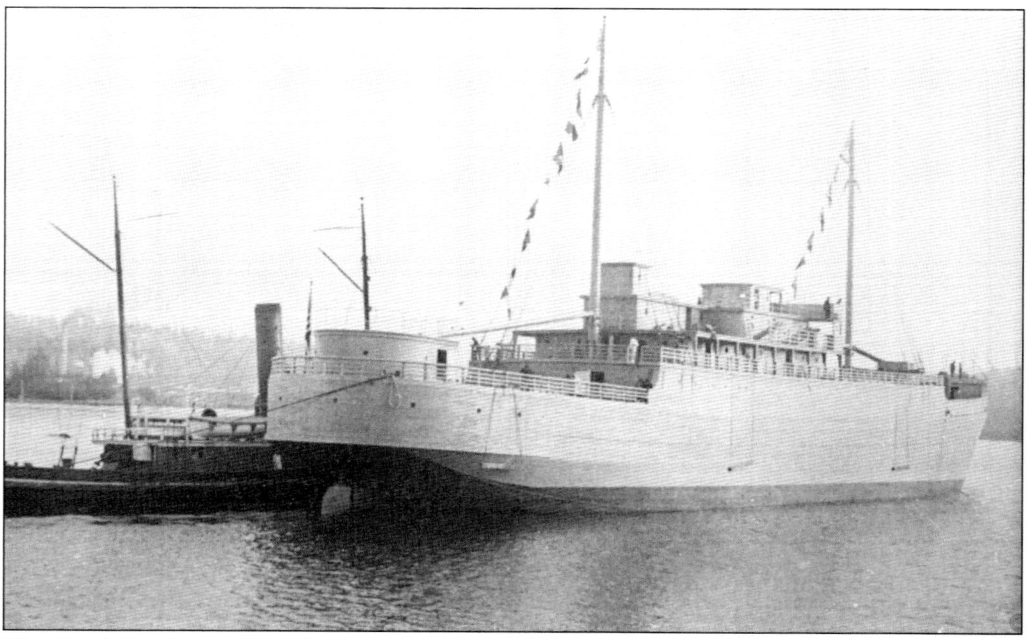

The *North Bend* was a Hough type steamer of 275 tons built in 1918 under a program to replace vessels lost to U-boats. Reportedly, Mrs. Woodrow Wilson suggested the name for this first ship in the nation's emergency fleet. Robert Banks's daughter Mary christened the USS *North Bend*. (CHMM 009-16.130.)

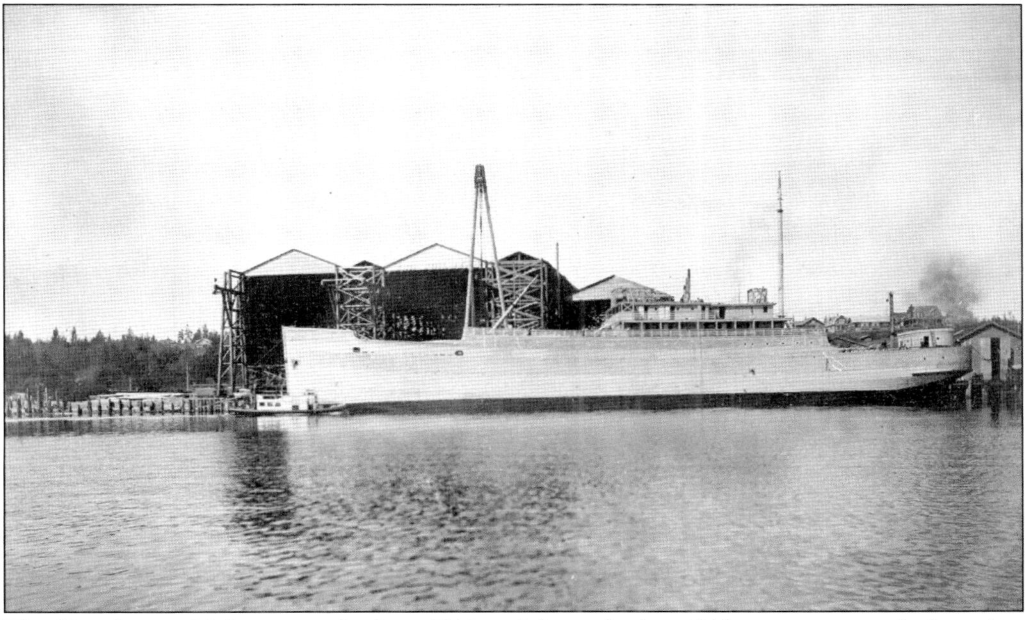

The Hough type *Kickapoo* was built in 1918 and dispatched in 1919 to carry war relief supplies after World War I. The *Kickapoo's* mission put her in the midst of hostilities between Whites and Reds during the Russian Civil War. Delivering both humanitarian aid and military goods to the Whites, she took sniper fire from the Reds while docked at Novorossisk. (CHMM 009-16.132.)

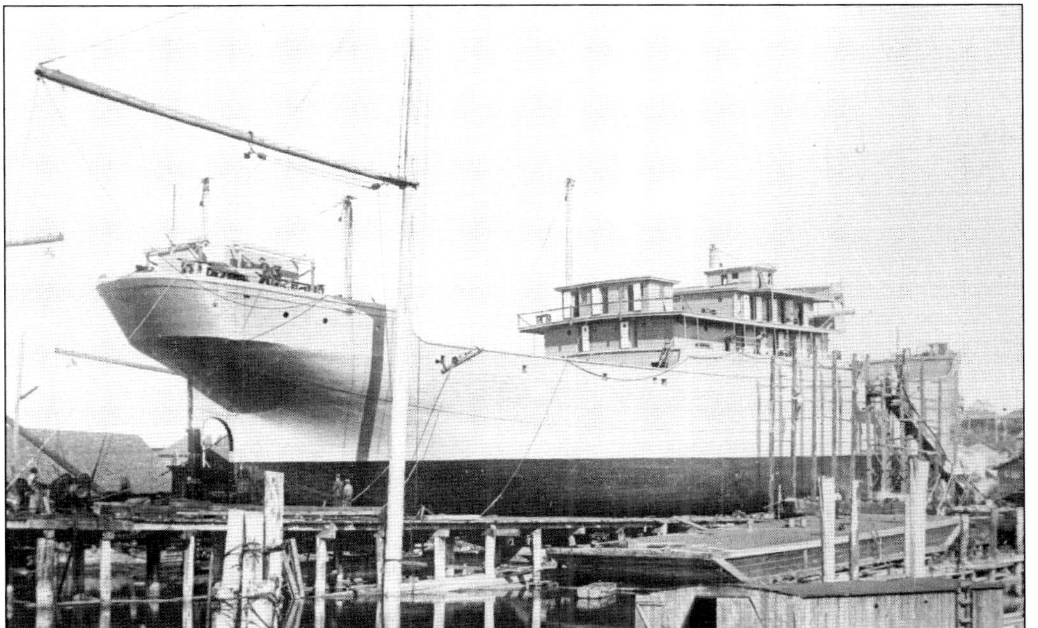

The *Fort Leavenworth*, a Ferris type steamer of 266 tons, was built in 1919, another vessel for the wartime emergency fleet. The war ended before she had an engine installed, so she was converted to a six-masted schooner. (CHMM 009-16.140B.)

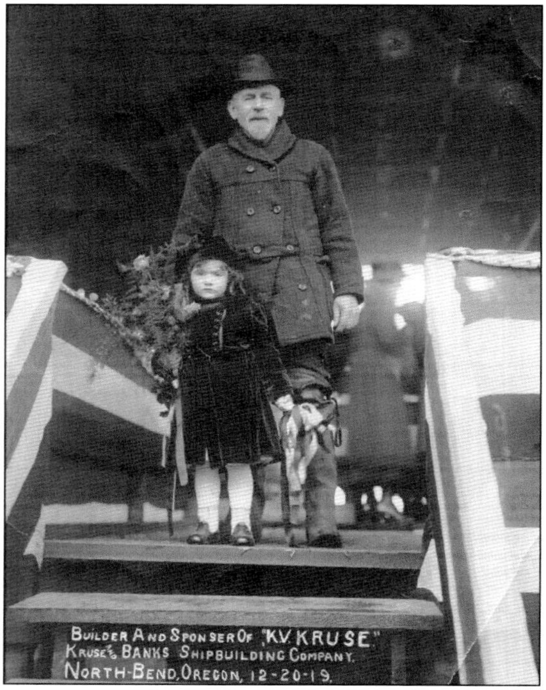

Virginia Conrad stands with her grandfather, master shipbuilder K. V. Kruse, at the December 20, 1919, launching of the graceful schooner *K. V. Kruse*. (Mary Banks Granger.)

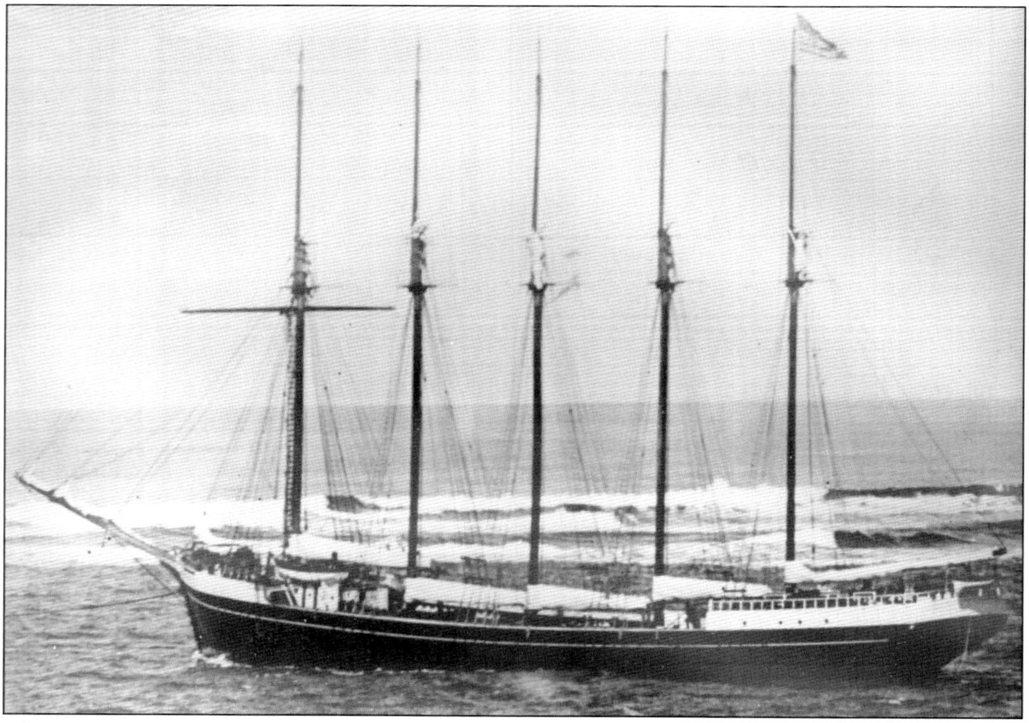

The five-masted schooner *K. V. Kruse*, the next-to-last tall ship built on Coos Bay, crosses the Coos Bay bar on her maiden voyage in 1920. She was sold in 1939 as a barge to a Canadian company and wrecked off British Columbia in 1940. (Mary Banks Granger.)

Mary Banks, daughter of shipbuilder Robert Banks, is shown at the launching of the steam schooner *Ryder Hanify*, on April 17, 1920. Built for the J. R. Hanify Company, her name later was changed to the *Joseph S*. She foundered in 1950. (Mary Banks Granger.)

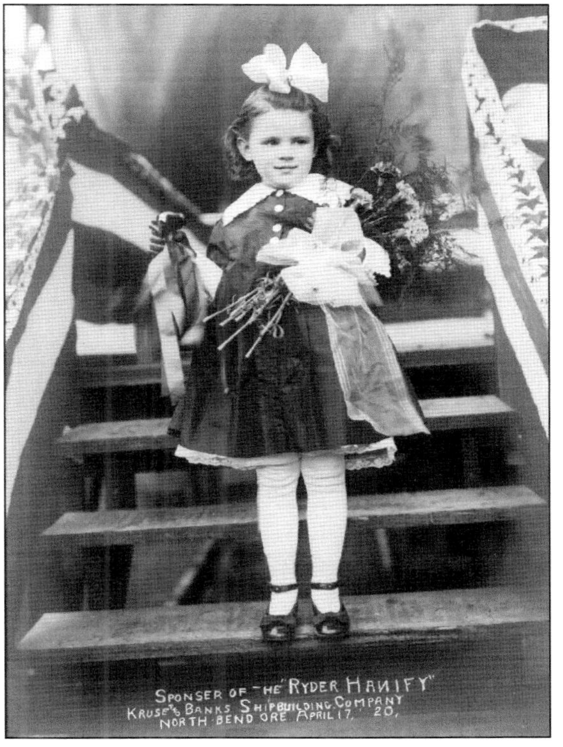

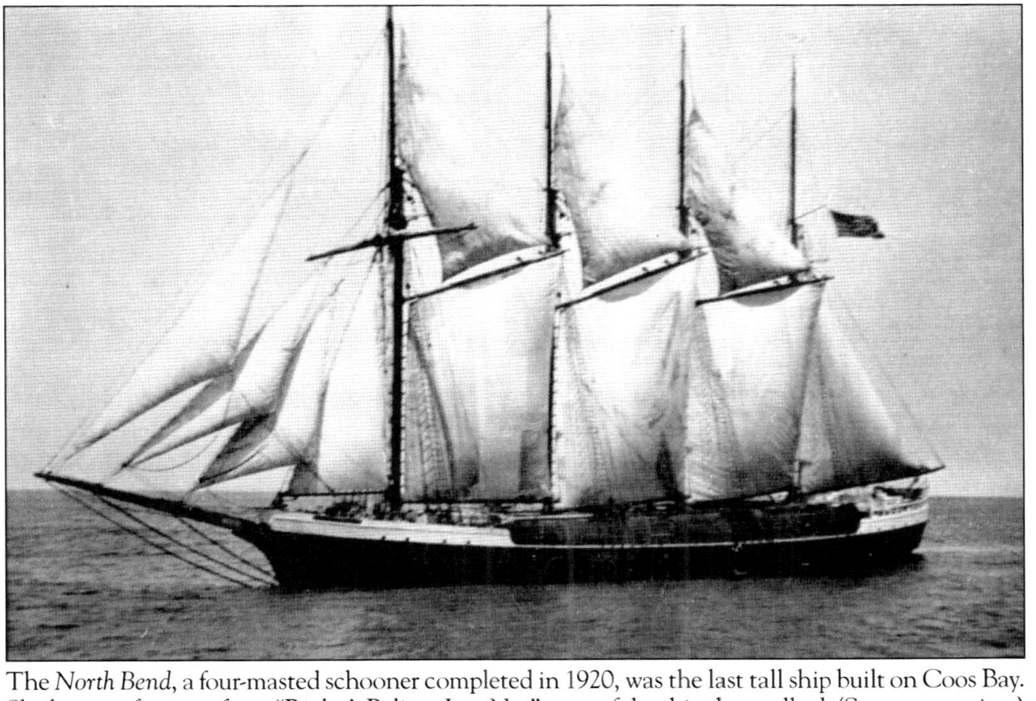

The *North Bend*, a four-masted schooner completed in 1920, was the last tall ship built on Coos Bay. She became famous after a "Ripley's Believe It or Not" story of the ship that walked. (See next caption.) She was being used as a barge on Coos Bay when she sunk in 1940. (CHMM 009-16.150.)

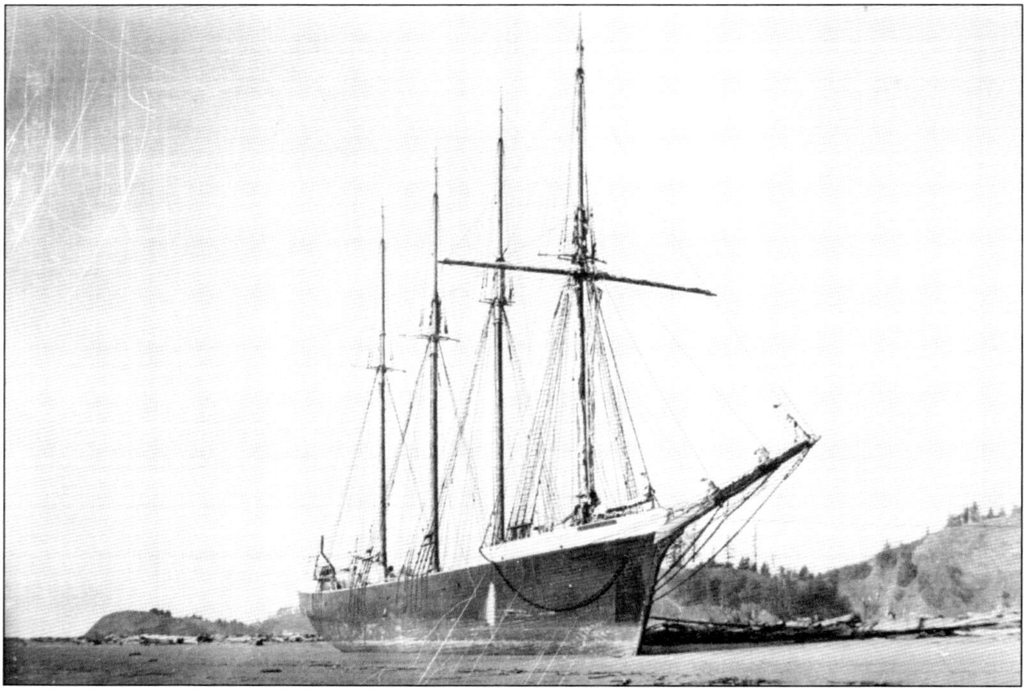

The *North Bend* grounded on Peacock Spit (near the mouth of the Columbia) in 1928. Efforts to re-float her failed. She was stripped and abandoned. After 13 months the tides and shifting sands re-floated her. Her undamaged hull traveled through 12,000 feet of sand. Once freed, however, there was no longer any demand for a sailing ship. After several years she was converted to a lumber barge. (CHMM 009-16.151.)

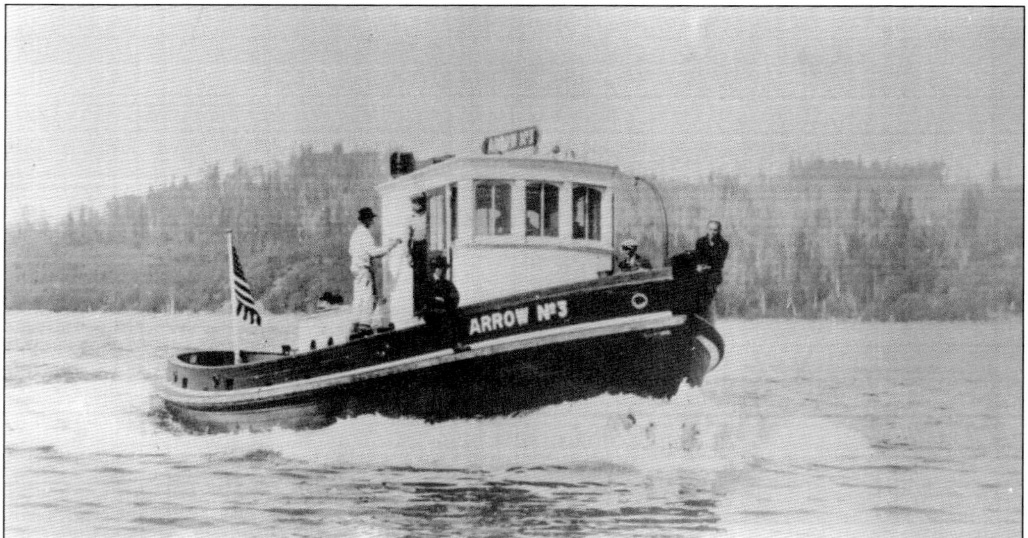

The tug *Arrow No. 3* is a 61-ton oil screw built in 1925. She was sent to Peacock Spit to help the stranded *North Bend* in 1928, but was unable to re-float the schooner. (CHMM 009-16.158C.)

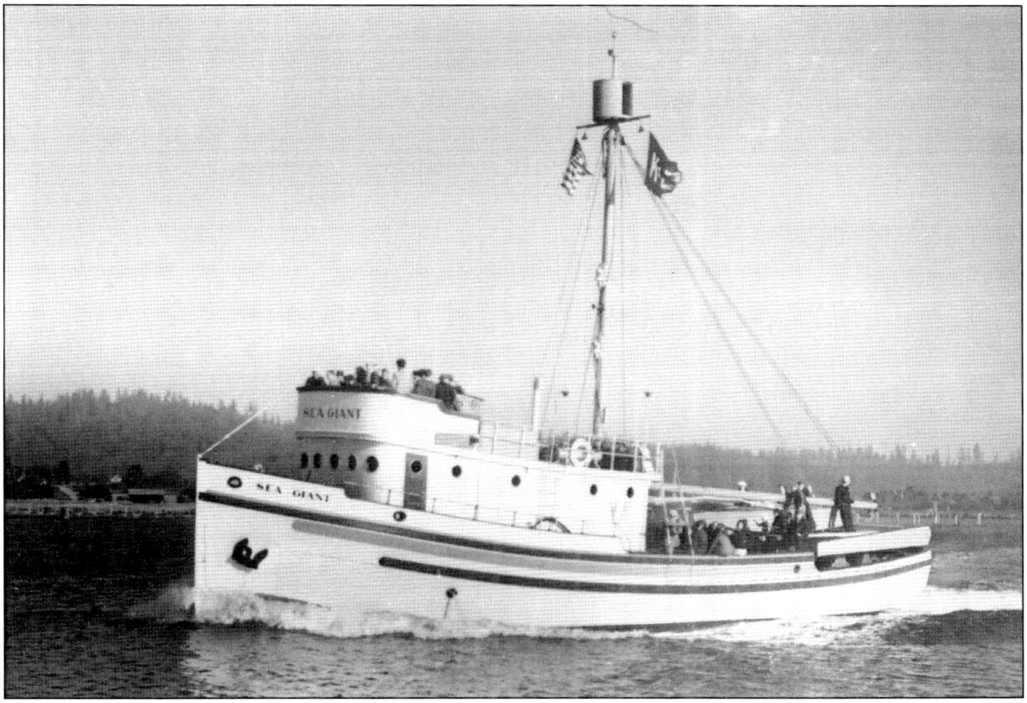

The 86-foot *Sea Giant*, Oregon's first purse seiner for the pilchard fishing industry, was built in 1936 for Robert Banks and John Graddis. (CHMM 009-16.166.)

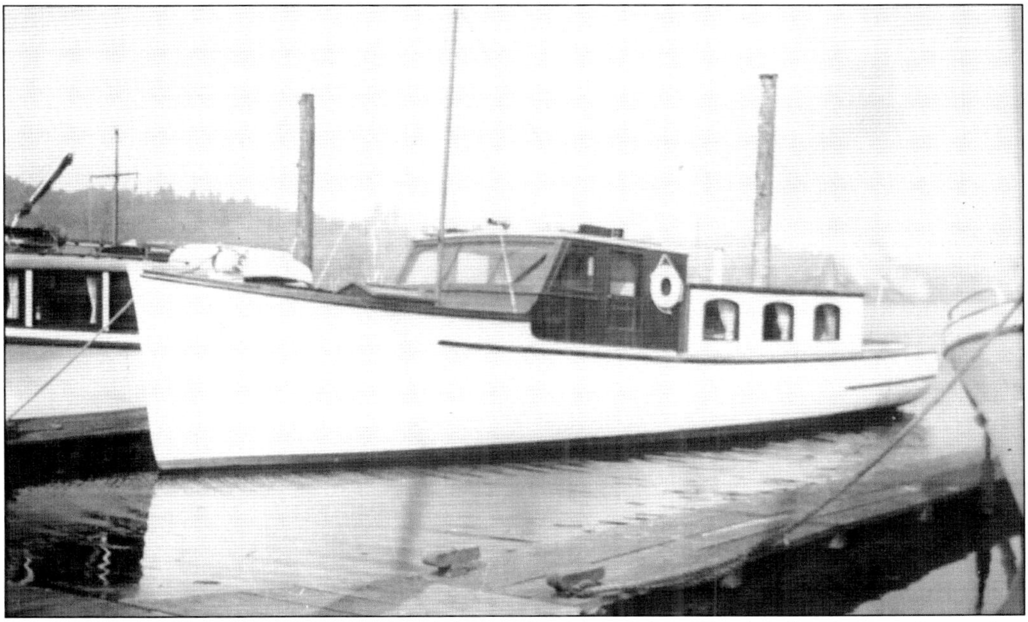

The private yacht *Arrora* was completed for Neil Banks, Robert Banks's brother, in September 1939. Neil Banks was a craftsman who worked on ships' interiors. He also built houses in Eureka, California. The *Arrora* was used on Puget Sound as a floating home after the shipyard closed. (CHMM 009-16.170.)

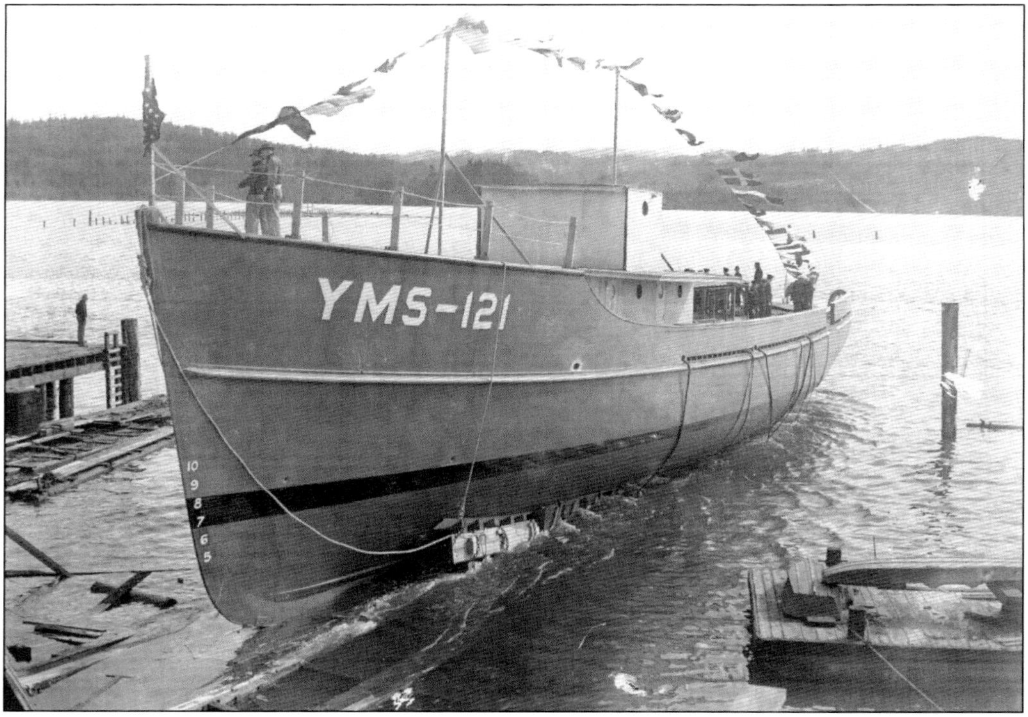

The *YMS-121* was a wooden minesweeper built for the U.S. Navy. Her hull was laid in 1941 and the vessel launched on May 14, 1942. She was one of eight minesweepers built by Kruse and Banks during the Second World War. A sister ship, *YMS-124*, was used for the filming of the 1943 war movie *Minesweeper* starring Richard Arlen. (CHMM 009-16.172.)

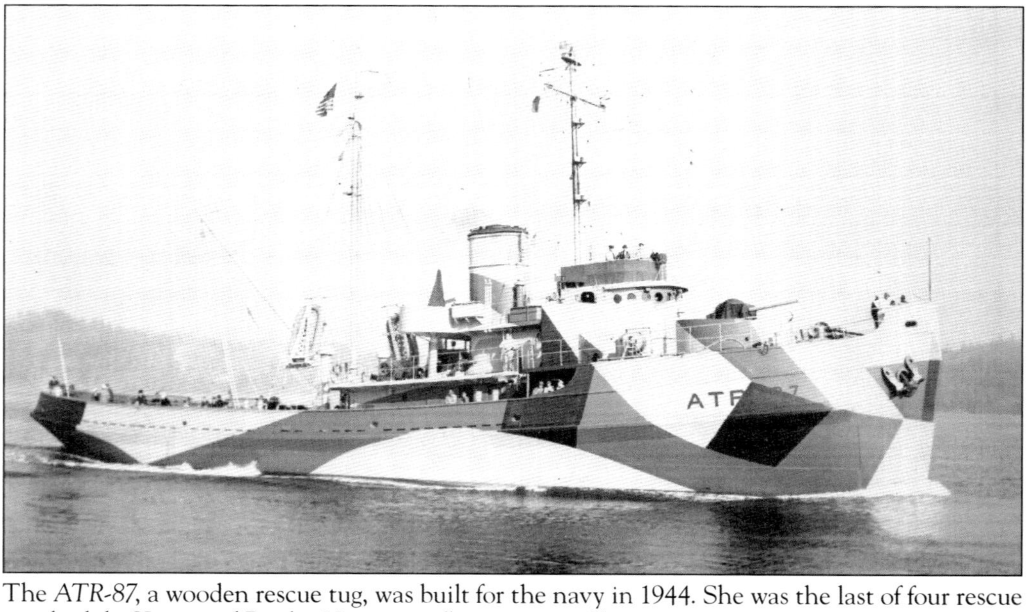

The *ATR-87*, a wooden rescue tug, was built for the navy in 1944. She was the last of four rescue tugs built by Kruse and Banks. Her camouflage paint and her weapons were added after launching. She saw action at Okinawa in 1945. (CHMM 009-16.190.)

Nine

Maturing

After World War II, North Bend prospered. Weyerhaeuser and Menasha expanded their waterfront activity. Timber cutting increased, and for a time the Port of Coos Bay was the world's major lumber exporter.

Housing developments like Oregon Homes and Skyline Homes and Apartments boosted housing stock in the late 1940s. The Edgewood Terrace development, started in 1959, added more. Among immediate post-war construction were the Hillcrest School, Clyde Allen's Humboldt building, and the brick First National Bank.

Weyerhaeuser's expanding operations during the 1950s created an employment surge. New churches were built and City Hall added a wing. The Port Theater opened and Keizer Hospital expanded. Local restaurants opened as well, including the Top Hat (now The Pancake Mill) across from Mill B on U.S. Highway 101, and the Dari-Treat store on Virginia (later a Dairy Queen).

Walter Kraus built a $500,000 medical facility on McPherson across from the hospital (today's School District 13 offices). A new Safeway at Meade Avenue, off Virginia, debuted in 1955. Dallas Troutman opened "The Emporium" in Safeway's former building.

Mercy Home, a nursing facility for the elderly, came in 1957 (renamed St. Catherine's in 1964) while the Mattechecks opened a $200,000 bowling alley. In 1959, an A&W drive-in came to Broadway at 16th and the Post Office completed a $65,000 building on McPherson.

Construction continued with a new junior high in 1960. Also in the 1960s, a new high school was built section by section and Kraus completed the Oregon coast's first covered mall, Pony Village. In the mid-1960s Albertson's food stores purchased land at dead man's curve (Broadway at Newmark) from Storey-Lynch Development. Soon Bi-Mart also built there.

The 1960s were years of destruction as well. Numerous downtown buildings were declared unsafe and knocked down.

The International Woodworkers of America built a union hall on Broadway in 1965–1966. In 1991, the union sold the building to the city for use as a community center. The annual holiday tree lighting and other events are held there.

Building continued (including the 1974 Coast Guard Air Station) until the early 1980s recession. Other construction, like the school district's computer technology center, dedicated in September 2003, resumed as North Bend entered the 21st century. Some more recent structures are pictured later in this chapter.

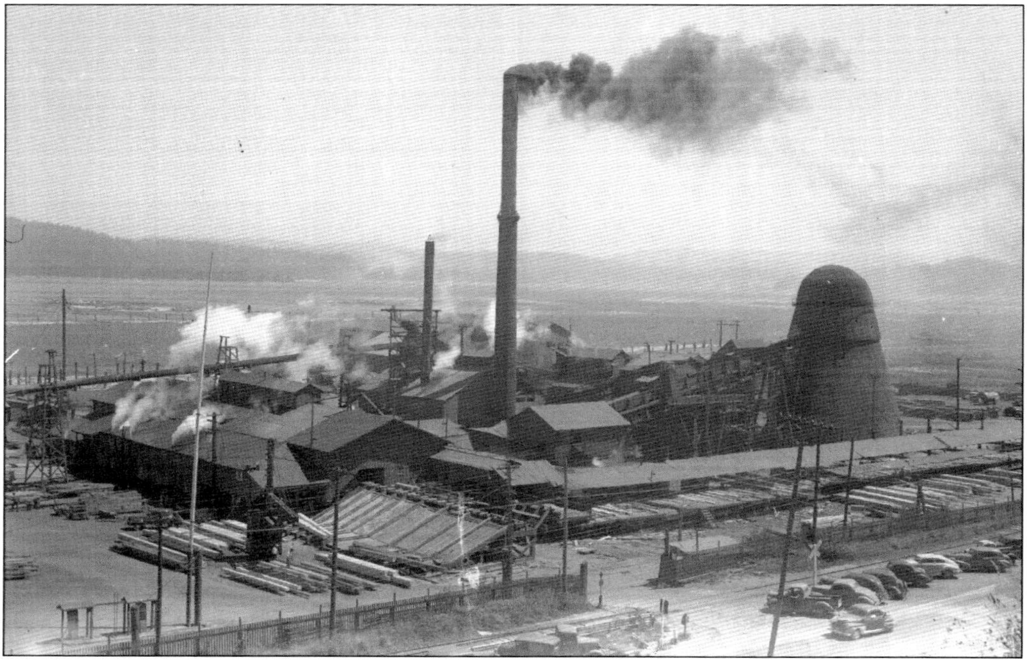

Mill B was located on the waterfront south of where Vermont Avenue comes through. Irwin and Lyons owned this mill for many years, moving machinery from their Empire mill in 1939 and installing it here. Irwin and Lyons sold to Menasha in 1954. Menasha sold to Weyerhaeuser. (CHMM 986-N59.)

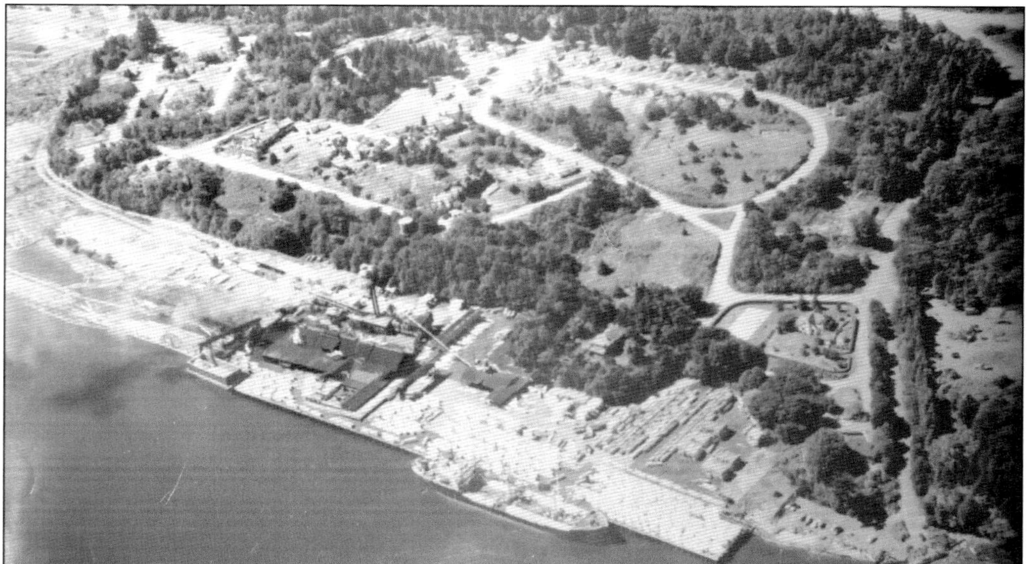

This aerial view shows the Coos Bay Logging Company mill, once Simpson's "old town" sawmill, with docks full of lumber awaiting shipment. A fire in December 1949 damaged the mill, and in January 1950, what remained was deliberately burned. The lots in Simpson Heights, a development begun in 1924, are largely vacant. Major housing construction occurred after World War II. (CHMM 009-16.1415.)

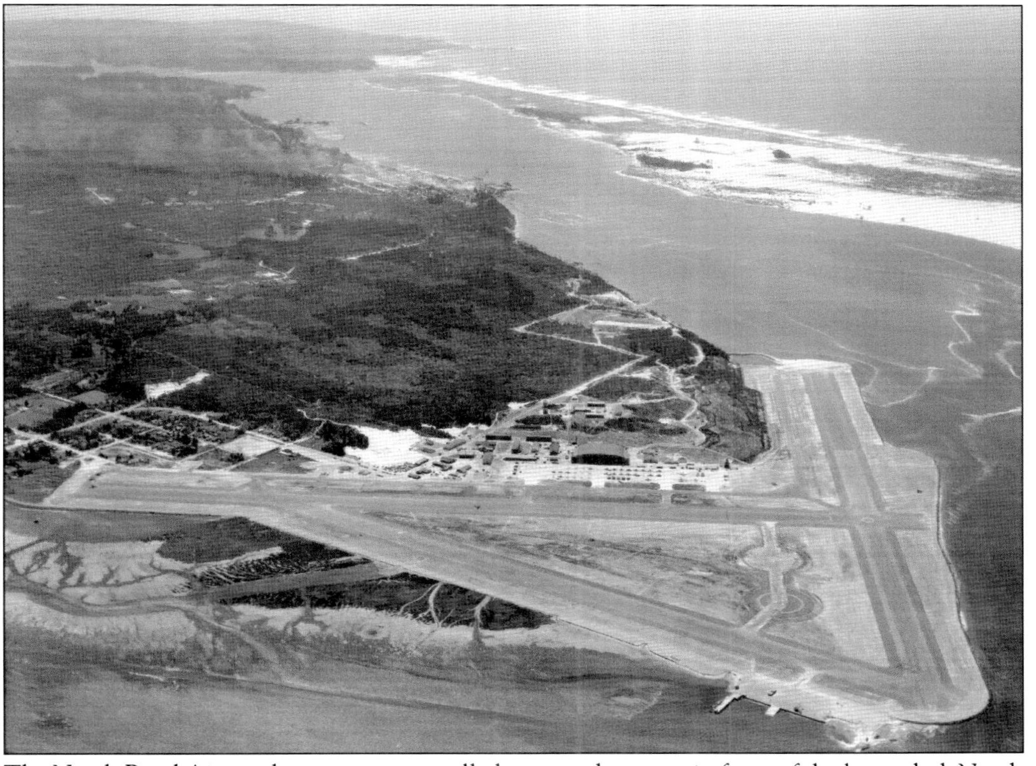

The North Bend Airport has numerous small planes on the apron in front of the large, dark North Bend hangar. The navy leased the airport during World War II. The Oregon Homes "Airport Heights" housing development has not yet begun. (CNB.)

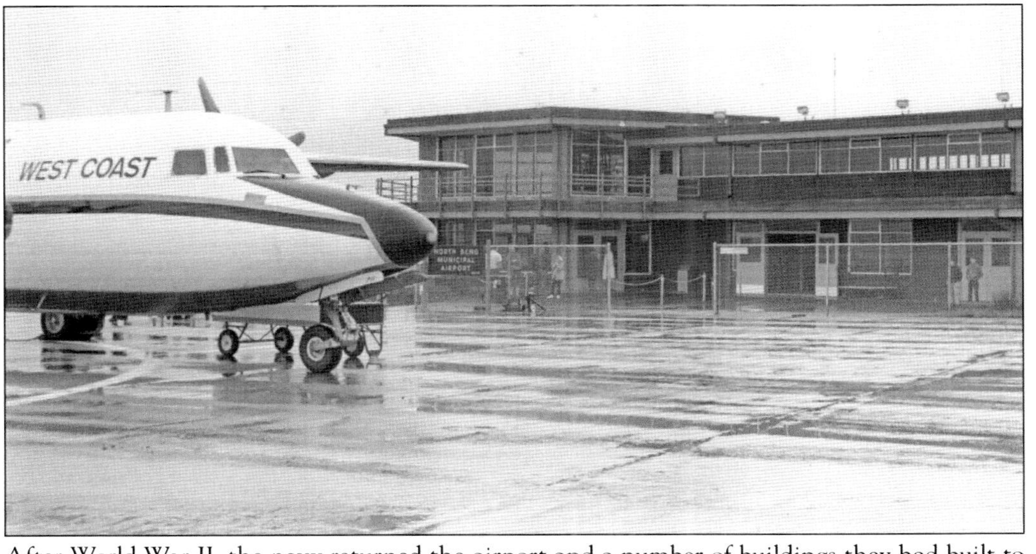

After World War II, the navy returned the airport and a number of buildings they had built to the city. In 1947, West Coast Airlines began service for passengers, mail, and freight. They flew north to Portland and south to San Francisco. A West Coast airplane sits at the new $196,000 North Bend Municipal Airport terminal built in 1963. (CHMM 989-P2a.)

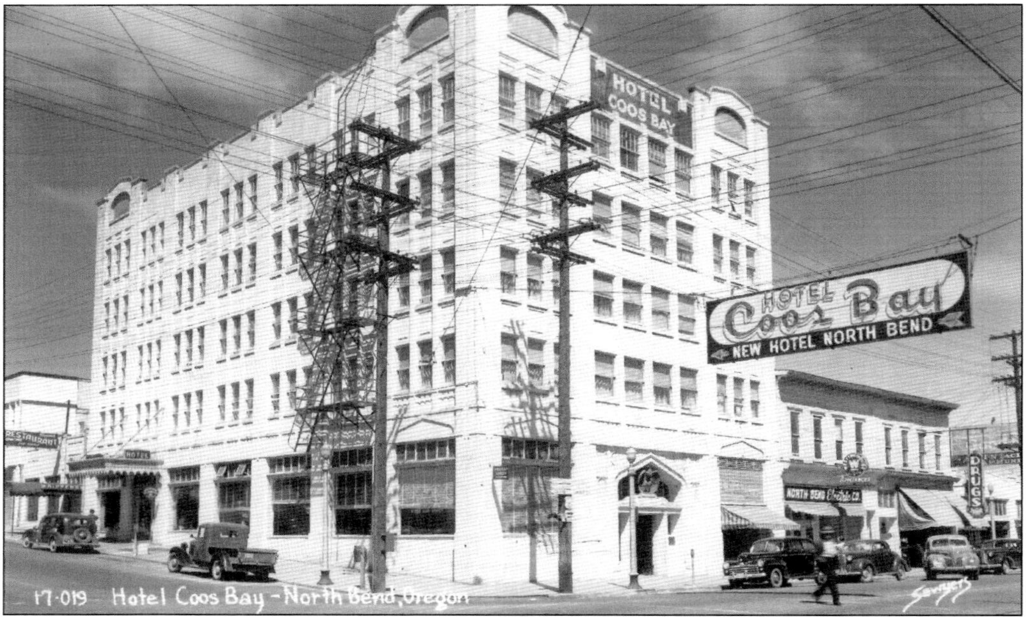

This is the Hotel Coos Bay in the late 1940s. The "over highway" sign also promotes the "new" Hotel North Bend, located at the airport, in a building formerly used by the U.S. Navy for bachelor officer quarters. In 1959, the Hotel Coos Bay reverted to its original name, Hotel North Bend. (CHMM 969-204g.)

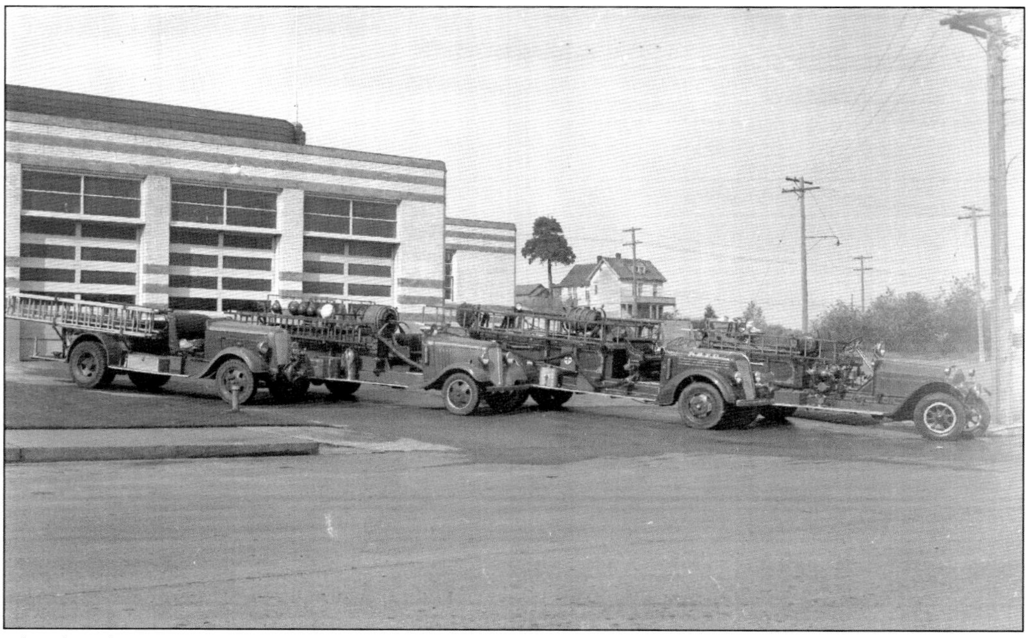

The fire department's equipment is displayed outside its home in the new City Hall. Pictured from left to right are a 1930 Reo, a 1933 Chevrolet, the 1937 Federal (which the department today maintains for parades), and the 1921 LaFrance. The photograph probably dates to 1939. (CHMM 992-N119.1.)

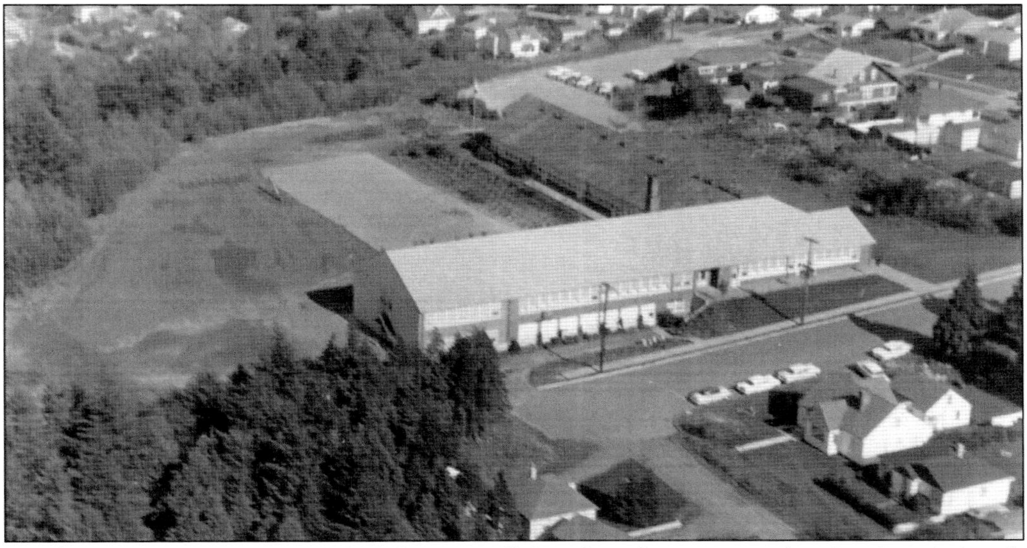

The $238,400 Hillcrest School, built by Tom Lillebo of Reedsport, opened in October 1948 with 14 classrooms for 400 students. It replaced the aging Central School for grades one to four. Since expanded, Hillcrest now serves all city elementary children, grades K to four, in the public school district. (CNB.)

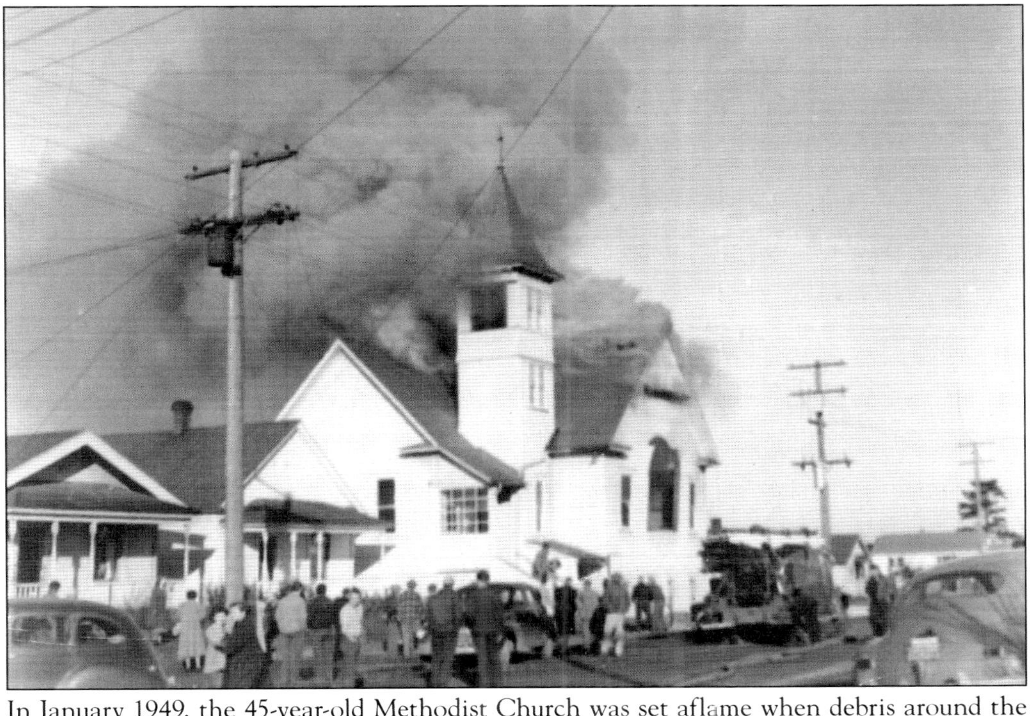

In January 1949, the 45-year-old Methodist Church was set aflame when debris around the furnace ignited. The Fire Department responded promptly and extinguished the blaze, but hot gasses collected under the roof and exploded, destroying the building. The Methodists built a new church at the crest of Meade Avenue. It opened in 1951 and continues in use. (NBFD.)

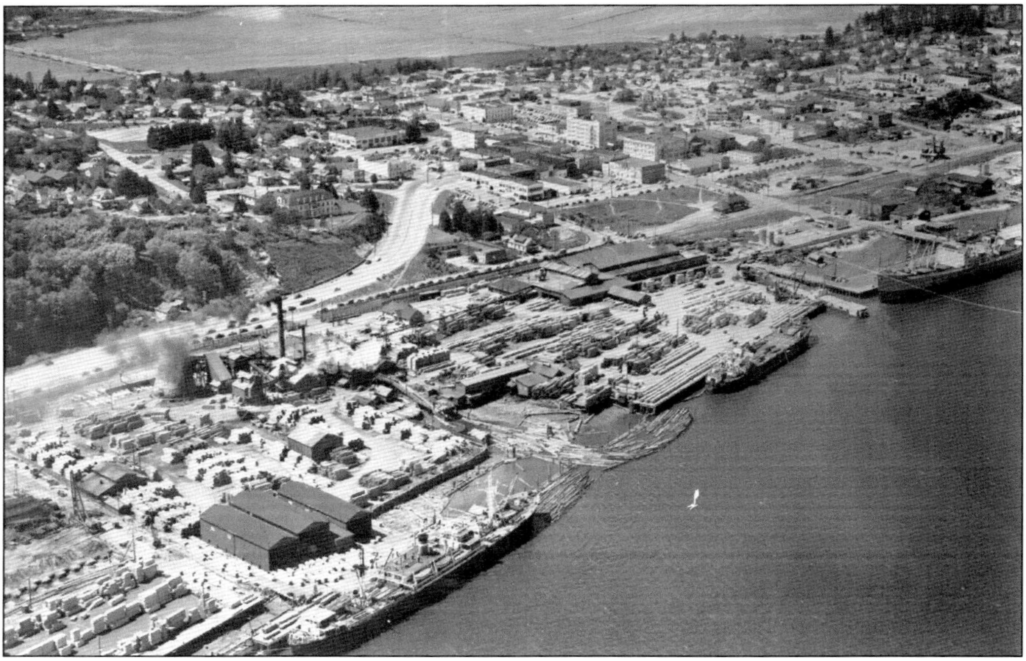

This late 1940s aerial view looking north shows the newly routed and surfaced U.S. Highway 101 as well as much of historic North Bend from the industrial waterfront and Mercy Hospital to the Hotel Oregon. The highway work was competed in late 1948. (CHMM 992-8-0880.)

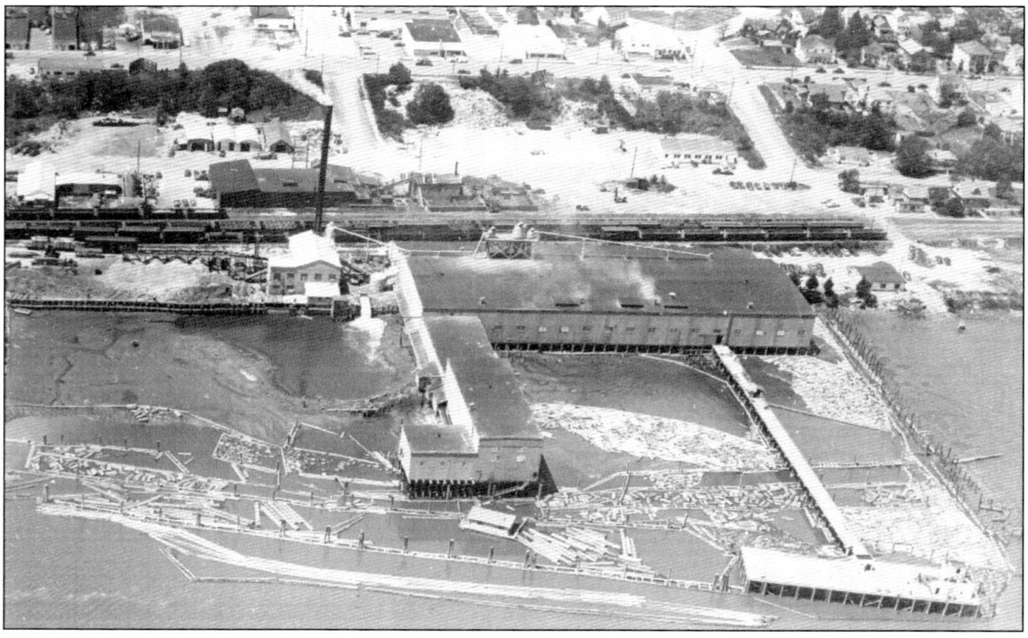

Menasha's Plywood Mill was built around 1949. It employed about 285 people when it closed in 1967. Menasha continued to operate a large pulp mill (built in 1960) that produced containerboard on the North Spit across the bay from North Bend. The pulp mill was sold to Weyerhaeuser in 1981 and closed in 2003. (CHMM 009-16.1512.)

The Weyerhaeuser sawmill and export dock facilities were on the bay at the southern end of North Bend. The $900,000 Weyerhaeuser mill opened in 1951, with a $10 million plywood plant added in 1962. The recession of the early 1980s, and other factors, caused the timber industry's decline. The mill closed in 1989. (CHMM 989-P51.)

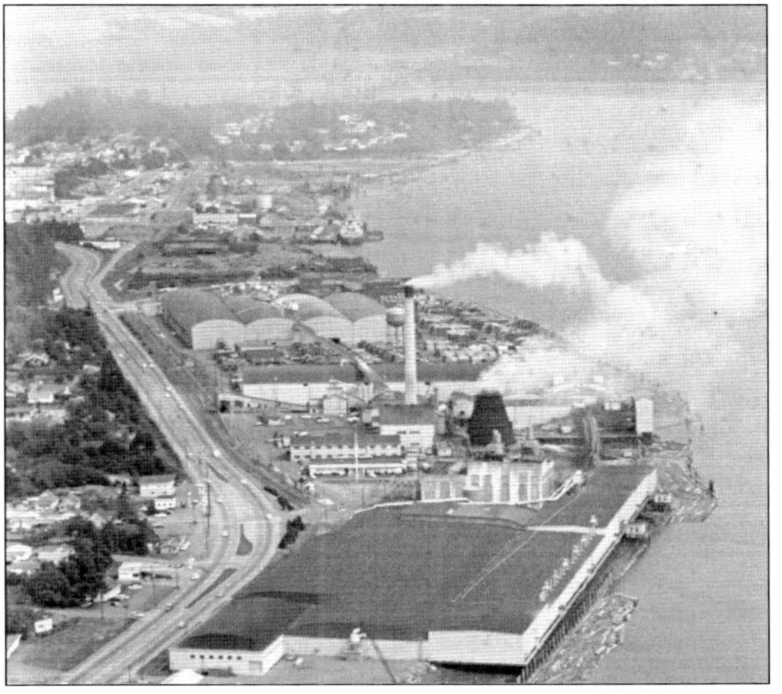

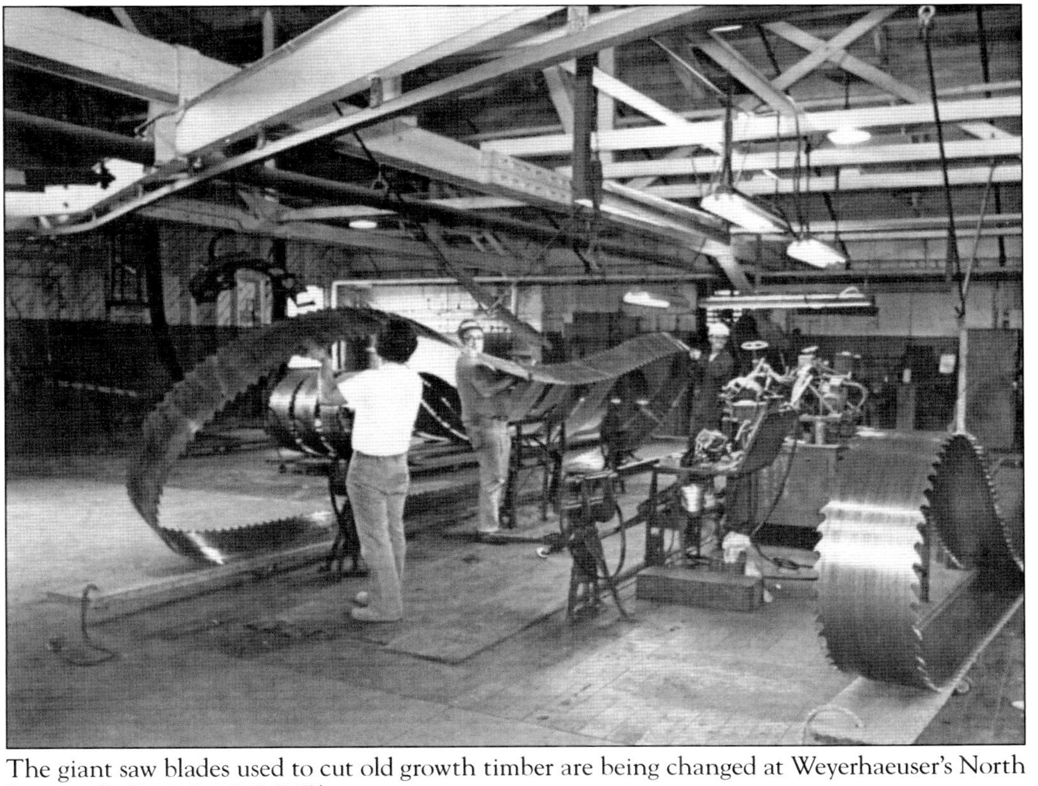

The giant saw blades used to cut old growth timber are being changed at Weyerhaeuser's North Bend mill. (CHMM 988-P85.)

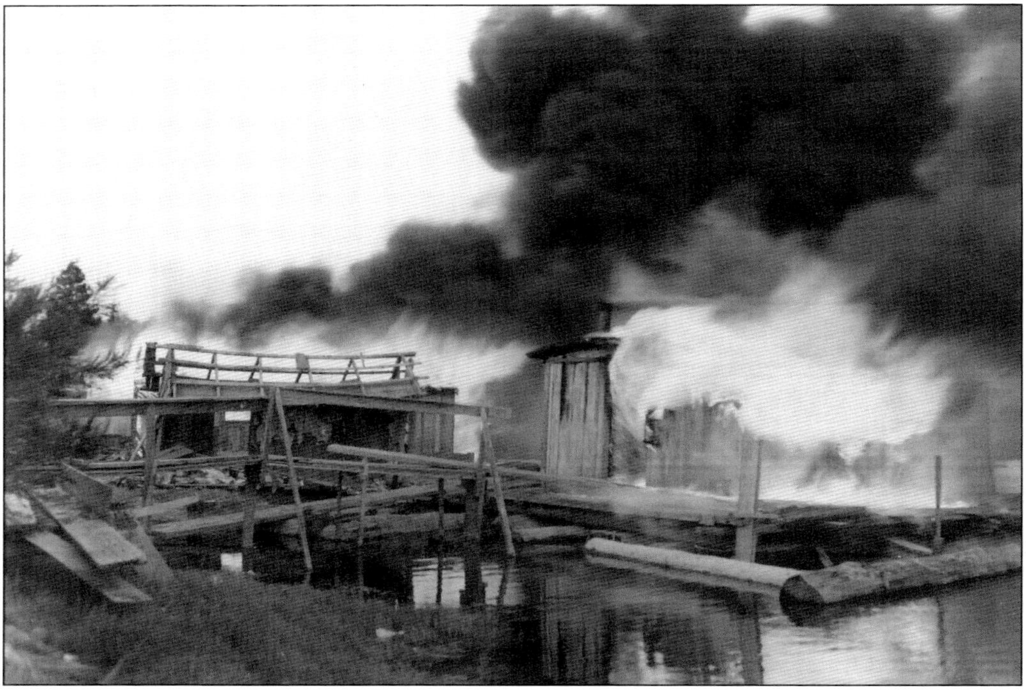

In the early 1950s deteriorating float houses along the North Bend waterfront were burned. Often tied to docks, or the remains of the Montana Avenue Bridge, some float houses had a reputation for illegal alcohol sales during Prohibition and for prostitution as well. At least two float houses, off Hamilton near the Montana Avenue Bridge, were pulled out and used as dwellings on land. (CNB.)

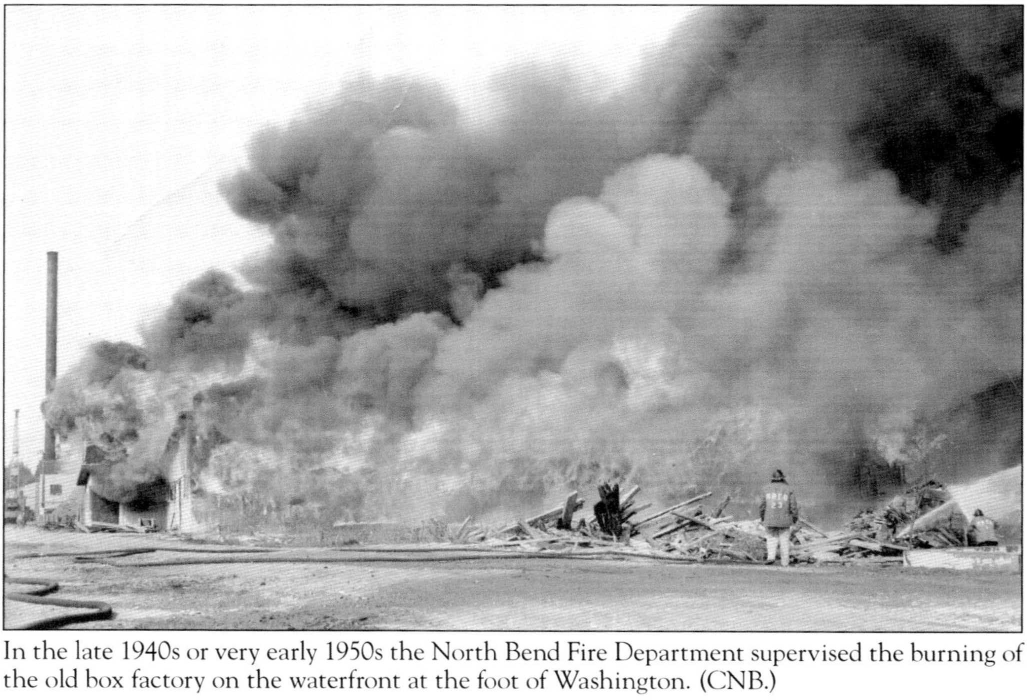

In the late 1940s or very early 1950s the North Bend Fire Department supervised the burning of the old box factory on the waterfront at the foot of Washington. (CNB.)

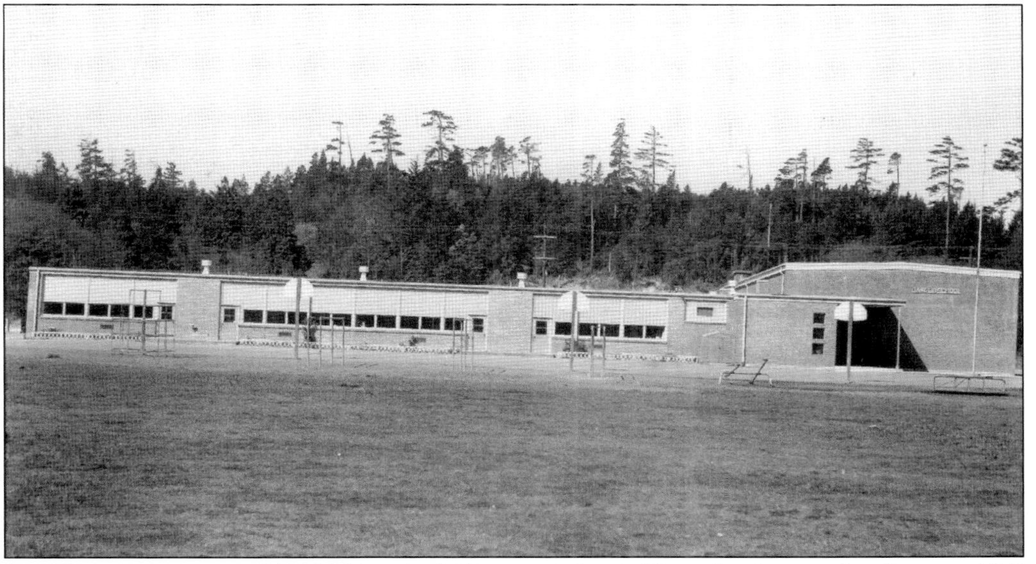

In 1951, voters approved $105,000 to build Bangor School. The school opened in January 1953 to serve children who had previously been double shifted at the Sunset elementary school (since 1949 housed in airport buildings, remaining from the navy's tenure. Sunset school closed about 1961). The new school served the postwar Oregon Homes "Airport Heights" subdivision, opened in 1949, as well as Bangor proper. Bangor school closed in 2003. (CNB.)

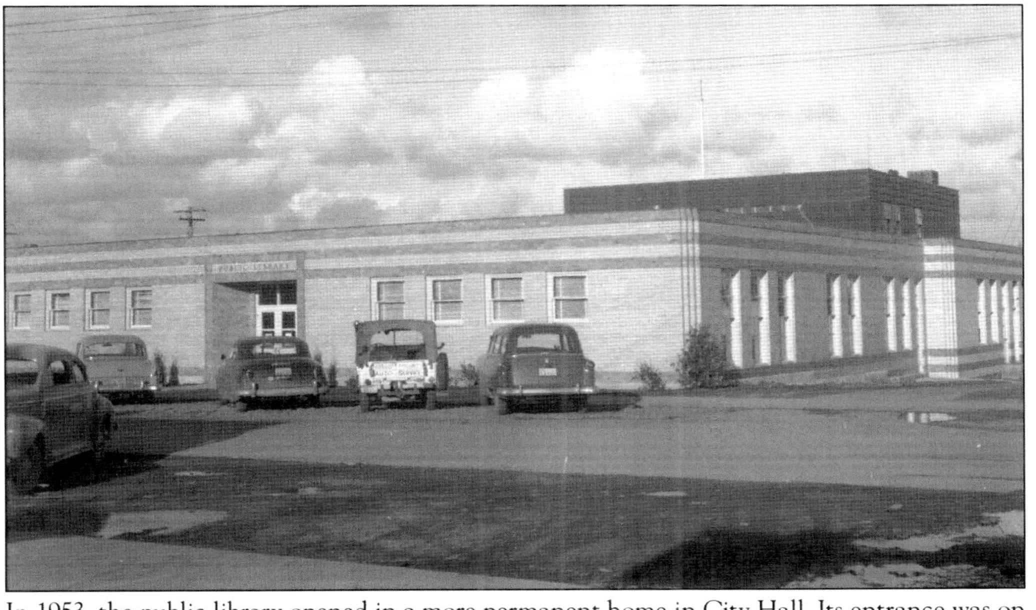

In 1953, the public library opened in a more permanent home in City Hall. Its entrance was on McPherson Avenue. Voters approved an $80,000 bond to build this addition. The city's first paid librarian, Mrs. Woodbury, aged 85 in 1953, took the bus from Santa Cruz to attend the opening. The library remained in City Hall until 1989. (CHMM 986-N814.1.)

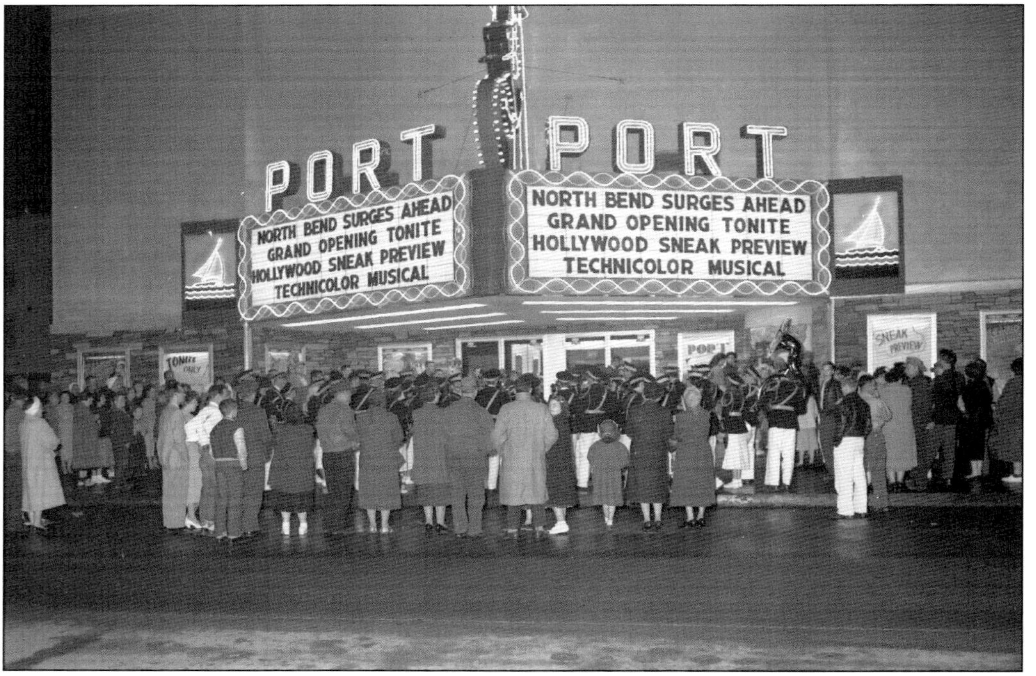

The Port Theater opened in late November 1953. The marquee announced that "North Bend Surges Ahead" with a sneak preview in Technicolor. The new 900-seat Cinemascope-ready theater cost $160,000. The Port, in an era soon dominated by television, only survived into the late 1980s. For a time it had both a large anchor and a miniature lighthouse sitting atop the marquee. (CHMM 995.26524.1.)

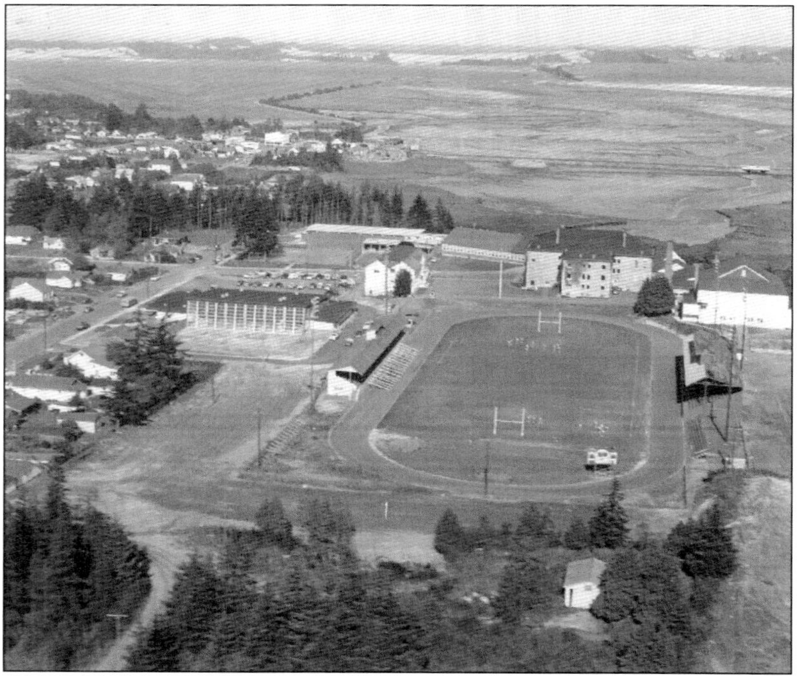

The new indoor swimming pool is shown near the high school and athletic field. When the pool opened in 1957, it was state of the art. The old high school building is central to the other buildings. The Westside School (left) was remodeled for a cafeteria, and the 1937 gymnasium is to the right. At top, the mud flats have not yet been filled for Pony Village. (CNB.)

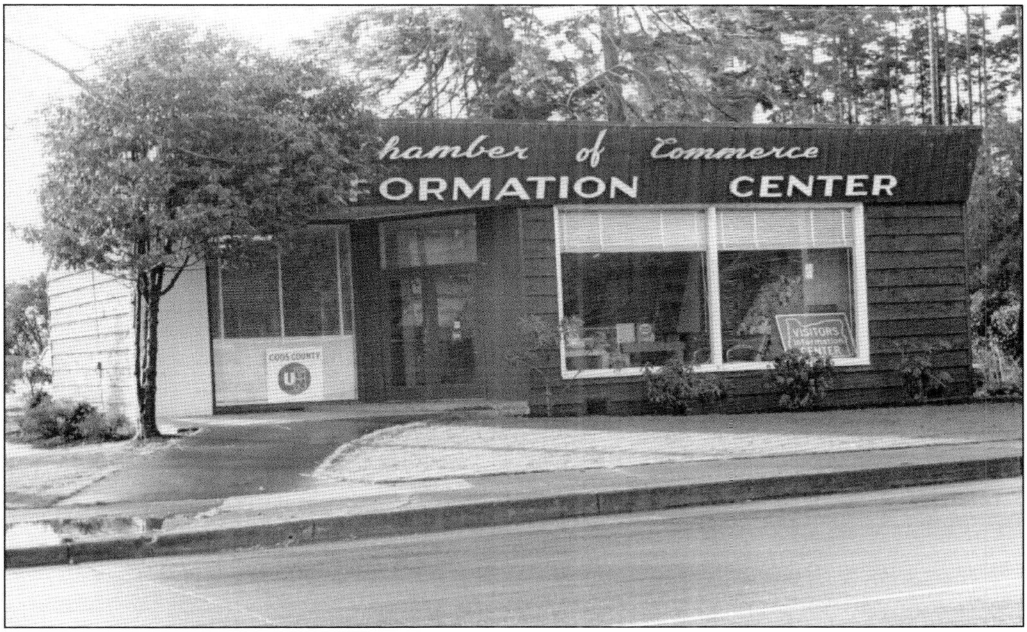

The North Bend Chamber of Commerce building was constructed about 1950. The North Bend Chamber merged with Coos Bay's chamber in 1980 to form the Bay Area Chamber of Commerce. The City of North Bend currently maintains the building as a tourist information center. (CNB.)

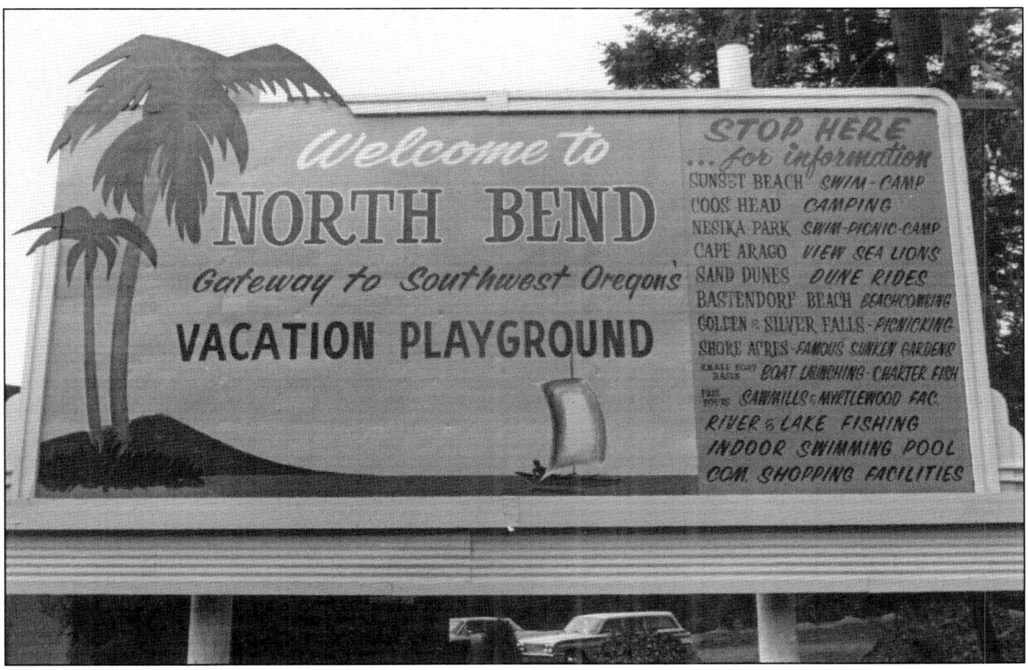

This sign greeted southbound drivers on U.S. Highway 101 just outside the North Bend Chamber of Commerce building. Encouraging tourists to visit and stay was, and remains, an important part of North Bend's economy. (CHMM 989-P40.0.)

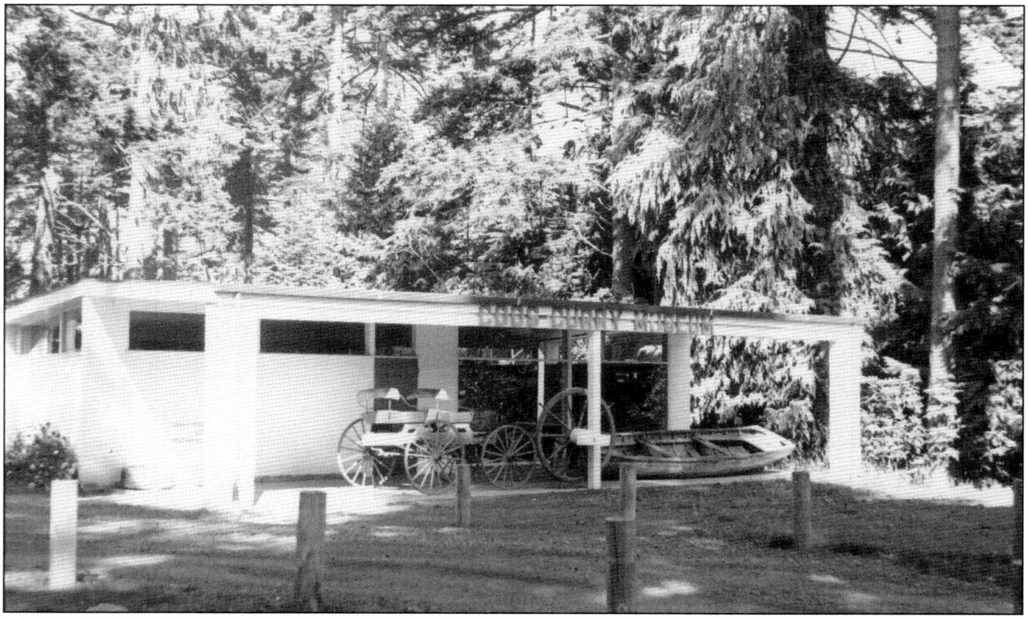

The Coos-Curry Pioneer and Historical Museum opened in Simpson Park in 1958. In 1977, the museum split with Curry County and dropped its limiting "pioneer" title to become the Coos Historical Museum. More recently, to emphasize the maritime heritage of the region, the name became the Coos Historical and Maritime Museum. (CHMM 010-1.11.)

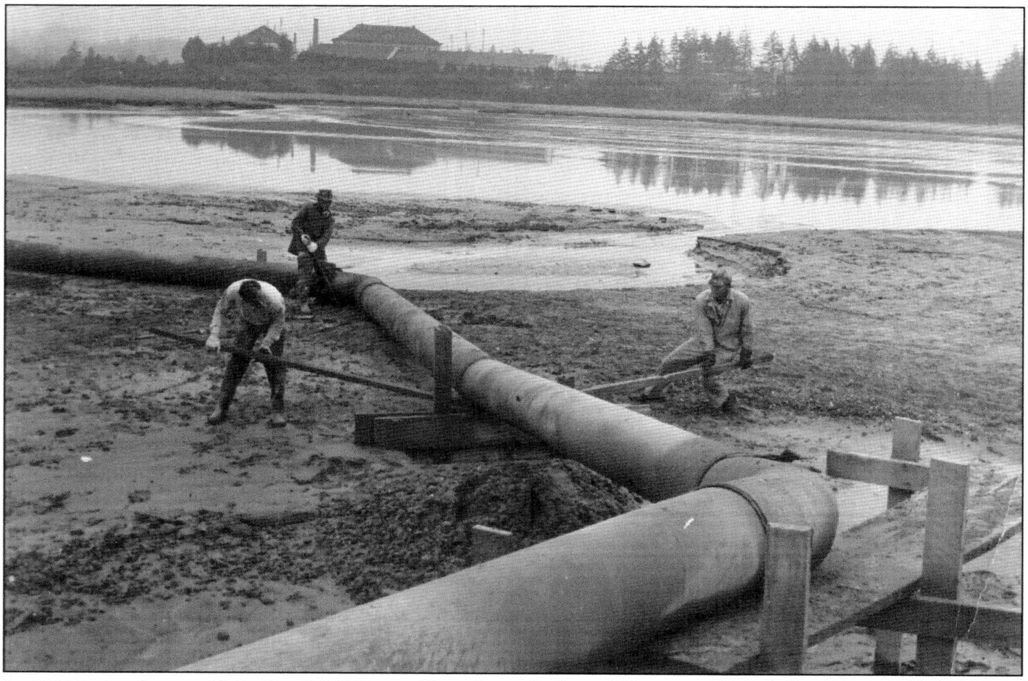

In 1958, dredge spoils helped fill Pony Slough and claim 35 acres of mud flats from tidal action. Walter Kraus's Pony Village project, the first covered mall on the Oregon Coast, was built on this fill. It was built in three parts. Kraus sold his mall for $1 million in 1962. (CHMM 989-P71.)

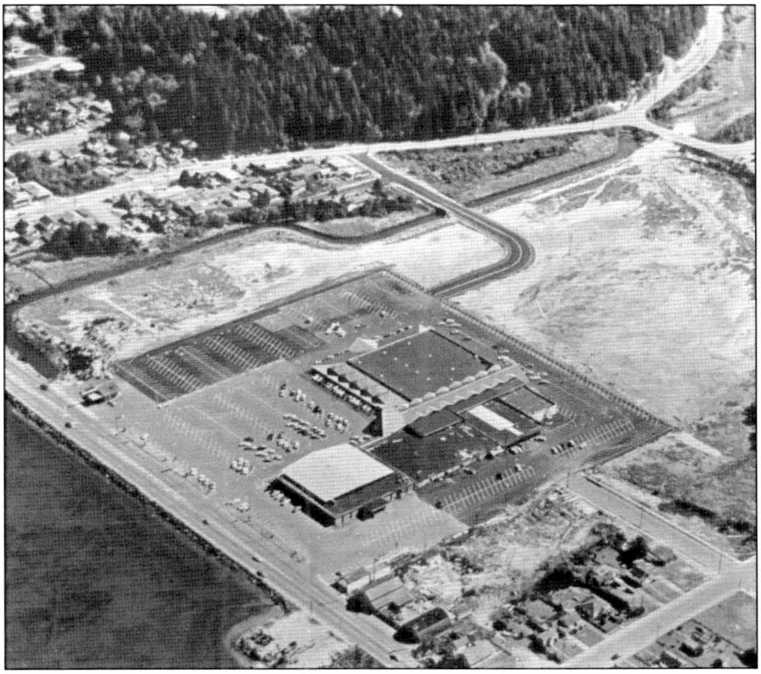

This is an aerial view of Pony Village Mall. Safeway, the first store to open in January 1960, has the white roof. Safeway's opening drew 4,000 people. The second phase added a Gold Bond redemption center, Sugar 'N Spice Bakery, and a Sprouse-Reitz variety store. Among the other early occupants of the mall were a Coast-to Coast store, Thrifty Drugs, Coastwise Finance, Village Coin Laundry, and Wardrobe Cleaners. (CHMM 989-P83b.)

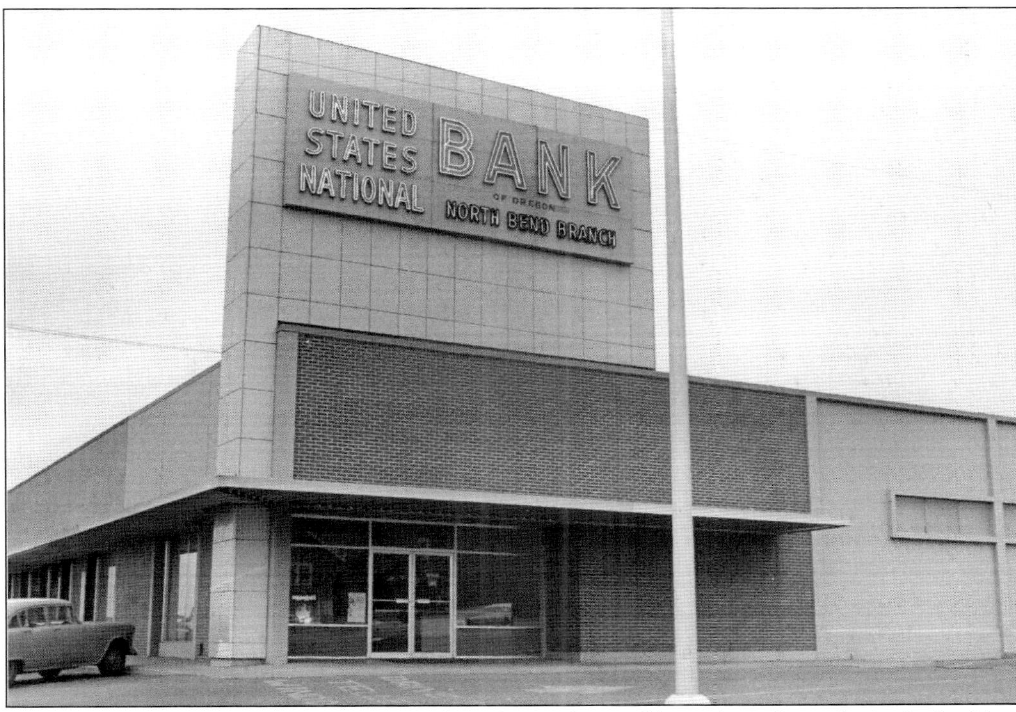

This was the first United States National Bank North Bend branch. Safeway built the building in 1955, moving from its downtown location. When Safeway located at Pony Village, the bank opened here in August 1960. Later tenants included McKay's Market, a roller skating rink, and currently, the South Coast Hospice thrift store. (CHMM 989-P11.)

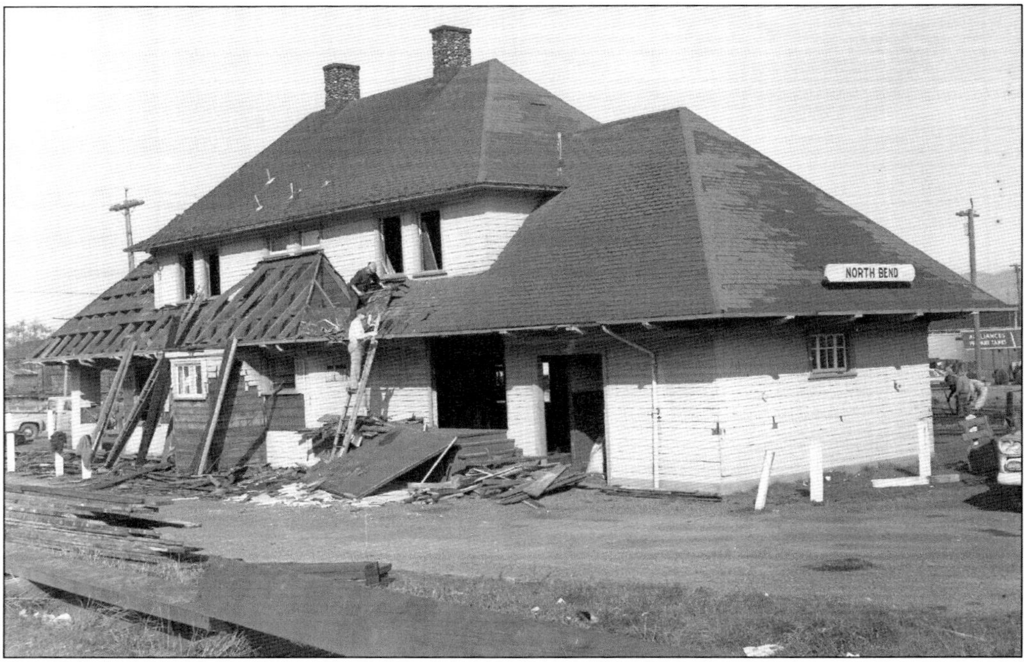

North Bend's 1916 passenger station was torn down in 1962. Passenger service ended in 1953. The station was just one of the structures that fell victim to "progress" in the 1960s. (CHMM 995-1.40316.2.)

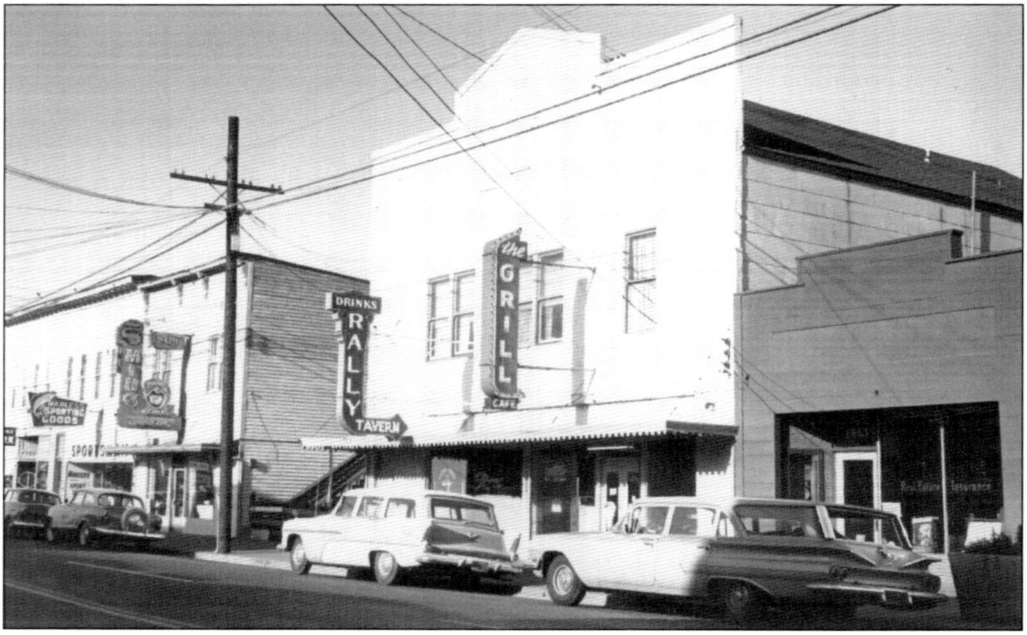

This photograph shows several downtown buildings on the east side of the 1900 block of Sherman Avenue, including the Rally Tavern and the Grill Café, which were torn down in the mid-1960s. There was no preservationist sentiment at the time and historic building after historic building from Mercy Hospital to Kinney High School were razed. (CHMM 989-P37.)

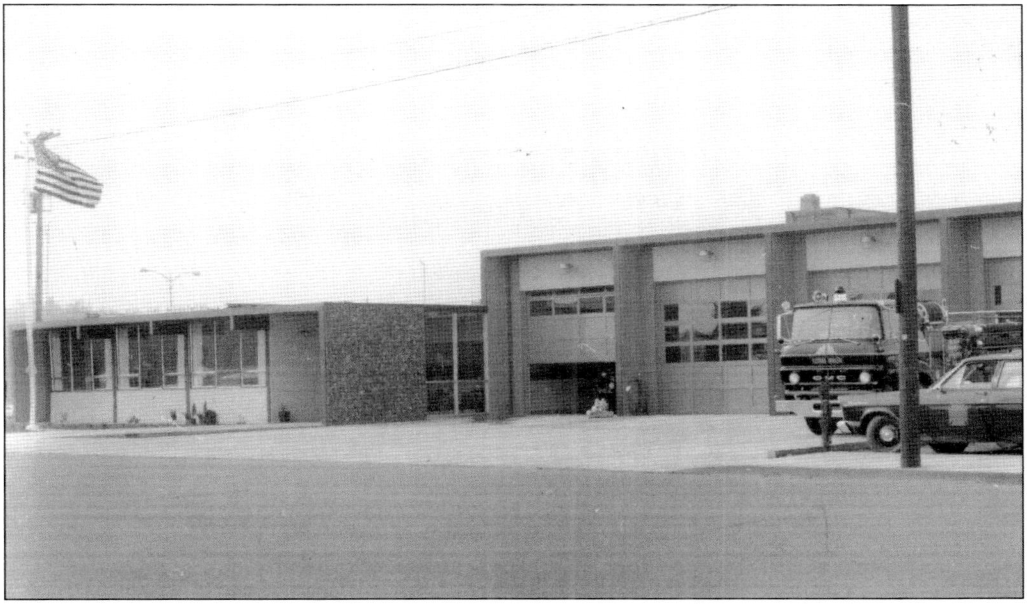

In 1964, construction of a new fire hall began at the corner of McPherson and California Avenues. Don Thompson constructed the $178,000 building. Framing timber was salvaged from the *Alaska Cedar's* December 1962 shipwreck. Opened in 1965, the building had garage space for vehicles, plus offices, sleeping quarters, kitchen, and meeting room. The vehicles shown are a 1963 GMC Coast engine and an early 1970s Ford station wagon. (CNB.)

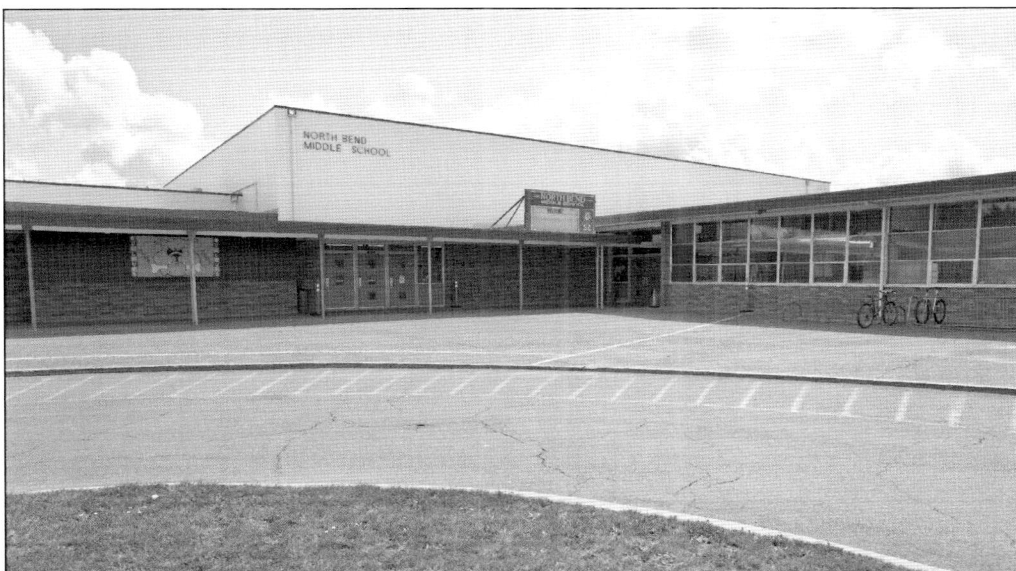

The middle school, built as the junior high, opened in 1960. Hamlin and Martin were the architects for this $825,000 construction by Todd Builders of Roseburg. Robert Bordner was principal. The building had 19 classrooms, cafeteria, music room, offices, and a gym also used for high school events. The "Bullpups" now are grades five to eight, but were seven and eight only in 1960. (Gary Sharp.)

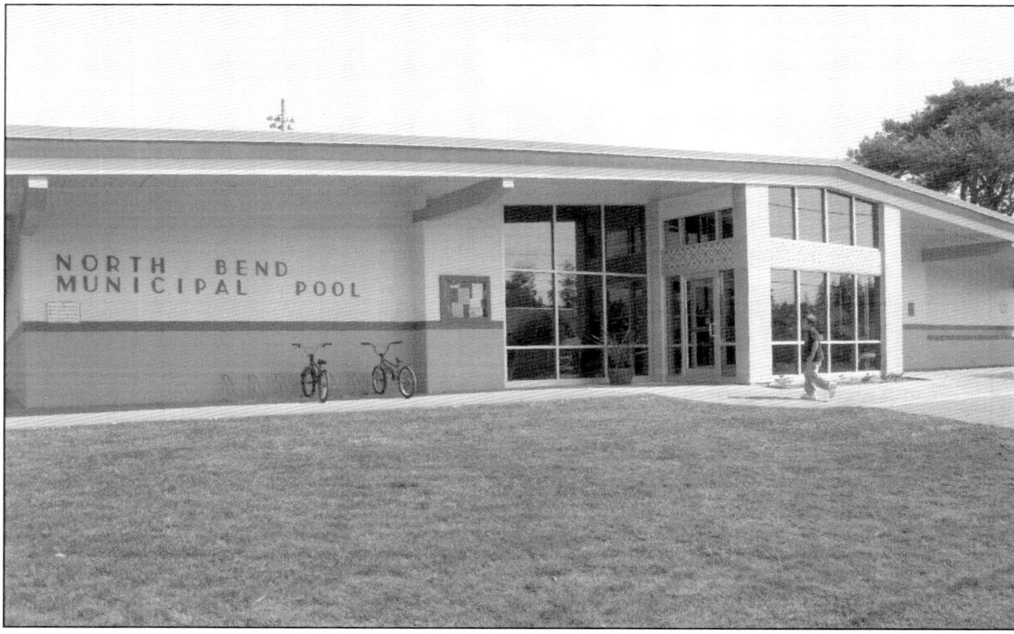

The city's award winning swimming pool opened in 1957. In 1955, voters approved a $325,000 construction bond for the indoor pool. It was administered by the school district for many years before financial problems caused the district to return it to the city. The city extensively refurbished the pool, including adding a new entrance, in 2009. (Gary Sharp.)

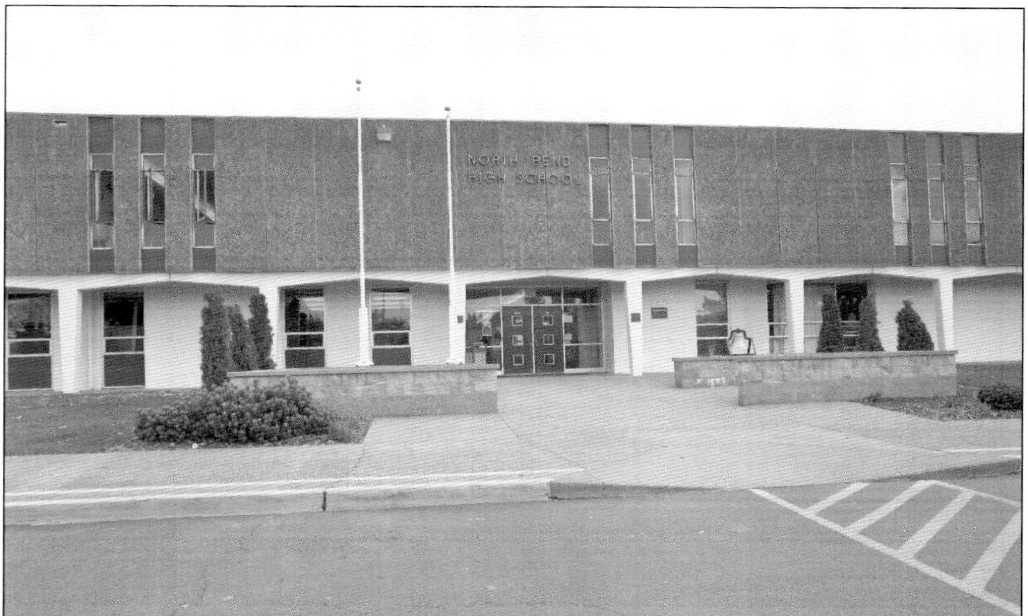

The North Bend High School acquired its newer buildings over several decades. "Bulldog" colors are brown and gold. In 1973, the athletic field was named for Victor L. Adams, controversial former coach and teacher. A new gymnasium was built in 1975 on the site of the 1937 structure. (Gary Sharp.)

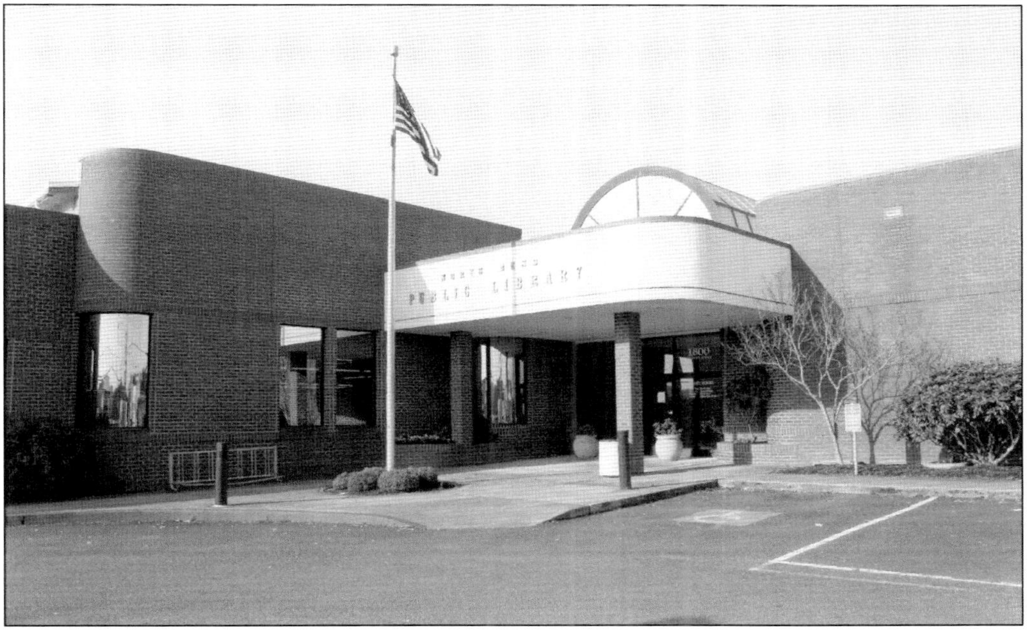

Richard Turi, local architect, drew plans for the new public library built in 1989. This launched his firm into a library specialty and over 20 other Oregon library projects came to North Bend. In 2001, a major addition expanded the North Bend children's library and the staff workspace. (Gary Sharp.)

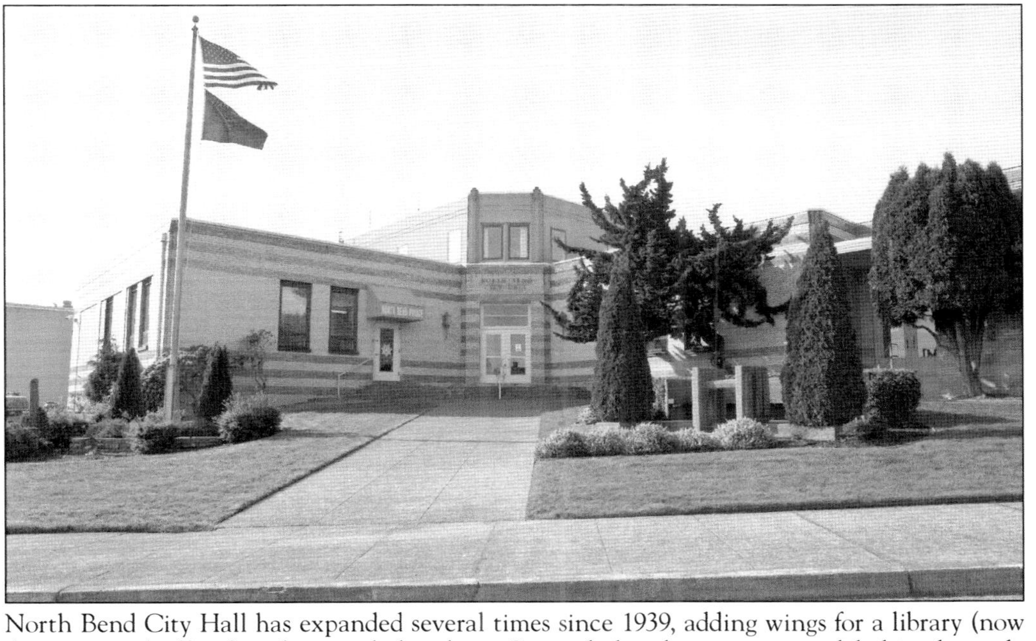

North Bend City Hall has expanded several times since 1939, adding wings for a library (now departmental offices) and council chambers. Council chambers were remodeled in the early 1990s. The most recent renovations, with architect Richard Turi, were done by Don Thompson Construction in 2006 and 2007. The police dispatch and communications center moved to a secure interior location, and police headquarters was updated. (Gary Sharp.)

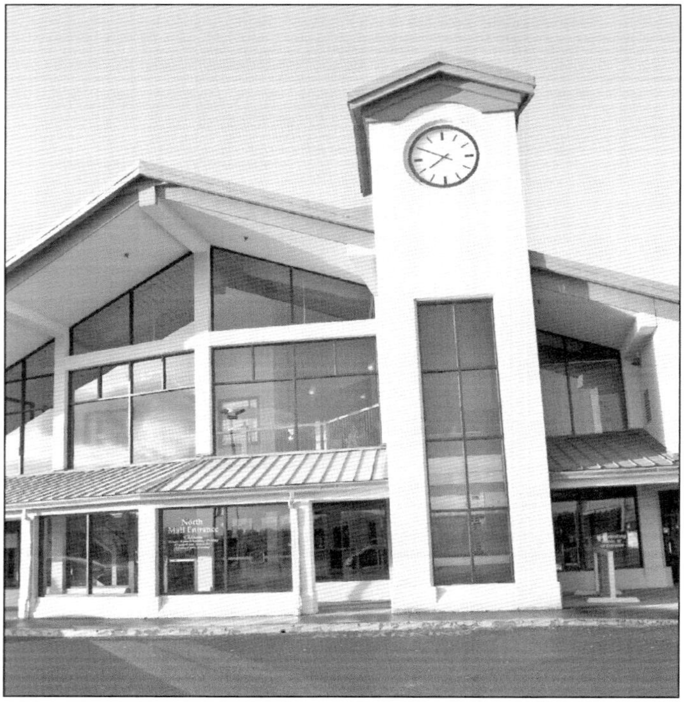

In 1999, Pony Village Mall underwent a major renovation that included building the clock tower and elevator. Baughman and Son, contractor, also put stucco over the entire wooden structure and added a new metal roof. In 2010 the mall's major tenants include Macy's (formerly The Bon,) JC Penney, Sears, and Ross. (Gary Sharp.)

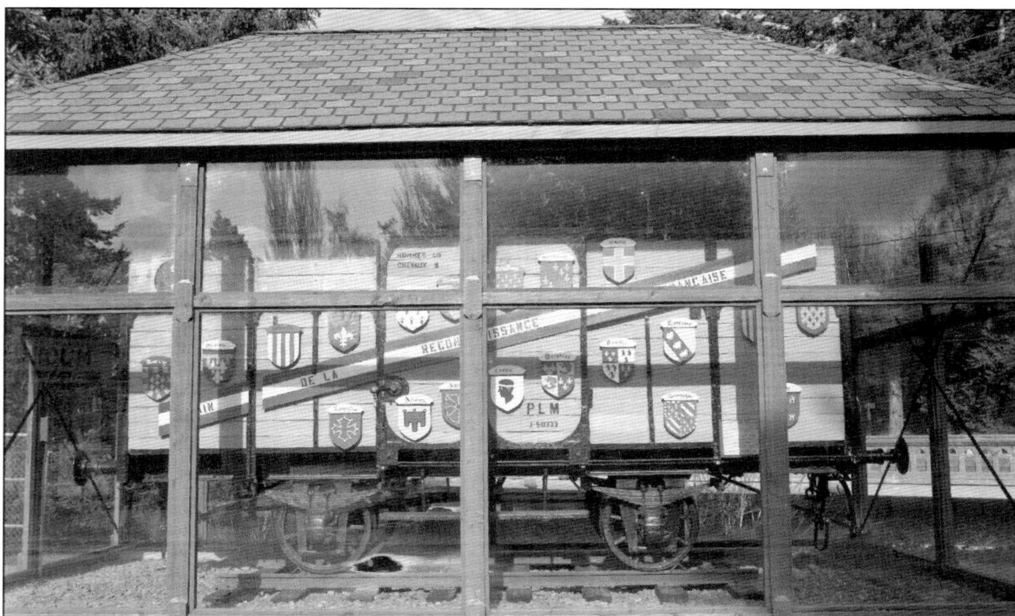

The Oregon "Merci Boxcar" was brought to North Bend in 2006 at the instigation of Mayor Rick Wetherell. After World War II, the grateful people of France sent each state in the United States a "40 and 8" railway car. During World War I, the boxcars held 40 soldiers or eight horses. Each decorated boxcar was filled with gifts to thank Americans for their wartime help. (Gary Sharp.)

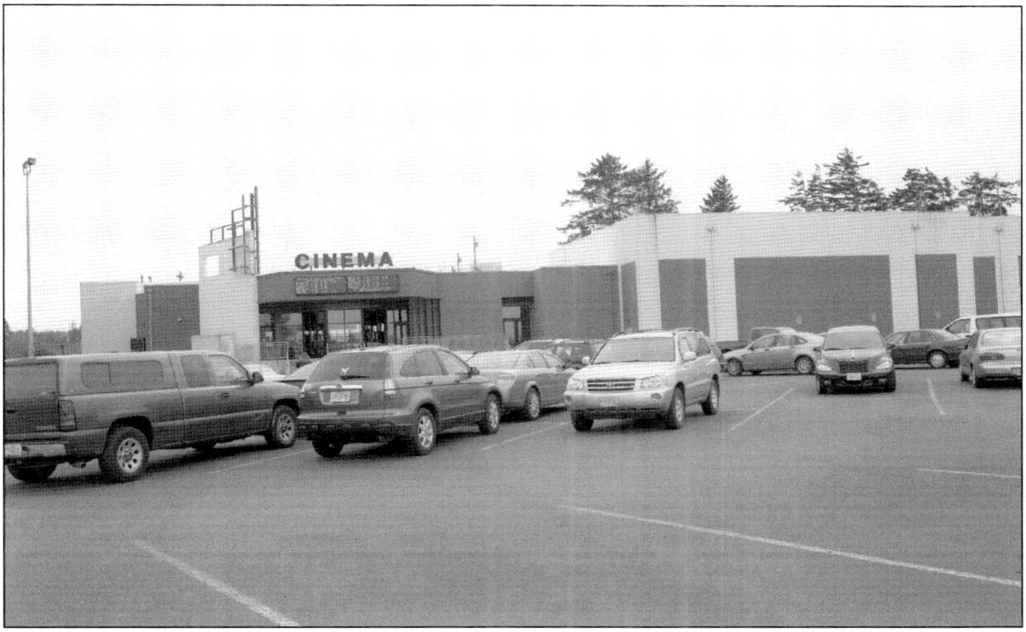

The Pony 4, a four-screen complex, opened without fanfare in December 1980. A local group—Theaters, Incorporated—owned it and later sold it to a national chain. A $3 million expansion was completed in early 2005, converting it to 11 screens. Seating capacity went from 628 to 1,622. (Gary Sharp.)

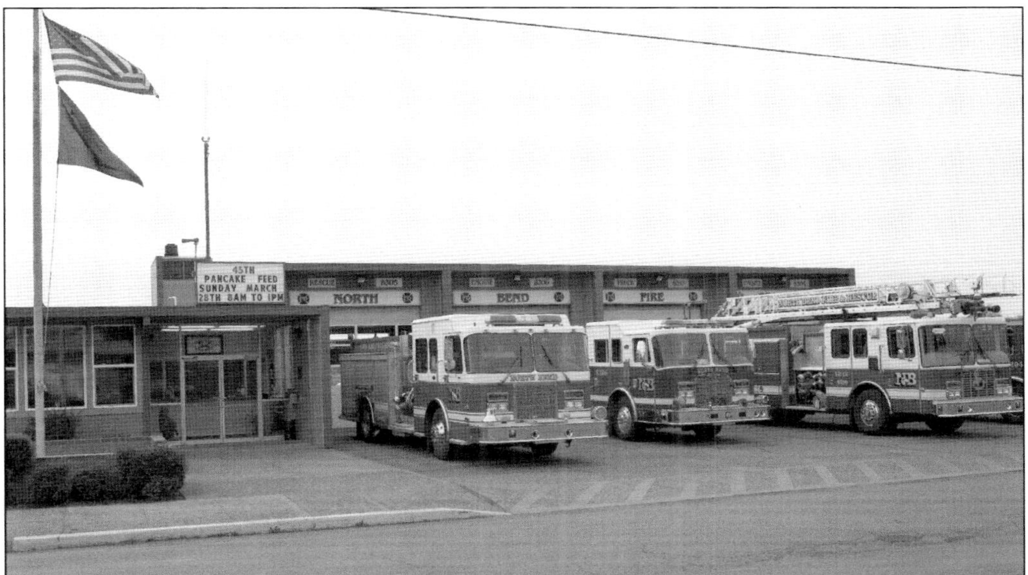

The North Bend Fire Department's chief is Scott Graham and assistant chief is Jim Brown. The department has four engines, a wildland vehicle, a fireboat, ladder truck, and airport rescue vehicle, among others. The equipment shown here in 2010 is, from left to right: a 2001 Simon Fire engine, a 2004 KME engine, and a 1995 Ferrah 75-foot-ladder truck. The department maintains two antique vehicles, a 1937 Federal and a 1949 Mack truck. (Gary Sharp.)

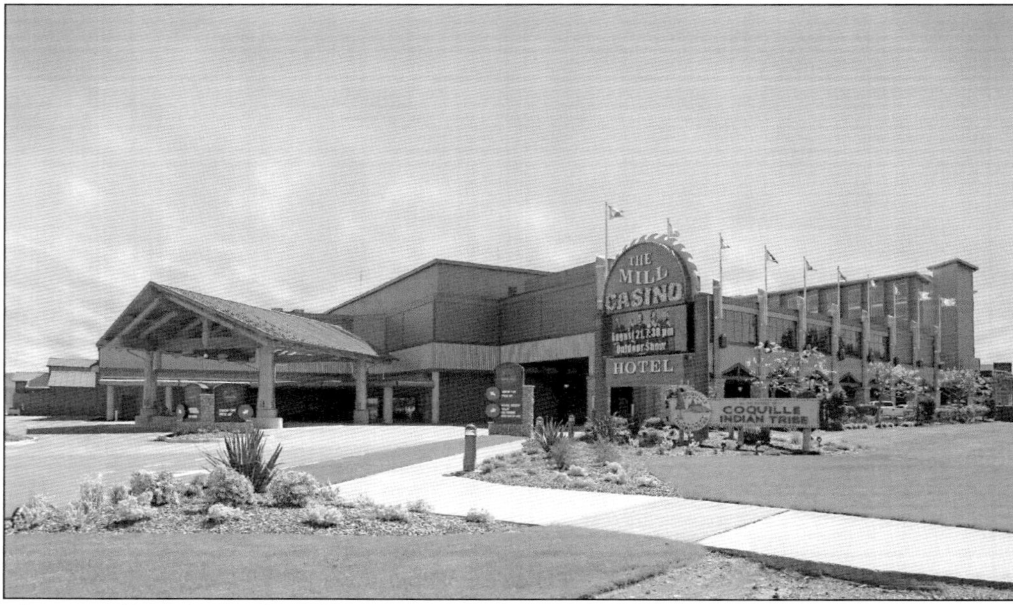

The Coquille Tribe purchased Weyerhaeuser's old mill site in 1995 and opened the Mill Casino and a 112-room hotel lodge there. In 2006, they added a large recreational vehicle park. In July 2008 they opened a seven-story 92-room hotel addition. Plans for their northern bay front property include retail stores and a waterfront walkway. (The Mill Casino, Hotel & RV Park.)

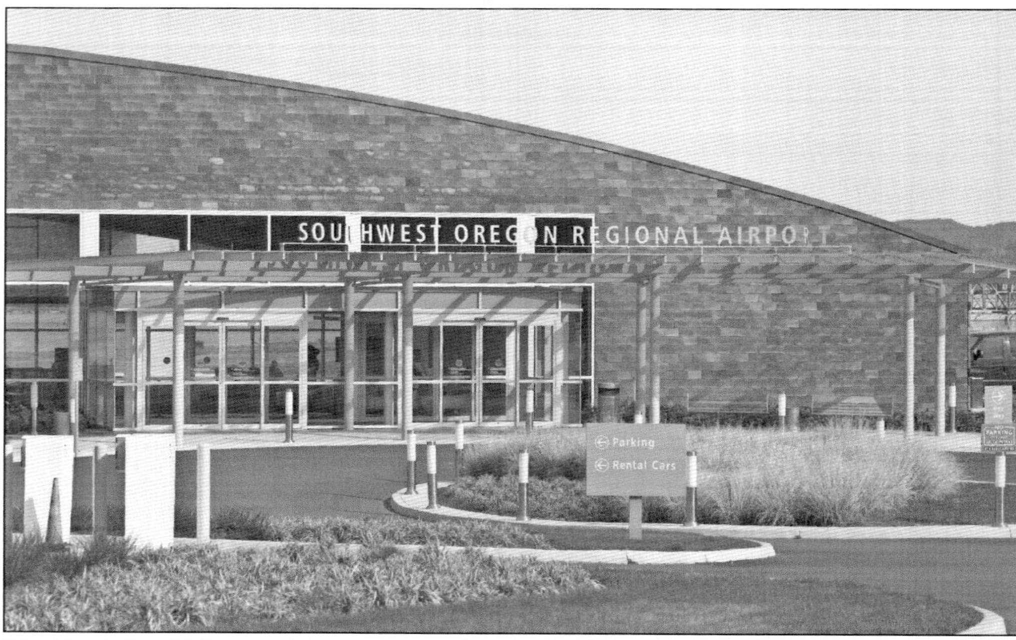

The North Bend Municipal Airport ownership shifted from the city to the Coos County Airport District in 2002. In 2006, the name was changed to Southwestern Oregon Regional Airport and in 2008 a new terminal was opened. From 1982 until 2008, Horizon Air, part of Alaska Airlines, served the airport. Since 2008 Skywest, a part of United Airlines, flies to Portland and San Francisco. (Gary Sharp.)

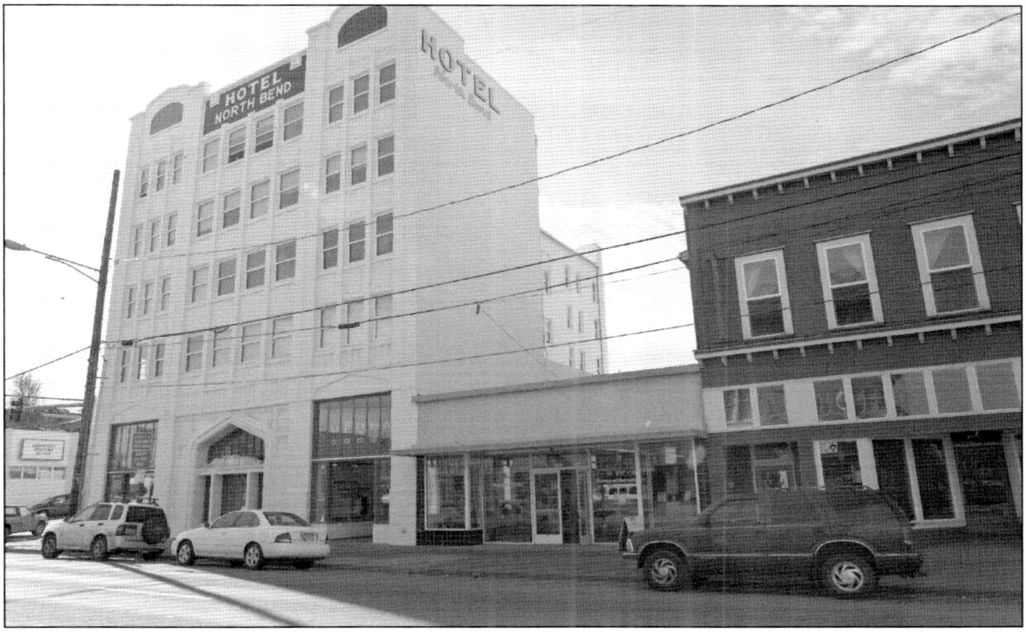

This is the completely refurbished Hotel North Bend. The project, undertaken by Umpqua Community Development Corporation and completed in 2009, provides low and moderate-income housing. The building is on the National Register of Historic Places. Wayne Schrunk's two rebuilt buildings, also completely modernized, stand adjacent. (Gary Sharp.)

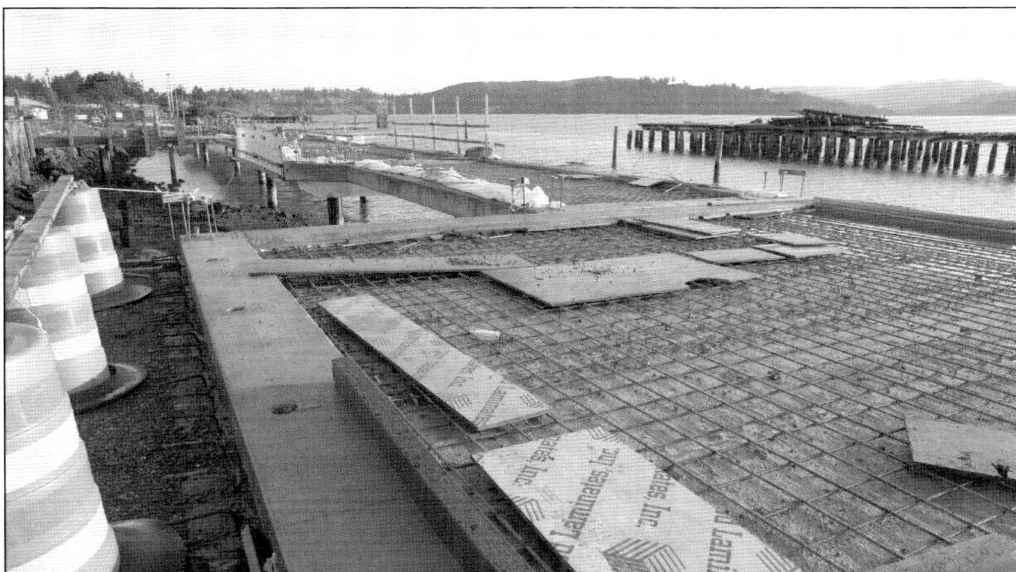

This photograph shows work nearing completion in spring 2010 on the new boardwalk, between Virginia and California Avenues, that helps restore North Bend's historic tie to the water. The $2 million project, built with a mix of federal and city urban renewal funds, began in late 2009 and finished in June 2010. Remains of the oft-rebuilt old wooden city dock are in the background. (Gary Sharp.)

Bibliography

Beck, David R. M. *Seeking Recognition: The Termination and Restoration of the Coos, Lower Umpqua, and Siuslaw Indians, 1855–1984*. Lincoln, Nebraska: University of Nebraska Press, 2009.

Beckham, Stephen Dow. *The Indians of Western Oregon: This Land Was Theirs*. Coos Bay, Oregon: Arago Books, 1977.

Douthit, Nathan. *The Coos Bay Region 1890–1944: Life on A Coastal Frontier.* 2nd edition. Coos Bay, Oregon: Coos County Historical Society, 2005.

Gorst, Wilbur H. *Vern C. Gorst: Pioneer and Grandad of United Air Lines*. Coos Bay, Oregon: Gorst Publications, 1979.

Hough, Louis A. *A Fleet to be Forgotten: The Wooden Freighters of World War One*. San Francisco: San Francisco Maritime History Press, 2009.

Lansing, William A. *Seeing the Forest for the Trees: Menasha Corporation and its One Hundred Year History in Coos Bay, Oregon 1905–2005*. Eugene, Oregon: Monroe Press, 2005.

Peterson, Emil R., and Alfred Powers. *A Century of Coos and Curry*. Coquille, Oregon: Coos-Curry Pioneer and Historical Association, 1977.

Wagner, Dick. "Consolidation 2002–2004: An Insider's Personal Account." North Bend, Oregon: February 2005. Typescript.

Wagner, Dick. *Louie Simpson's North Bend*. North Bend, Oregon: The North Bend News, 1986.

Wagner, Dick and Judy. *North Bend Between the World Wars: 1919–1941*. North Bend, Oregon: Bygones, 2005.

Wagner, Judith and Richard. *L. J.: The Uncommon Life of Louis Jerome Simpson*. North Bend, Oregon: Bygones, 2003.

————. *Instigator: The Troubled Life of Lorenzo Dow Kinney*. North Bend, Oregon: Wegferd Publications, 2008.

West, Victor Jr. "Asa M. Simpson's Shipyard, North Bend." North Bend, Oregon. Typescript.

Weybright, Nancy M. "The No Beginning Possibly One Hundred Year History of Coos County School District 13." North Bend, Oregon: 1981–1982. Typescript.

Youst, Lionel. *She's Tricky Like Coyote: Annie Miner Peterson, an Oregon Coast Indian Woman*. Norman, Oklahoma: University of Oklahoma Press, 1997.

ABOUT THE ORGANIZATION

The Coos Historical and Maritime Museum in the North Bend–Coos Bay area is the source of many images in this book. Its collections include more than 200,000 images and more than 45,000 artifacts pertaining to the cultural history of Oregon's south coast. Museum field trips, events, exhibits, and award-winning education programs are undertaken in partnership with tribes or area nonprofit organizations, and provide an excellent orientation to the history of this somewhat remote area.

Currently the Coos Historical and Maritime Museum is raising funds for construction of a new waterfront facility to improve its capacity for service. The museum has outgrown the small building it has occupied since 1958; the new 19,000-square-foot building and adjacent plaza are designed for a range of community services. In addition to supporting existing and planned programs and activities, the facility will greatly expand opportunities for innovative partnerships and cultural events.

The museum thanks the authors for donating all royalties from this book to the new facility project.

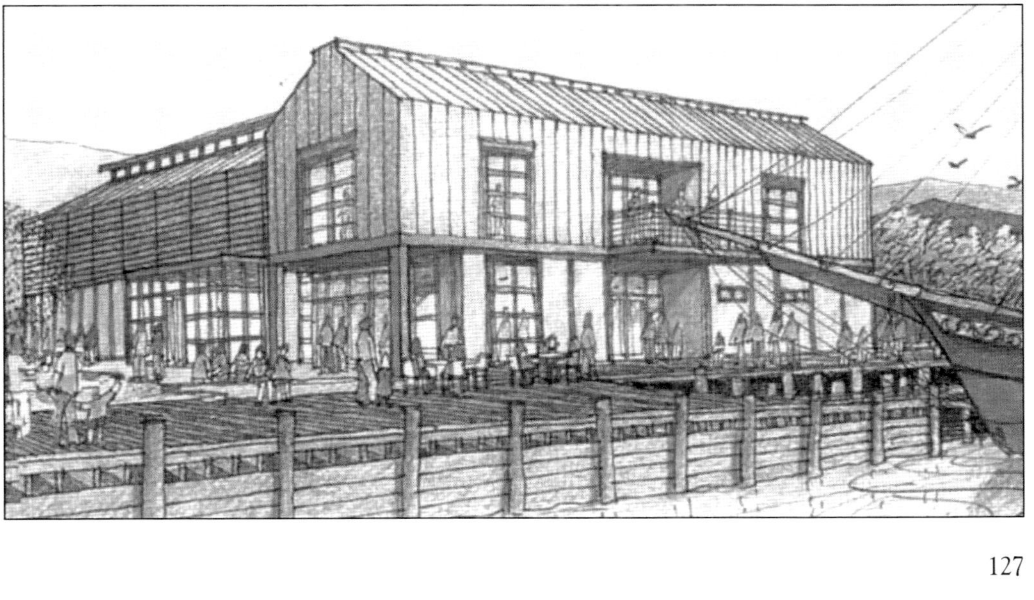

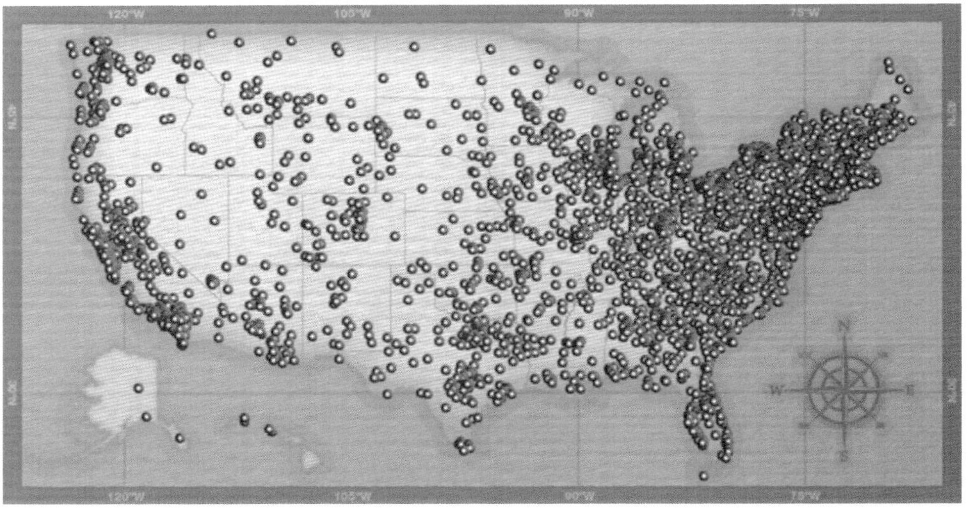